Body and Sexuality

Theology and Religious Studies
Agnes M. Brazal, *Series Editor*

The Theology and Religious Studies Series aims to provide
a space for the dissemination of works that stimulate critical
reflections on the faith towards a better response to the signs of
the times. As the Church and other faith groups stand to benefit
from the expertise of those in other fields in engaging with the
changing situation, this series welcomes new theological inquiries
that dialogue with recent studies and findings in other academic
disciplines, as well as with insights arising from thoughtful
debate and discussion in the public sphere.

Body and Sexuality

Theological-Pastoral
Perspectives of Women in Asia

Agnes M. Brazal
Andrea Lizares Si

EDITORS

ATENEO DE MANILA
UNIVERSITY PRESS

ATENEO DE MANILA UNIVERSITY PRESS
Bellarmine Hall, Katipunan Avenue
Loyola Heights, Quezon City
P.O. Box 154, 1099 Manila, Philippines
Tel.: (632) 426-59-84 / Fax (632) 426-59-09
E-mail: unipress@admu.edu.ph
Website: www.ateneopress.org

Book design by Victor Santos
Cover art work by Joanna Ruiz
On the cover: *Orchid Sundok* by AnnaFer, 1999

The editors and publisher wish to acknowledge with gratitude the help
of artist Anna Fer for the cover concept and design.

Grateful acknowledgment is also made for permission to reprint
"The Passion of the Womb: Women Re-living the Eucharist" by Astrid Lobo Gajiwala,
from *Body, Bread and Blood*, edited by Francis Gonsalves, SJ (Delhi: ISPCK, 2000).

The views expressed here are those of the individual authors and not necessarily of the Ecclesia of Women in Asia and the editors.

The National Library of the Philippines CIP Data

Recommended entry:

Body and sexuality : theological-pastoral perspectives of
    women in Asia / edited by Agnes M. Brazal, Andrea
    Lizares Si. – Quezon City: Ateneo de Manila University
    Press, c2007
        p. ; cm

    1. Body, Human–Religious aspects–Catholic Church.
2. Body, Human–Philosophy.   3. Women–Religious
aspects–Catholic Church.   I. Brazal, Agnes M.   II. Si, Andrea
Lizares.   III. Title : Theological-pastoral perspectives of
women in Asia.

BX1795.B63 261.8357 2007 P065000003
ISBN 978-971-550-516-1

Contents

Preface and Acknowledgments   **vii**

Introduction   **x**

I   **Shifting Foundations and Methodologies**

■ 1   *Body, Self and Sexual Identity:*   **1**
Reflections on the Current Evidence
CHRISTINE E. GUDORF

■ 2   *Revisioning Eros for Asian Feminist Theologizing:*   **34**
Some Pointers from Tantric Philosophy
PUSHPA JOSEPH, FMM

II   **Body and Sexuality: Asian Societies/World**

■ 3   *Em-body-ing Theology: Theological Reflections on the*   **60**
Experience of Filipina Domestic Workers in Hong Kong
GEMMA TULUD CRUZ

■ 4   *Theological Reflection on Sex Work*   **75**
THERESA YIH-LAN TSOU, SSS

■ 5   *Ecological Approach Towards Redefining Sexuality of Women*   **90**
DZINTRA ILISHKO

III   **Body and Scriptures**

■ 6   *Gender Identity and Ezekiel 16*   **104**
JULIA ONG SIU YIN, IJS

■ 7   *Pauline Body in 1 Corinthians:*   **120**
A Metaphor of Whole Human Being
and of Christian Community
NOZOMI MIURA, RSCJ

■ 8   *Re-imaging Woman and Reshaping her Destiny*   **139**
An Indian Feminist Reading of the Bent Body (Lk 13: 10-17)
EVELYN MONTEIRO, SCC

■ 9   *The Body: A Testimony to Discipleship*   **153**
(John 19: 25-27)
MARY CECILIA CLAPAROLS, RA

IV   **Body and Sacraments**

■ 10   *Re-imaging the Body of Christ:*   **172**
Women's Body as Gospel Proclamation
ANTOINETTE GUTZLER, MM

■ 11   *The Passion of the Womb:*   **187**
Women Re-living the Eucharist
ASTRID LOBO GAJIWALA

■ 12   *Reflections on the Spirituality of Ageing Korean Women:*   **201**
The Empowerment of the Sacred in their Body-Image and Inner Life
HAN SOON HEE, RSCJ

V   **Sexuality and Church Leadership**

■ 13   *Facing the Reality of Clergy Sexual Misconduct*   **216**
in the Church: A Step Toward Justice and Healing
LEONILA V. BERMISA, MM

■ 14   *Queer Revisions of Christianity*   **234**
SHARON A. BONG

VI   **Images of God's Body**

■ 15   *Bodily Representations of Hindu Goddesses: A Feminist Perspective*   **252**
A. METTI, SCC

■ 16   *The Universe as Body or Womb of God:*   **273**
Theologizing on Difference and Interdependence
JEANE C. PERACULLO

Index   **291**

Editors and Contributors   **299**

Preface and Acknowledgments

The essays in this collection were prepared for and mostly presented at the Second Biennial Conference of the Ecclesia of Women in Asia (EWA 2), held at St. Charles Borromeo Sisters' Syantikara House in Yogyakarta from November 16 to 19, 2004. It brought together forty-eight women to discuss "Body and Sexuality: Theological-Pastoral Perspectives of Women in Asia," the theme of the conference. The women—religious/single/married, professors/pastoral and grassroots workers, ecumenical partners, feminists—came from Australia, Bangladesh, China, India, Indonesia, Japan, Korea, Malaysia, Mongolia, Myanmar, Pakistan, Philippines, Singapore, Sri Lanka, Taiwan, Thailand and Vietnam. Guest participants from the United States, Germany, and Latvia also attended. This anthology is a bound memory of this insightful and fruitful meeting.

In the opening address, Agnes M. Brazal, EWA Coordinator and Professor of Theology at the Maryhill School of Theology, Philippines, invited the participants to explore how body and sexuality have been experienced and constructed in the Asian context, keeping in mind that these constructions are "shaped by power dynamics in society." She underlined our responsibility to recover stories of women resisting oppressive discourses to "unloose the body," and use these stories to re-weave the strands of faith handed down to the community. Observing that many Asian theologians have "skirted the issue," she described the conference as a "free space" and a "laboratory of ideas" on a topic in which women's voices have long been muted.

The gathering was significant in its successful attempt to challenge Asian women theologians to come together and write on this theme, as can be seen from this collection. It was likewise EWA's hope that the papers presented at the conference would contribute towards deepening or challenging Asian churches' theological reflection on women and sexuality in relation to the issue of "family." The Federation of Asian Bishops' Conference, in its Eighth Plenary Assembly last August 2004, focused on the theme "The Asian Family towards a Culture of Integral Life" (FABC Papers No. 111). FABC pledged to devote its energies and resources to promoting this thrust in the next four years; this book is part of EWA's contribution to this process.

The EWA 2 and thereafter this collection of essays came to fruition upon the initiative of the organizing group, the Ecclesia of Women in Asia. EWA is a forum of Catholic women doing theology in Asia on the academic, pastoral and grassroots levels. Conceived in a conference on the post-synodal document *Ecclesia in Asia* in Pune, India, in 2001, EWA was born a year after in 2002, when fifty-five women theologians from seventeen Asian nations gathered for a four-day conference in Bangkok. Organized around the theme "Ecclesia of Women in Asia: Gathering the Voices of the Silenced, " it aimed to bring together Catholic women theologians in Asia so that they may be seen and heard. It was there that EWA was born.

EWA's vision is the development of theologizing from Asian women's perspectives and the recognition of Asian Catholic women theologians as colleagues in theological discussions within the Church and academe. Its mission is to encourage and assist Catholic women in or from Asia to engage in research, reflection and writing towards theologizing that: 1) is inculturated and contextualized in Asian realities; 2) is built on the religious experience and praxis of the socially excluded; 3) promotes gender mutuality and integrity of creation; and 4) fosters dialogue with other disciplines and faiths.

Towards this end, the EWA aims to: 1) organize conferences that encourage the writing of original and creative theological papers for publication; 2) foster communication and discussion among Catholic women theologians through a cyberspace group and a website; 3) dialogue with feminist grassroots/theological movements and women from other faiths; and 4) conduct other such programs and activities as shall help in the attainment of our vision.

Aside from organizing conferences, setting up a website (http://geocities.com/ecclesiaofwomen) and an e-group, and clarifying our Vision-Mission, the EWA has also published the essays from its 2002 conference as the *Ecclesia of Women in Asia: Gathering the Voices of the Silenced* (Delhi: ISPCK, 2005). A selection of sixteen articles from this collection had been translated into German and published as *Das Schweigen Brechen: Asiatische Theologinnen Ringen um die Befreinde Dimension des Galubens* (Freiburg: Herder, 2005). In addition, Evelyn Monteiro and Agnes Brazal represented the EWA in the Eighth FABC Plenary Assembly not only to share women theologians' perspectives, but also to make the bishops aware of the existence of this forum of Catholic women theologians.

Thus, it all began in Pune, India, with a dream. But it is not enough to simply dream. EWA would not have lived on and this publication would not have been realized, without women of kindred spirits who not only share the dream, but also contribute to re-weaving it, in particular, the members of the Continuity Committee who have worked to keep EWA alive: Agnes M. Brazal, 2004 EWA Coordinator, Pushpa Joseph, 2003 EWA Coordinator; Andrea Lizares Si, PRO/Webmistress; Evelyn Monteiro and Antoinette Gutzler, editors of the EWA 1 book; Christine Burke, EWA 2 Program Coordinator; Nunuk Murniati and Intan Darmawati, EWA 2 hosts; Sanae Masuda, caretaker of our funds; and Theresa Tsou. Acting as EWA consultant is Annette Meuthrath, in-charge of South Asia desk, Institute of Missiology, Missio. Thanks to the wonders of information technology, especially email, the group has been able to sustain friendship, solidarity and sense of mission through all this time.

The editors would also like to acknowledge Astrid Lobo and Virginia Saldanha who wrote the press releases for the EWA 2 conference. Excerpts from these releases have been integrated into this preface and in the introduction. Last but not least, special thanks to the Institute of Missiology, Aachen, Germany, Comité Catholique contre la Faim et pour le Développement (CCFD) and the Swiss Catholic Lenten Fund (SCLF), whose invaluable financial assistance made possible the EWA 2 conference and supported this publication.

Introduction

One is not born, but rather becomes, a woman.

—Simone de Beauvoir

Many people used to think of the body as something given, and with divinely pre-ordained meanings; meanings that Marxists, feminists and post-structuralist discourses have revealed to be largely socially constructed. Body is produced...shaped by power dynamics in society.[1] Bodies have been named, contrasted/linked with each other, with nature, with sources of social and supernatural powers, and ranked accordingly. Normal/abnormal, pure/impure, beautiful/ugly— these labels on bodies have been used to establish the dominance of particular social groups.

Patriarchal societies have generally produced docile, decorous and useful women's bodies. The Eighth plenary assembly of the Federation of Asian Bishops' Conference (FABC) affirms that: "[t]he world view of patriarchy lies deep in the cultural and religious subconscious of Asia and dominates politics, economics, human relationships, childrearing views and practices, stereotypes about men and women, community roles, etc."[2] These meanings inscribed in women's body and sexuality have varied, based not only on gender but also class, race, caste, age, sexual orientation and religious status. Christianity and the other religions of Asia have been major constitutive forces as well in the history of Asian women's bodies. Colonialism, neocolonialism, and the networked world are other significant forces in defining bodies of Asian women.

But this body is not just acted upon. It is also a medium of action in the world, a medium of power and resistance. Thus, it is important as well to recover the stories of women both in the past and today who resist oppressive discourses to "unloose the body," stories of women defining their own bodies and sexuality in alternative humanizing ways. These stories, including those hidden in the *interstices* of sacred texts and heritage, will be like strands of thread which, with our hands and creativity, we can use to re-weave the faith that has been handed down to us, in fresh novel ways.

Focusing on the theme "Body and Sexuality" as seen from different theological and pastoral perspectives, this collection explores how body and sexuality have been defined in various Asian contexts and critically reflects on these in the light of the faith tradition. Many of the essays in this anthology not only engage in deconstruction, but also attempt to reconstruct theologies of body and sexuality that are built on the rich cultural heritage of Asia. In line with the interdisciplinary and interfaith thrust of the Ecclesia of Women in Asia, they exhibit openness to dialogue with the changing world and other religious traditions.

The first two essays which were presented as main papers in the conference focus on *Shifting Foundations and Methodologies.* Christine Gudorf, award-winning author of *Body, Sex and Pleasure: Reconstructing Christian Sexual Ethics*, and Professor of Religious Studies at Florida International University, USA, presented her paper on body, self, and sexual identity. Gudorf dwelt at length on postmodernity's insistence that the body is inscribed, in an attempt to make the participants self-conscious about how their selves were constructed, and so enable a rebuilding. How should we interpret postmodernity's insistence that the body is constructed, or inscribed? Is the body the self? What about the body and rights? Does the self have complete control of its body, or can that control be usurped in some situations? These were some of the compelling questions she chose to answer in a stimulating paper that drew from science, psychology, culture, and the simple experience of being human.

The second essay of Pushpa Joseph, teaching and post-doctoral Fellow in Christian Studies at the University of Chennai, India, linked the creative powers of Eros with the divine energy of Sakti in Tantric philosophy. She proposed a Sakti Theology with its rousing of all the energies one can discover in one's body, emotions and mind, as an alternative to the excessive intellectualism of patriarchal theologies. Based on an egalitarian foundation that recognizes both intense connectedness and distinct identity, this Sakti theology advocates "power with" as opposed to patriarchal "power over" relationships.

The rest of the articles in this anthology were presented as papers during the conference itself, in workshop groups, or offered later by friends who failed to make it to the conference.

Body and Sexuality: Asian Societies/World reflects on the theological challenges posed by the inscription of domestic work in the bodies of Filipina migrant workers in Hong Kong, the "right to sex work" in the context of Taiwan, and the need to acknowledge Bodiliness from an ecological, feminist and multicultural perspective.

Body and Scriptures explores the metaphorical "woman" in the marriage imagery of Ezekiel 16, and how readers in Singapore identified with the characters depending on their gender. This is followed by a discussion of the body ethics of Paul in 1 Corinthians and how an East Asian concept of the body possesses striking similarities with Paul's concept of *sōma*. The story of the bent woman in Luke 13:10–17 read from an Indian feminist liberationist perspective is the focus of the third article while the last essay highlights the body as a language of resistance expressed in the silent testimony of the women in John 19:25.

Two of the papers on *Body and Sacraments* touch on women as *imago Christi*. The first asserts that that "body" is integral to "Christic-ness" and the Gospel can only be good news to Asia if the "Christic-ness" of women is neither violated nor denied. The second dwells on the broken bodies and spilt blood of women's Eucharistic lives to question a communion ritual that prevents those who faithfully set the table from setting the agenda. A third essay gives center stage to ageing women in Korea, suggesting a spirituality of imperfection that empowers elderly women to embrace new visions of themselves.

Sexuality and Church Leadership consists of an article on clergy sexual misconduct in the Philippines and an evaluation of the Church's response, and another on the lesbian body with its dialectical tension between sex and gender to critically assess Pope John Paul II's Letter to Women.

Images of God's Body features two pieces: the first deconstructs oppressive facets while appropriating liberative elements of Hindu Goddess myths, as well as underscores the challenges these pose to Christian God-language and ritual; the second explores the image of the world as God's womb, which in many Asian religions is a powerful symbol suggesting hidden growth and creative power.

While all of the articles in this collection recognize how women's bodies have been defined and constructed by patriarchal societies, some—more strongly than others—affirm the significance of women's bodily difference which must be redefined in a way that does not romanticize nor constrict women's options. Ilishko (guest participant) critiques early radical and liberal feminists' rejection or denial of women's bodily reality. Ecofeminists favor reclaiming women's bodies and their biologically linked roles that avoid both alienation from and identification with the body. Women's bodily experience of menstruation /birthing /breastfeeding /menopause...being gifted a womb...are likewise highlighted or appropriated in the theological reflections of Lobo on how women live the Eucharist in their daily life and of Peracullo on her imaging the world as God's womb.

It was not the aim of the conference to arrive at a consensus on the topics discussed, but simply to start a conversation, and stimulate further reflections. It is hoped, nevertheless, that this compilation will provide a helpful overview of what Asian Catholic women today are thinking regarding the subject of body and sexuality, and how they are creatively reconstructing theology using Asian cultural resources.

NOTES

1   Michel Foucault, *Power/Knowledge: Selected Interviews and Other Writings 1972–1977* (New York: Pantheon Books, 1980), 51–52, 58–59.
2   Federation of Asian Bishops' Conference, "The Asian Family towards a Culture of Integral Life," FABC Papers No. 111 (Hong Kong: FABC, 2004), 16.

BIBLIOGRAPHY

Federation of Asian Bishops' Conference. "The Asian Family towards a Culture of Integral Life." FABC Papers No. 111. Hong Kong: FABC, 2004.
Foucault, Michel. *Power/Knowledge: Selected Interviews and Other Writings 1972–1977*. New York: Pantheon Books, 1980.

I

Shifting Foundations
and Methodologies

Body, Self and Sexual Identity

Reflections on the Current Evidence

Christine E. Gudorf

1

For centuries within Christianity, the term "body" brought to mind not the embodiment of Christ in the Incarnation, nor even God's deliberate creation of the human body, but instead associations with sin, lust, temptation and excess. Neither was the body understood as the locus of the self; rather the self was identified with the soul struggling to save itself from the snares of the body.

The proliferation of this negative approach to the human body deformed Christian spirituality, marriage and sexuality, and had profoundly destructive effects on Christian charity and social justice. For if I am to live in constant suspicion of my body, careful to rein in its every appetite and deaden my ears to its voice, then I will not take seriously the demands that other bodies make on me. If bodies do not matter, then damage to bodies will not be taken seriously. In fact, we all know how bodily pain and suffering are presented as a good thing that unites us to the sufferings of Jesus Christ on the cross.

In the face of such teachings, the Christian imperative to love the neighbor as did the Good Samaritan can fade. We become like the priest and the Levite, concerned with things sacred and not to be bothered with a crime victim. I have no doubt that the American bishops' long silence and inaction around clergy pedophilia was due to interpreting it as violation of celibacy vows, and not as violation of the boys themselves. Bodies do not matter, but vows do. This is undoubtedly why we hardly hear sermons against wife-beating and other forms of domestic violence. It also explains why for centuries the church has ignored the economic, social and political oppression that drives women to prostitution, not to mention national and international trafficking in women, in favor of holding individual women responsible should any show themselves in the confessional. Blaming the victim is standard fare when we broach issues of the body.

Today I do not want to dwell on this history, but to examine what issues we face as Catholic women working on issues of body. The culture of postmodernity which is seeping into all corners of the world brings many positive but also some negative and very ambiguous aspects. How should we interpret postmodernity's insistence that the body is constructed, or inscribed? Is the body the self? What about the body and rights? Does the self have complete control of its body, or can that control be usurped in some situations?

The body is inscribed—by one's genes, one's culture, one's choices, and one's environment. The fact that the body is inscribed does not differentiate the body from the self, for selves are also inscribed. Our families, our friends, the institutions with which we have associated— everything in our experience has inscribed itself in some way into our selves. While we can refuse a specific inscription or two, we are more likely to only edit a very few of our environmental inscriptions. Ours is not the final word on what is inscribed into our selves; many of us have aspects of our selves that we would rather have obliterated. Sometimes our only option is to decide how.

Is the body the self? Yes, but not the whole self. When we examine the lives of people who have suffered ongoing pain in the body—victims of torture, chronic illness or chronic abuse—we find that maintaining some minimal sense of self is all that is possible. Pain takes over one's life as well as one's self. Theft of one's body is theft of one's self for the most part.[1]

And yet not completely. For all the trafficked women that give in to drugs and despair, for all the beaten wives and children who resign themselves to abuse, for all the victims of torture in the world who retreat into madness so as to avoid the pain, there is always a handful who find the resources—from within or without—to call up a self that overcomes the pain and resists the theft of himself/herself.

It is critical to accept the unity of the body and the self because we know that all damage done to bodies affects the self as well. But hope depends upon a recognition of the fact that the self can transcend body. This transcendence is not to be understood in terms of opposition, as in soul/body dualism. Rather, the body is the locus of the self, which the self can move beyond. Thus, we sometimes see in the dying an emotional and spiritual acceptance of death before we see the body die, and we recognize in that acceptance the transcendence of the self. Of course, it often happens that the body dies before there is emotional and spiritual acceptance of death; we interpret this as tragic.

For women, the issue of body is especially fraught in that women have been largely objectified as bodies only: bodies to be taken in sex, bodies to bear children, bodies to work in households, fields and sweatshops. It is no accident that the great majority of writing on bodies today is being done by feminists who are asking questions not only about the relation of body and soul, but of body and self.[2]

There is a general agreement among scholars that the contemporary Western notion of the self emerged only within the modern period. One of the clearest and best known descriptions of the process of that emergence is Charles Taylor's *Sources of the Self*.[3] Four of Taylor's descriptors of the modern self, summarized here by Robert Di Vito are: "1) the modern sense that human dignity lies in self-sufficiency and self-containment, achieved through radical disengagement from one's personal and social location in the world, 2) the modern feeling of personal unity and of having sharply defined personal boundaries, 3) the modern belief in 'inner depths,' and 4) the modern conviction that our humanity depends upon a capacity for autonomous and self-legislative action."[4] One premise of this article is that if the modern self is distinguished from the pre-modern self by these four criteria, the postmodern self now developing seems to be distinguished from the modern self especially by a new <u>absence</u> of (2) the feeling of personal unity and sharp boundaries of the self and (3) the belief in "inner depths" of a person, at the same time that (1) self-sufficiency and (4) autonomy as marks of the self continue to strengthen.

Within Christianity, modern understandings of the self have been varied, ranging from a focus on the self in relationship, to a focus on the moral self, often depicted as conscience, to the most traditional understanding of the self as soul. All of these are constructed in ways that reflect to differing degrees the body/soul dualism that has characterized Western thought. Perhaps the closest identification between self and body in Western understandings is the recent secular understanding of the self as self-consciousness and as located within, sometimes even co-terminus with, the brain.

It is interesting to explore to what extent self-references using "soul" language may have sometimes prefigured modern usage. When the mystic Marguerite Porete wrote The Mirror of Simple Souls[5] she presented "this simple soul" as her core self, a self-conscious self that yearns for union with God, relates to other persons for whom it feels love, responsibility and compassion, and grows historically through those relationships. Marguerite's Soul is in an extended dialogue with the teaching voices of Love and Reason, and is called in different directions by them, very much like depictions of personal conscience as aware of and responsive to conflicting voices that pressure it. In what follows I have assumed that while the self can be explored from various perspectives privileging different aspects of the self, our self identity— our central concept of ourselves, viewed from whatever standpoint— develops from the continuous interaction of historicity, relationality, and transcendental freedom as self-consciously experienced within the body of an individual human person. Sexual identity is one part of self-identity, a part that I will later argue seems to be declining in importance.

How is the self related to the body? In the contemporary Western world many have abandoned the dualist understanding of the self in favor of a more materialist conception. Our Bodies, Ourselves[6] the book title/slogan of the American women's movement, was originally intended as a riposte to the dualism model, an insistence that our selves are affected by what happens to our bodies, that physical abuse and neglect do damage the self as well as the body, and that knowledge and control of one's body <u>are</u> essential to the construction of self-hood. Classical dualism (Stoic or Christian variety) and the materialist *Our Bodies, Ourselves* view of self both focus on control of the body, the difference being that under dualism the focus is on controlling <u>what</u> the body does (good or evil), while in feminist materialism the focus is on <u>who</u> controls the body. In the Christian dualist model, the body begins as Other, and only when it has been thoroughly subordinated to the soul-self could it possibly become part of the self. Usually it remained a potential threat to the soul-self, only temporarily tamed by prayer and ascetic discipline.

While I do not believe that the phrase *Our Bodies, Ourselves* was intended to assert that the body constitutes the <u>entire</u> self, in the current phase of post-modernist culture, the claim that our bodies are us, extends the popular metaphor of physical brain as self to include all of the physical body, and also all reflex knowledge. The self has come to be understood as created not only through its own agency, through its own choices for good or evil, but also through the reflex knowledge of itself that it received from others who observed its agency or lack of agency, and its responses to that reflex knowledge.

Discussions of body and self connect to a number of other recent debates within academia, including those around the self as relational, and even more current, the debate between social constructionists and those described as essentialists, who argue for a givenness within all human persons. The relationality of the self is proved and is no longer hypothesis—certainly within contemporary Catholic thought. The development of the self is dependent upon relationships with others, including God, family and friends, the larger society, the natural world, and also relationship with oneself through reflection. This is a social constructionist stance, nuanced by insistence on transcendental freedom in humans and by the varied ability of particular bodies to convey data specific to agency. These, in turn, constitute a kind of residual givenness within a largely constructionist model.

In attempting to describe the relation between body and self in modernist and postmodernist terms, I will first review evidence of a strong link between body and self, then turn to evidence for the self as transcending body, before a preliminary attempt to integrate the evidence. As a feminist, I believe that we begin reflection based on experience, always limited by one's relational history. I am a middle class, late middle aged, white American wife, mother and grandmother, all of which inevitably skew my perspective on both body and self.

EVIDENCE FOR THE BODY AS SELF

Racial Bodies as Exceptions to Disembodied Christian Selves

Other than sex, race has probably been the body characteristic which has most influenced self historically. One's skin, hair and eye color, and the shape of one's body features proclaimed from what people and geographical location one came. Like sex, one's race was inalienable, an assignment that lasted a lifetime.

Racial and ethnic societies and their religions have often added to the biological signs of race, further marking bodies with signs such as male and female circumcision, ear and nose piercing, styles of beardedness, shaved faces or pates, distinctive hair styles, body-scarring and tattoos, and innumerable styles of dress and undress—all of these designating a body's membership in particular racial/ethnic groups. In some societies the <u>unmarked</u> body has also designated group membership.

The racial body has had a strong influence on individual consciousness of self whenever groups have come in contact with other races. Within Christian history there has been a dialectic between the dualist distrust of all bodies hence the call to convert all soul-selves, and an assumption that some bodies—e.g., those marked by another race, such as Moors, later Africans and Native Americans—were unsavable. We see this in the 1540s debate between Catholic clerics Bartolome de las Casas, who argued that the Indians were apt Christians, already practicing much of the gospel, and Juan Sepulveda, who declared that they were what Aristotle described as natural slaves incapable of responsibility for their own lives and salvation. Even las Casas asserted for a time that the true natural slaves were the Africans as their bodies survive enslavement better than the Indians.

During the centuries of slavery in the United States, many opposed the conversion of slaves, arguing that physical characteristics that distinguish Africans from their owners were evidence that the selves in these groups were different and lesser, despite the fact that the marginality of the body to Christian understandings of the soul-self should have led to the imputation of little or no significance to body differences.

Physical and Sexual Abuse as Demonstrating Body/Soul Connections

In the last quarter century there has been a plethora of research testifying to how abuse of the body (both physical and sexual) affects self-identity. Studies show that serious malnourishment during certain stages of fetal development mentally retards children.[7] Other studies show that crack users and children born addicted from crack-using mothers are hard-wired for addiction, so that the pathways of their brains seek out and maintain states of extreme excitation, to the detriment of their relationships and life choices. Children born of heroin addicts have delayed growth and motor development and permanent behavior abnormalities.[8]

Abuse provides even more examples. Whether we look at studies of the effects of rape, child sexual abuse, physical abuse of children, torture of political or military prisoners, or battlefield exposure on children, we see similar destructive patterns in the victims. These include fear, lack of trust, inability to form intimate relationships, and a generalized failure to protect oneself from future abuse because of deep-seated understandings of self as unworthy of protection and as incapable of being protected.[9] Victims are prone to depression and despair, and often demonstrate numbness to their own pain as well as to the pain of others. Treating others well becomes difficult or impossible when we have no way of knowing what will cause them pain. Moral teachings such as "Love your neighbor as yourself," or "Do unto others as you would like them do to you," assume that we feel our own pain and recognize what will cause pain to others. But if we do <u>not</u> feel our own pain, we lack a critical component of the capacity for moral agency.

We have become accustomed to seeing patterns not only of dysfunction but of self-destruction in the lives of persons who have suffered abusive body trauma.[10] Many of these abused persons pursue alcohol or drugs as paths to mind-numbing escape, well aware of and sometimes even welcoming the death-dealing potential of these escapes.

We have also become familiar with the opposite case: that is, the victim who attempts to deny his own victimization by taking on the abuser role and victimizing others. For reasons involving gender socialization and biological hormonal patterns, the latter are more typically male than female, though both responses are found in each sex.[11] For related gender socialization reasons, those females who become abusers themselves are much more likely to choose verbal and emotional abuse than physical or sexual abuse.

There is a clear and simple logic to both these responses to physical and sexual abuse. The parent who beats a child unnecessarily, the torturer who mutilates and threatens, the rapist who invades the victim's body—all are saying to their victims in their every touch: "You are not in control of your body; I am. I do to you what I will, not what you will. I make you feel what I want, not what you want. What you feel, what you want, what you will, does not count." Often the abuser teaches these lessons verbally as well as through touch. When the abuse is long-lasting or repeated, this message is virtually impossible to resist, for it is true in that it corresponds to the experience and memories of the victim.

The vast majority of our self-identity—our own concept of who we are—is reflex knowledge, reflected back to us from others. So there is real danger that the victim will learn the lesson of the abuser, because we are both programmed and accustomed to taking in reflex knowledge about ourselves and using it to construct our self-identity. This is also why abuse by persons we trust—a parent or relative, a pastor, a teacher, a psychiatrist—is the most damaging to the victim's self: their messages we are accustomed to trust completely, so they have greater access to our sense of self.

If victims do learn the abuser's lesson, they will not take responsibility for their lives, for in their experience, others are always in charge, and opposition is futile, even dangerous. Furthermore, after long periods of abuse, many victims dismiss or suppress feelings and desires which they cannot act upon and which others do not respond to. When we no longer recognize our feelings and desires, we have nothing to guide us in setting a course for ourselves. We drift, and become targets for the desires of others.

While the self continues to develop throughout the entirety of human life, it is most vulnerable to abuse during the formative years of infancy, childhood and youth, when the most basic elements of self-identity are being constructed. Resistance to abuse and recovery from abuse are always possible, but are usually much more difficult for children, especially when the abuse involved trusted persons as abusers, was extended over long periods, or was particularly severe (painful).

The research on this point is clear: abuse of the body by another, especially for children, wounds the self. But we must be careful in interpreting this research. It would be wrong, for example, to conclude from this evidence that ascetic practices, even when painful, damage the self. For so long as those practices are freely chosen by the self, and especially if they are also administered by the self, they do not send the abuser's message to the self, do not deny the self's control of the body, do not claim control for another, and do not dismiss the self's desires and feelings. When they are self-inflicted, even painful ascetic practices may be, as often claimed, methods of realizing, and focusing the attention of the self on the deep feelings and desires of the self.[12]

Chronic Illness and Disability

No one who has ever spent time with a chronically ill person doubts that chronic physical pain has a negative effect on the self. As Elaine Scarry pointed out in *The Body in Pain: The Making and Unmaking of the World*, pain focuses our attention inward, making it difficult to attend to any Other, to the world outside our body.[13] Pain narrows our world to our own body, making us insensitive to, even uncaring of, Others and their pain. This is a primary reason why the Catholic Church has directed physicians to use pain-killers to reduce or eliminate pain in the dying, so that dying persons can attend to the work of the self— resolving relationships with Others, attending to familial and career responsibilities, settling personal affairs, making peace with God.[14] At the same time the Catholic Church has set a limit on the use of pain-killers—avoiding unconsciousness whenever possible—until this work of the self is complete.

One of the things many parents and nurses realized long before science confirmed it in the last decades is the ability of touch to alleviate pain. A number of controlled studies have demonstrated the ability of therapeutic touch to relieve not only chronic pain, but also pain in childbirth.[15] The parent who kisses a bump or a scrape to make it better actually can make it feel better, because touch releases pain blocking endorphins into the bloodstream. Nurses in hospitals and nursing homes know that holding the hand of a person in pain, rubbing patients' backs or legs, or stroking their shoulder, alleviates some of the pain.

Education studies show that elementary school students learn best in classrooms where they feel secure and cherished, where kindergarten children take turns sitting in teacher's lap for story time, where teachers walk among the desks of older students, patting a head or shoulder in encouragement as children work.[16] It is often assumed that as children age in elementary school the intimacy of teacher to student touch should decrease. But the needs of older children to be touched are not less than those of the young. The difference is that the self of these older children is more formed, has clearer boundaries, and those boundaries need to be respected. This does not mean we should not touch older children who actually may be much more in need of supportive touch. It only means that with older children we must take more care to ensure that our touch is welcome. Even with young children, touch should never be imposed against the child's will except in short term emergency situations where the child's safety is at stake. Permission to touch can be asked and granted in a variety of ways, verbal and non-verbal, but as children age permission should be increasingly explicit and verbal. Obviously, such touch should always be non-genital and non-demanding, and it should be reciprocal. There is something wrong in a situation in which teachers touch children but children are not allowed to touch teachers. Once a relationship that includes supportive touch is established, consent can be assumed until there are verbal or nonverbal revocations of that consent.

Studies show that the sick and elderly who are touched and stroked not only have lower levels of pain, they also experience less depression and have higher levels of verbal interaction with others.[17] In the US, many old persons whose children have died or moved away are forced to replace spontaneous hugs of affection with the more impersonal touch of barbers, beauticians and physical therapists. The body connects us to others in a variety of very different ways, and since our sense of self is grounded in relationship to others, the experiences of the body, both positive and negative, influence our self-identity. What does it say about our self-worth, if the only way we are touched is by people we pay?

SUPPORT FOR SELF AS TRANSCENDING BODY

Though we have seen a great deal of data on conditions and circumstances in which body experience strongly influences, both positively and negatively, the formation of self, there is also a great deal of data that suggests the usefulness of retaining some degree of body-transcendence as found in the earlier Christian dualist model of self.

Physical Disability

The sick and physically disabled increasingly refuse to be identified with their disabled bodies. For one, "Persons With AIDS" (PWAs) prefer this term instead of "AIDS victims" or "AIDS patients" because they are primarily persons, who only accidentally happen to have contracted AIDS. Physically disabled persons often use metaphors that evoke traditional soul imagery as when, for example, a wheelchair-bound grandmother in my parish insists: "My legs can't walk but I can still dance with joy!" Many assert that disability in some spheres is usually compensated in some other area of human life, so that the disability does not diminish the self. For instance, the severe disabilities of author Helen Keller, physicist Stephen Hawking, and even quadriplegic actor Christopher Reeves failed to diminish them.

One may easily agree that the body can be transcended and does not necessarily determine the self. But we must recognize that while the body does not determine the self, it does ground the self. The impact that bodily disability has on the self seems to be dependent upon both the type of bodily disability and the context in which the disability is lived out. Alzheimer's, for example, gradually obliterates the self as it destroys the relationships and memories that constitute and maintain self-identity.

On the other hand, context is also critical to the possibility of body transcendence. A paraplegic child without access to both a wheelchair and a world with wheelchair ramps will have limited material resources for transcending the disability even though her own personal energy and commitment may be superior to that of more privileged paraplegics. Mild or moderate mental retardation is generally less disabling in agricultural societies, where physical health and strength are more important for both employment and participation in everyday social life than the literacy and abstract thought so necessary in our own highly technical society. The point here is that granting that the self transcends the body in some ways does not necessarily root transcendence in the human will or any other aspect of the self. Transcendence may be grounded in a combination of factors, many of which are social and environmental.

Aging
Aging is another bodily experience which affects self-hood and to which individuals and societies respond very differently. In youth-oriented cultures such as our own, aging persons use a variety of aids, from hair dye, cosmetic surgery, Viagra, joint replacements and other surgeries and treatments to deny or disguise the changes that age brings to the body. In some other cultures, age is still considered (though less and less) to confer dignity and authority. Persons anticipate grandparenthood and relish the day they are referred to as "greybeards" for the status of elder thus conferred on them. They feel little impulse to transcend the aging process, and seem to feel less fear of death than their counterparts in youth-oriented societies.

To the extent that humans experience aging as limitation—and I think we all do at some level as we need glasses or stronger lenses to read or drive, as our sexual drive or capacity gradually decreases, as we find ourselves cat-napping during the day, unable to pull all-nighters of work or partying or to drive non-stop through the night—the concept of transcendence over the body has increasing value for helping us sustain the energy for living a full life.

Sexual Victimization

Within the women's movement, advocates for sexual victims agree on the value of the concept of body transcendence. For while they insist that abuse of the body negatively affects the self, they also protest any cult of victimhood. To be victimized does not create a victim-self. The self can not only survive victimization, it can utilize the experience to grow. Their argument resembles St. Augustine's on faith and doubt: that one who has never doubted cannot have strong faith, for faith becomes strong by overcoming doubt. Sexual victimization creates a doubt about the self, its worth, its strength, its role. Overcoming that doubt, claiming control of one's body and one's life, often creates a much stronger self—and certainly greater self-knowledge of—and faith in—that strong self than would have occurred without the experience of abuse.

Race

Even in the area of race, there are now signs of the possibility of transcendence. For over 15 years in the US, rising numbers of persons refuse to fill out the race question on census, health, and other licensing forms. Ads in movie theaters and newspapers argue that race is a category without scientific basis, one that should be rejected and ignored. In multiracial nations growing numbers refuse to identify with only one part of their biological and cultural heritage. Recently one of my students told me, "I'm Cuban-American. Nationality is easy, because all of my grandparents are Cuban. But one grandmother is Jewish, married to a grandfather of Catholic Spanish descent. My other grandmother was brown-skinned with African features, and her husband was half-Chinese. What does that make me?"

At the same time that interracial populations continue to grow, there is some evidence that, in deference to capitalist values, race is giving way to class as the basis for exclusion. For example, African Americans with Ivy League educations and million-dollar incomes increasingly claim to have never experienced racial discrimination. Such examples are not limited to the developed world. On the other hand, religious and other cultural differences seem increasingly difficult to transcend.

THE BODY AND SEXUAL IDENTITY

All of these examples suggest that the body cannot simply be denied or ignored by the self—it must be addressed in virtually every area and stage of life. What happens to the body affects the self. But the body does not determine the self.

For Christians, the very word "body" is sexually freighted. While the concept of bodily transcendence may have originated in the doctrine of the Resurrection, the experiential context for theological interpretations of transcendence of the body included negative attitudes toward sexuality, reinforced by the adoption of vowed celibacy as the preferred vocation and required for any form of ministry.

Books such as Peter Brown's *The Body and Society*[18] teach that Gnostic aversion to physicality and materiality was not the only basis for much of the early advocacy of virginity in the church. Virginity was a conscious rejection of the then current model of marriage in favor of a singleness that represented freedom in Christ to accept the charisms of the Spirit and develop them in new activities and associations. This seems to have been especially true for women, who, being more constrained by the restrictions of marriage, had more to gain from virginity.

This historical pattern is also relevant to the rapid acceptance of artificial contraception in the twentieth century. Contraception offers women the freedom to pursue the charisms of the Spirit, to develop more than their maternal housewifely gifts. A great deal of data shows that most working mothers would like to combine an important role as childcare-giver with activities outside the home, that allow them both social participation and contribution, as well as economic independence. Relatively effective modern contraception has helped ensure that pursuing a variety of the charisms of the Spirit as a female need not always require virginity.

Because the Christian theological tradition was largely written by men, and celibate men at that, the treatment of body—of sexuality— and self usually focused not on fertility, but on sexual desire. Today in the Western Catholic Church, there is popular rejection of much of previous pastoral and theological teaching on sexual desire because of a popular experientially based expansion of Augustine's third blessing of marriage, the sacramental bond. Christian tradition of the past emphasized the first two blessings of marriage, offspring and avoidance of sin, and tended to describe the sacramental bond as an indissoluble cooperative agreement oriented to the shared rearing of children. Today many Catholic couples understand the sacramental bond primarily in terms of intimacy and emotional commitment, which are at least initially based in the marital experience of shared sexual delight. They readily identify with what Gallagher, Mahoney, Wilczak and Rousseau wrote in *Embodied in Love*[19] about marital sex functioning as a school for love. Gallagher et al. described marital sex as an experience of opening one's body and by implication one's spirit—becoming vulnerable—to the spouse, and being rewarded with overwhelming pleasure for taking that risk. That pleasure is joyful, and like all joy, overflows onto others around the couple, making the couple more open to each other, to their children, to friends and neighbors. One reason sexual pleasure has this capacity to expand love is, as Patricia Jung explains, it "awakens us to our own loveliness and worth," to self-love, as well as helping to sustain relationships.[20]

Shared sexual pleasure creates a trust and openness that allows emotional sharing, which in turn helps us to know and be known by the spouse. When we are intimately known by the Other who continues to love and cherish us, we can develop the courage to accept moral challenges, such as helping the spouse perfect himself/herself (a very sensitive business!) and we can reach out to comfort each other in life's inevitable tragedies.

Today there is a general understanding among Christians that we should not approach sexual desire as something to be renounced or denied, but rather as something like a premoral good. Sexual desire can clearly be misused, as in pornography, some types of sexual violence (other types not being related to sexual desire at all), seduction or sexual harassment. But sexual desire is understood as a general good, because it can produce physical pleasure, relational bonding, and the gift of children.

Sexual desire can also be sublimated. Sexual desire is one form of eroticism, of sensuality, an outpouring of human energy, of zest for life. Sublimation of sexual desire can transform the energy in sexual desire into other forms of creative energy: art, science, community service, even theology—magnificent human achievements that enrich community life. This is one reason why it would be a mistake to shift from a moral and spiritual preference for virginity to an insistence, as found in Judaic, Islamic and Hindu traditions, on marriage and procreation as normative vocations. The Spirit gives a variety of gifts, a variety of calls. The monastic vocation is a valuable call, and the capacity to live it is a communally as well as personally valuable gift. The body—here in the form of sexual desire—should not be denied or renounced, nor should sublimation be made normative. Humans should exercise a great deal of freedom in determining how we interpret the role of our bodies in a response to the call of the Spirit, both as individual selves and as members of particular cultures under particular historical circumstances.

There are also moral pressures on us in the employment of sexual desire. The ecological crisis today, due both to the increase in global population and to profligate resource use by rich parts of that population, suggests that human sexual desire should be less and less identified with procreation. A certain amount of de-linking of self from physical roles such as motherhood and fatherhood is called for. Couples who in the past would understand their own social significance as resting on their being the parents of a dozen children, ought therefore to be persuaded to ground their self-identity in a combination of roles, not simply parenthood. This demographic transition is a daunting one in poor nations where there are fewer alternative roles available from which to construct the self.

THE SEXUAL SELF

Until the twentieth century, virtually everyone in the world understood that when a child was born, its genitalia indicated what we now distinguish as sex, gender and sexual orientation. If the child had a penis, it was understood that it was a male, would take on the social roles accepted for males in that society, and would be sexually attracted to females.

During the twentieth century, these three deductions from genitalia were challenged. First gender was separated from genitalia through anthropologists' study of other societies in which the roles assigned to males and females were very different from those assignments in our society. We came to see gender as constructed, as society-specific. The women's movement, in which women successfully adopted roles hitherto restricted to men, greatly accelerated the dissemination of this understanding. Second, sexual orientation was separated from genitalia. Beginning with Alfred Kinsey,[21] through the work of Evelyn Hooker,[22] and many others, homosexuality came to be understood not as deviance, but as an alternative orientation, which many scientists now believe is based on a genetic predisposition differentially affected by environment. Having a penis neither disqualifies one from being a nurse or a housewife, nor ensures that one will be sexually attracted to females. Note that both of these steps involved de-linking body from one part of sexual identity. One's body does not in any direct way determine gender or orientation.

Most of us have accepted these two revisions in previous understandings of sexuality. We understand sex to refer to biological sex, gender to refer to roles based on social interpretations of sex, and sexual orientation to refer to sexual attraction to the same or other sex. However, we have not yet learned adequate language to deal with the latest challenge, which undermines the single remaining direct link between body and sexual identity: sex. Biologists, influenced by the new openness on gender and orientation, have gradually come to concede that sex is not simple, either, and is much more open-ended than commonly believed. What we call sex—maleness or femaleness— is actually composed of six different biological components, which do not always fall into the dimorphic patterns of maleness and femaleness. Neither is there any clarity as to the priority of these factors in deciding sex—some people decide sex based on the genitalia, others based on chromosomal sex, and yet others on the sex of the brain (which often influences the sexual identity that is experienced by the person). Within the scientific community of the US we find all these different ways of assigning sex based on biological criteria. But even <u>within</u> these criteria there is no clear dimorphic pattern. For example, while the majority of humans are either XX or XY, there are many millions of humans whose chromosomal pattern is XO, XYY, XXY, XXX and even very rarely XXXX. Whether we look at hormone levels or the effect of hormones on the brain (brain sex), we see a spectrum stretching between two poles. Both the dimorphic paradigm for understanding sex, and the understanding of sex as biologically given rather than socially constructed, are eroding. The most persuasive evidence of this is the scientific evidence, but the social evidence is also amassing. Youth culture in the West is increasingly unisex in appearance, and global media spread this culture. Female models, often understood as physically ideal women, increasingly have the bodies, haircuts, and often the clothes of young males. Cross-dressing is hip among entertainers, even some sports figures. On the beach in Miami, Rio, Maui, and the Riviera one frequently sees transsexuals in various stages of the transformation process. Media language has adapted: among the politically correct, the phrase "gay, lesbian, transsexual and transgendered persons" now rolls off the tip of the tongue.

Thus at the same time that the human body is less and less understood as a given and more and more as open to (re)construction, so the sex of the human body is independently undergoing a similar transformation from given to constructed in our social understanding. This transfer of sex from the category of biologically given to socially constructed further reduces the impact of body on sexual identity.

LATE MODERN CULTURE

Late modern society, especially youth culture, is, I think, groping for a new understanding of the relationship of body to identity. Youth, who are still constructing their self-identities within the reflex process began in infancy, certainly understand the body as central to the self they project at any given moment. Thus we see the multicolored and avant-garde cuts of hair on youth all over the world; metal rings hanging from eyebrows, tongues, noses, ears, navels, and other more private parts of the body; and scars or tattoos on shoulders, ankles, breasts and buttocks. In developed nations, we also see young men and women crowding the gyms to change their physiques.

On the other hand, the body is not so much the source that influences the formation of self-identity, or even sexual identity, as it was in the past. It is now more the slate upon which one expresses one's self of the moment. While the body is not a *tabula rasa*, it is increasingly understood as a medium for communication rather than as either a communicating self or as an (ideally) dependent appendage of the moral self.

The meaning of the body is changing, with serious consequences for sexual identity. Increasingly, we have come to understand the body as constructed, as both sculpted and engineered. We do some of the sculpting ourselves, and rely on professionals to do the engineering—surgeons, physical trainers, cosmeticians, tattoo artists, nutritionists, hair stylists, etc. I have a mother with two artificial knees, a son with a kidney transplant and a testicular prosthesis, a sister-in-law with two hip replacements, a sister with breast implants, and a second cousin who is a male to female transsexual! If the Enlightenment led to the Age of Science and the recognition of humans as co-creators of the <u>world</u>, we now have come to see ourselves as co-creators of our very <u>selves</u>, including our bodies. As this understanding spread, it was inevitable that perceptions of sex, based as they were on the givenness of the body, would be eroded.

Today, while the embodiedness of every human person remains, fewer and fewer aspects of that body are accepted as they are. We have claimed the right and ability to control many aspects of health, physical ability/disability, sexuality, and appearance, and are, in genetic surgery, probably on the verge of being able to engineer our children or grandchildren to a much greater extent. Science fiction seems only a generation ahead of our technology, pushing us in a direction where the self is still linked to a body, but where bodies may be exchanged at will, the way we are increasingly exchanging body parts and incorporating manufactured parts (pacemakers, artificial hearts, plastic joints and skin) today.

It seems to me that the first and fourth of Taylor's aspects of the modern self (radical disengagement from the personal and social location in the world, and the modern conviction that our humanity depends upon capacity for autonomous and self-legislative action) have, if they have changed at all, probably strengthened in the late modern/postmodern period. But youth today do not have nearly so strong a sense of personal unity and defined boundaries, nor are they as sure as previous modern generations that all of us have "inner depths."

I suspect that the shift toward experiencing the body as constructed has a great deal to do with lessening the sense of personal unity and well defined personal boundaries. It is difficult to maintain strong personal boundaries when we are at the same time incorporating into ourselves, parts of other people, mechanical parts, as well as varying mind-altering substances (tranquilizers, anti-depressants, and a host of other psychiatric drugs). Nor are these changes limited to small elites in a few parts of the world; many of them, including artificial body parts, are gradually becoming standard treatment even in poor war-torn countries of Africa and Asia. Moreover, how can we maintain impermeable boundaries while turning the reconstruction and maintenance of our bodies and minds over to a variety of experts, from plastic surgeons to physical trainers to therapists?

In the shift from premodernity to modernity, human beings developed stronger individual boundaries, insulating themselves from the extended family and other communities in which they had been embedded. Oddly enough, those same boundaries, are becoming more and more permeable—not to personal or communal relations, but to impersonal, instrumental relations.

At the same time, the sense that human beings have "inner depths" seems to be seriously eroding, also under the influence of instrumentalism. For example, if we look at the development of the human rights tradition over the last 200–300 years, it is apparent that until recently, human rights were understood as terms referring to the inner depths of the human person, as an inalienable quality of dignity and worth. Today human rights are increasingly understood as a useful convention, as an instrument for achieving justice and social stability for humans but as lacking any clear and consistent foundation.

As we have come to understand the human person as more open to construction, and less as having a given character, we have become less and less able to define the "inner depths" and thus less and less sure that they exist. Some aspects of late modern technological culture support such doubt—intolerance for boredom, solitude and quiet, extreme distractibility and short attention spans. To the extent that the body now serves as an advertisement of the momentary self, understandings of inner depths are likely to collapse into the "next self" which will also be advertised by the body. So much is it taken for granted that persons can, do, and should express in and on the body all that they are, that sometimes one hears expressions not only of wonder, but of anger and betrayal, upon the discovery of covert depths in friends and acquaintances.

Constructionist experiences of body and constructionist models of self provoke specific, complex questions for theology and moral theology, some of which have been long debated within the church. We are all familiar with bioethical discussions concerning possible limits to human reconstruction. Can humanity's status as co-creator with God authorize a germ-line therapy that transforms not only ourselves, but our descendants? What other moral limits, if any, might exist on human authority to reconstruct the created nature of human beings?

Similarly, questions of the continuity of the self have long been central to discussions of divorce; ministers, priests, lawyers and judges hear couples who report that one or the other spouse has become a stranger, not the person to whom the vows were made. Today this argument has become more common, and more persuasive, not only in the context of marriage, but in a variety of other relationships throughout the lifespan.

If the body is plastic in the sense of being radically reconstructable and the sexual self is reversible within all the sexual categories of sex, gender and sexual orientation, then the question arises as to whether the self is continuous or discontinuous. When I was young the question of the continuity of the self within religious studies was primarily focused on resurrection and reincarnation. Did the resurrected Jesus have the same self as before? Would we? And what aspects of a former self would be reincarnated in the new self within an eastern system of reincarnation? But the relevant time span in the question of the continuity of the self has now drastically shortened. My students ask how they can be sure that they are the same self from month to month, or even from one location to another. Some of my Indonesian students say that they are different persons in their villages than they are at university in Java. One US student stopped going to confession because it was always a different person confessing the sin than had committed the sin. At one level, this sounds like a combination of rationalization, science fiction and perhaps mental illness. But many of these students of mine lived through serious life transitions that propel such questions. Some were refugees on fragile rafts on which many died before reaching the US. Others tell of parents or siblings who survived months of torture in their native lands, only to emerge as different persons altogether. Some saw parents go through tough divorces that led to radically new life paths, even seemingly new personalities. They understand human relationality to mean that new relations and conditions will change the self. They ask at what point does the change become so great that this is a different self?

This is a much broader question than fundamental option theology. If fundamental option understands the self as developmental, as an onion with many layers, this new postmodern self is like nothing organic. This self is like a contemporary movie made up of multiple short vignettes. There is no core, the vignettes are not necessarily in chronological order, and they may have entirely different characters in them. Unlike fundamental option, where a "break" in the self is understood in terms of a fundamental shift toward or away from God (the good), in the postmodern example the new path is not necessarily better or worse morally than the old one; it is "merely" radically different, in ways that cause the self to become radically different.

At a moral level, this possibility that the embodied person is not continuous, but a series of discontinuous selves, is uncomfortable. To many it will seem too like schizophrenia. More to the point, what would religious conversion mean to a series of selves? Which of the selves is saved? What could salvation mean?

As if these questions are not daunting enough, there is another whole set of challenges to our understanding of the relationship of body to self, especially to the moral, relational self, coming from scholars such as Linda Holler, in her *Erotic Touch: The Role of Touch in Moral Agency*. Holler's survey of research on autistic persons and accident victims with frontal lobe brain damage shows that moral judgment is profoundly impaired when the sensory and affective mechanisms of the brain dysfunction, such that one cannot access the feelings of others. Holler argues that we have in fact misunderstood—ignored— the mutual interaction between our bodies and our moral, relational selves. The body does not merely act out the self; the body sets the initial constraints on the development of the self and is then physically affected by the conditions, decisions and choices of the self.

Holler explains that autistic persons experience physical touch as disturbing, even seriously painful. Because they are overly sensitive to all sensory stimuli, autistics are unable to physically connect with others—often unable to make even eye contact comfortably—so that they have no access to the feelings of others. They thus have little ability to take in the reactions of others to their own behavior or to make clear demands on others to get their needs met. They are symbols, says Holler, of the isolated individual that contemporary thinkers have critiqued in Cartesian thought. Their isolation is a serious obstacle to the ordinary process of moral development. Without access to the feelings of others, even the most basic of moral teachings fails to instruct.

Holler also cites Antonio Damasio's work *Descartes' Error*[23] to explain how frontal lobe-damaged patients have lost the ability to connect emotions with situations. Holler points out that there are many persons with mild degrees of autism who "pass" in our society, just as there are many with frontal lobe disorders.

Other kinds of variation in sensitivity to others appear to be not biologically based, but socialized.[24] Recent research shows that when given pictures of people's faces showing various emotions, American females score much higher at reading the emotions portrayed than do American males.[25] Interestingly enough, while women displayed equal ability in deciphering both positive and negative emotions, men scored almost as well as the women in recognizing positive emotions, but very poorly on recognizing negative emotions. It is not clear how this lesser male sensitivity to emotion in others is learned, but since male infants are touched less than females, and father-son touching in our culture is minimal compared to mother-daughter touching, we have some clues for further exploration.[26]

CONCLUSIONS

Is there any way to integrate all these observations into a cohesive picture of the relationship of body and self? Clearly, body grounds the self, but does not exhaust the self, which can develop an element, even a strong and prominent one, of transcendence over the body. Beyond this, here are a number of tentative observations:

1. Oddly enough, it is in the area of sexuality, which has thoroughly convulsed so many late modern societies, that the conclusion is perhaps the clearest. If none of the sexual aspects of the self are intrinsic to self-identity, but are in fact accidental in the sense of being reversible or capable of reconstruction, then it makes no sense to base moral rules upon these aspects. Acts which are mutually pleasurable, responsible and performed out of love do not become evil because one of the partners takes on a new sex, gender or orientation. Sexuality is an area of life in which the same Christian moral guidelines should apply as are applied in other areas of life. At the same time, vows should be kept whenever possible.

2. While I am willing to entertain the possibility of discontinuous selves in some circumstances, it seems to me that human beings have a radical capacity for change. Many people play out one role and begin a very different one with total aplomb: chairman of the board types who retire to a fishing lake, bereft empty nest homemakers who go to law school and become prosecutors, widows and widowers who remarry persons totally unlike their beloved dead spouses then lead very different lives, migrants who adopt whole new cultures and mores, paroled murderers who open half-way houses for ex-cons. Changed self is not by itself an indication of different self. We should not take our symbols—like baptismal immersion and new names—too literally. The conversions we see in the lives of many of the saints were radical changes, but an important part of the life of the saint was accepting responsibility for the self that he or she had been before conversion.

3. This brings up the major danger with the idea of discontinuous selves: it could undermine social responsibility. If I am a new self, then <u>am</u> I no longer bound by the promises made by my former self and the responsibilities that self accepted? It would be a mistake to argue that the sacramental system—reconciliation, for example—requires continuous self—for anthropology must ground theology, and not the reverse. But the common human good is one important aspect of anthropology. We now have too many abandoned children all over the world, not to mention other commitments which need to be kept. Human relationality requires that we be able to trust each other to keep our promises, to accept our responsibilities. The bottom line here must be that if we do understand ourselves as taking on new selves, at least some of the most basic kinds of person to person responsibilities must transfer to the new self.

Unfortunately emphasis on this kind of promise-keeping has not always been a strong point in the history of the church. Too many converts were, and sometimes in polygynous societies today still are, allowed to abandon their spouses and children as no longer the responsibility of the new self they became in baptism. This history is echoed in some US dioceses today when Catholic bishops remind married priests that they can have their vocations back if they will abandon their families.

4. What kind of situations might justify understanding the selves of a single body as discontinuous? If the self is formed through a social process involving reflex knowledge, it is maintained both by memory and by continuing relationships, which seem to be interlinked. The elderly may be more vulnerable to Alzheimer's when they have smaller and less interactive social circles. Conversely, the deterioration of memory and all its associated processes seems to be delayed in Alzheimer's patients who have sustained interaction with persons of whom they have long memories. Our selves are to some extent both what we think (have thought) we are and what other people think (have thought) we are. Thus large scale, persistent memory loss, especially when coupled with loss of basic relations of the self, could constitute the conditions for the emergence of a new self.

5. How should we understand the self in the case of patients with Alzheimer's? Those of us who have dealt with Alzheimer's know that this disease does not merely cause its victims to regress to earlier stages in their lives, but it can alter the basic personality structure, making calm and pacific persons, aggressive; fearless adventurers, fearful and paranoid. We can disagree as to whether the new "self" is rooted in suppressed aspects of the old self, or whether it is produced by the random damage of the disease process in the brain. But we do not understand it as the same self no matter how long it endures, anymore than we regard the nonsensical ravings of someone coming out of anesthesia as indicating a new self. In these cases, we normally speak of the death or absence of the self, as if there is no new self at all. This is apt language for rapidly progressing cases of Alzheimer's, in which the altered self quickly loses speech and the ability to communicate altogether, leaving many families and caretakers without a way to understand the human person slowly deteriorating before them.

In the cases of persons who have undergone severe trauma to the brain resulting in radically different emotions and behaviors, we can read the evidence as indicating either a second self or a damaged self. In the cases described by Damasio we would be hard put to describe the post-trauma self as equal to but different from the former self—the latter self is clearly defective, unable to function successfully because of diminished capacity to receive communications and/or to process incoming data and respond appropriately. But there are many other cases which are not nearly so clear-cut. We need much more information on the relationship between the mechanisms of the brain, human emotions, and human behavior. We need such information for purposes of pastoral care and applied ethics.

6. Perhaps the biggest challenge to both contemporary moral theology and education today is the autistics. The dominant model of moral education is a process of conscience formation which takes for granted that the self whose conscience is in formation, accurately reads sensory input from his/her own body and the verbal and nonverbal signals of others. But autistics cannot access information on the emotional impact

of their decisions and actions on others, and consequently, must base a large part of their moral decisions on external rules. We must rethink the process of the construction of human selves with more attention to the differences of bodies, more mindful that there may well be more than one model of construction—even adequate construction—at work. In some ways, the autistic self is like the pre-modern self, more focused on the external than the internal, on the social rather than the personal. Within a pluralist system of morality, one that recognizes more than one method of moral development, a more pre-modern self is not necessarily a moral disadvantage. Modernity has certainly had no monopoly on sainthood.

Right now, the evidence indicates that the body does set definite limits on the initial formation of the self, that ideally tactile nurture during the earliest years correlates with the development of those physical mechanisms that support the intellectual, emotional and moral capacities of the emergent self, and that interaction with others is necessary to develop those capacities. The largest absent piece of biological/psychological evidence for development of the self relates to aging and death, however. We can hope in the next decade or so to discover to what extent the data—now inconclusive—supports a common religious assumption that the process of advanced aging includes a gradual withdrawal from human relationships and the concerns of this world and the development of a more inward, spiritual focus.

NOTES

1   Elaine Scarry, *The Body in Pain: The Making and Unmaking of the World* (New York and Oxford: Oxford University Press, 1985).

2   Katie Conboy, Nadia Medina, and Sarah Stanbury, eds., *Writing on the Body: Female Embodiment and Feminist Theory* (New York: Columbia University Press, 1997); Jean Arthurs and Jean Grimshaw, eds., *Women's Bodies: Discipline and Transgression* (London and New York: Cassell, 1999); Judith Butler, *Bodies That Matter: On the Discursive Limits of "Sex"* (New York: Routledge, 1993); James B. Nelson, *Body Theology* (Louisville, KY: Westminster/John Knox, 1992); Caroline Walker Bynum, *Fragmentation and Redemption: Essays on Gender and the Human Body in Medieval Religion* (New York: Zone, 1992).

3   Charles Taylor, *Sources of the Self: The Making of the Modern Identity* (Cambridge, MA: Harvard University Press, 1989).

4   Robert A. Di Vito, "Old Testament Anthropology and the Construction of Personal Identity," *Catholic Biblical Quarterly* 61 (1999): 217–39, citing Taylor, *Sources*, 111–26.

5   Marguerite Porete, *The Mirror of Simple Souls*, trans. Ellen K. Babinsky (New York: Paulist, 1993).

6   Boston Women's Health Book Collective, *Our Bodies, Ourselves* (New York: Simon and Shuster, 1969) as well as the 1976 second edition and the 1984 *The New Our Bodies, Ourselves*.

7   M. L. Oster-Granite, F. F. Ebner, "Developmental Processes and the Pathophysiology of Mental Retardation," *Mental Retardation and Developmental Disabilities Research Reviews* 2, no. 4 (1996): 197–208; H. A. Delemarre-van de Waal, "Environmental Factors Influencing Growth and Pubertal Development," *Environmental Health Perspectives* 101, no. 2 (1993): 39–44.

8   Dianne Dunagan and Danni Odom-Winn, "Crack Kids" in *School: What to Do/How to Do It* (Freeport, NY: Educational Activities, 1991); R. A. Bashore, J. S. Ketchum, K. J. Staisch, C. T. Barrett, and E. G. Zimmerman, "Heroin Addiction and Pregnancy," *Western Journal of Medicine* 134, no. 6 (1981): 506–14. The effects of drugs and alcohol on the fetus are complex; some animal studies show deleterious effects not directly from drugs or alcohol, but from the malnutrition they induce: H. L. Bartley, I. R. Coyle, and G. Singer, "The Effects of Alcohol Induced Malnutrition in Pregnancy on Offspring Brain and Behavioral Development," *Pharmacology, Biochemistry and Behavior* 19, no. 3 (Sept. 1983): 513–18.

9   Diana E. H. Russell, *The Secret Trauma: Incest in the Lives of Girls and Women* (New York: Basic Books, 1988), 172–73.

10 L. Young, "Sexual Abuse and the Problem of Embodiment," *Child Abuse and Neglect* 16 (1992): 89–100; R. Krugman, J. Bays, D. Chadwick, C. Levitt, M. McHugh, and J. Whitworth, "Guidelines for the Evaluation of Sexual Abuse

of Children," *Pediatrics* 87 (1991): 254–60. For more complete treatment, see Chapter 6 of my *Body, Sex and Pleasure: Reconstructing Christian Sexual Ethics* (Cleveland, Ohio: Pilgrim, 1994).

[11] Men in most cultures, certainly in the West, are socialized to dominate women and children. But there is more than socialization at work. Persons of both sexes exposed to stress or threat produce higher levels of adrenalin and cortisol. But males also produce testicular testosterone, which quickens and heightens aggression. Daniel Goleman, "The Experience of Touch: Research Points to a Key Role in Growth," *New York Times Magazine*, 2 February 1988.

[12] Edith Wyschograd, *Saints and Postmodernism: Revisioning Moral Philosophy* (Chicago: University of Chicago Press, 1990), 37–41.

[13] Scarry, *The Body in Pain*.

[14] Sacred Congregation for the Doctrine of the Faith, "Declaration on Euthanasia," 5 May 1980, in *Bioethics: An Anthology*, ed., Helga Kuhse and Peter Singer (Massachusetts: Blackwell, 1999).

[15] P. Simkin and M. O'Hara, "Nonpharmacologic Relief of Pain During Labor: Systematic Reviews of Five Methods," *American Journal of Obstetrics and Gynecology* 186, no. 5 (May 2002): 131–59; S. Gormally, L. Wertheim, R. Alkawaf, N. Calinoiu, S. N. Young, "Contact and Nutrient Caregiving Effects on Newborn Pain Responses," *Developmental Medicine and Child Neurology* 43, no. 1 (January 2001): ·28–38; D. W. Smith, P. Arnstein, K. C. Rosa, and C. Wells-Federman, "Effects of Integrating Therapeutic Touch into a Cognitive Behavioral Pain Management Program. Report of a Pilot Clinical Trial," *Journal of Holistic Nursing* 20, no. 4 (December 2002): 367–87; and D. S. Wilkinson, P. L. Knox, J. E. Chapman, T. L. Johnson, N. Barbour, Y. Miles and A. Reel, "The Clinical Effectiveness of Healing Touch," *Journal of Alternative and Complementary Medicine* 8, no. 1 (February 2002): 33–47.

[16] Kevin Wheldall, et al., "A Touch of Reinforcement: The Effects of Contingent Teacher Touch on the Classroom Behavior of Young Children," *Educational Review* 38, no. 3 (1986): 207–16; Tiffany Field, "Preschoolers in America are Touched Less and are More Aggressive than Preschoolers in France," *Early Childhood Development and Care* 151 (April 1999): 11–17; Marlene Greenspan, "Therapeutic Touch and Healing Meditation: A Threesome with Education," *Early Childhood Development and Care* 98 (1994): 121–29; Tiffany Field et al., "Touching in Infant, Toddler and Preschool Nurseries," *Early Childhood Development and Care* 98 (1994):113–20.

[17] Christine M. Rinck et al., "Interpersonal Touch among Residents of Homes for the Elderly," *Journal of Communication* 30, no. 2 (Spring 1980): 44–47; Martin S. Remland et al., "Interpersonal Distance, Body Orientation, and Touch: Effects of Culture, Gender and Age," *Journal of Social Psychology* 135, no. 3 (June 1995): 281–97 and Beverly G. Willison and Robert L. Masson, "The Role of Touch in Therapy: An Adjunct to Communication," *Journal of*

Counseling and Development 64, no. 8 (April 1996): 497–500.

[18] Peter Brown, *The Body and Society: Men, Women and Sexual Renunciation in Early Christianity* (New York: Columbia University, 1988).

[19] Charles A. Gallagher, George A. Maloney, Mary F. Rousseau and Paul F. Wilczak, *Embodied in Love: Sacramental Spirituality and Sexual Intimacy* (New York: Crossroad, 1986).

[20] Patricia Beatty Jung, "Sanctifying Women's Pleasure," in *Good Sex: Feminist Perspectives from the World's Religions*, ed. Patricia B. Jung et al. (New Brunswick, NJ: Rutgers University, 2001).

[21] Alfred Kinsey, W. B. Pomeroy, and C. E. Martin, *Sexual Behavior in the Human Male* (Philadelphia: Saunders, 1948); Alfred C. Kinsey, W. Pomeroy, C. E. Martin and P. Gebhard, *Sexual Behavior in the Human Female* (Philadelphia: Saunders, 1953).

[22] Evelyn Hooker, "The Adjustment of the Male Overt Homosexual," *Journal of Projective Techniques* 21 (1957): 18–31.

[23] Antonio Damasio, *Descartes' Error: Emotion, Reason and the Human Brain* (New York: G. P. Putnam's Sons, 1994).

[24] Leslie Brody, *Gender, Emotion, and the Family* (Cambridge, MA: Harvard University Press, 1999).

[25] Julian F. Thayer and Bjorn H. Johnsen, "Sex Differences in Judgement of Facial Affect: A Multivariate Analysis of Recognition Errors," *Scandinavian Journal of Psychology* 41, no. 3 (Sept. 2000): 243–46.

[26] See also Stanley E. Jones, "Sex Differences in Communication," *Western Journal of Speech Communication* 50, no. 3 (Summer 1986): 227–41; Robert E. Salt "Affectionate Touch Between Fathers and Preadolescent Sons," *Journal of Marriage and Family* 53, no. 3 (Aug. 1991): 545–54.

BIBLIOGRAPHY

Arthurs, Jean and Jean Grimshaw, eds. *Women's Bodies: Discipline and Transgression.* London and New York: Cassell, 1999.

Bartley, H. L., I. R. Coyle, and G. Singer. "The Effects of Alcohol Induced Malnutrition in Pregnancy on Offspring Brain and Behavioral Development." *Pharmacology, Biochemistry and Behavior* 19, no. 3 (Sept. 1983): 513–18.

Bashore, R. A., J. S. Ketchum, K. J. Staisch, C. T. Barrett, and E. G. Zimmerman. "Heroin Addiction and Pregnancy." *Western Journal of Medicine* 134, no. 6 (1981): 506–14.

Beatty Jung, Patricia. "Sanctifying Women's Pleasure." In *Good Sex: Feminist Perspectives from the World's Religions*, 77-95. Edited by Patricia B. Jung, Mary E. Hunt and Radhika Balakrishna. New Brunswick, NJ: Rutgers University, 2001.

Boston Women's Health Book Collective. *Our Bodies, Ourselves.* New York: Simon and Shuster, 1969, 1976 and 1984 editions.

Brody, Leslie. *Gender, Emotion, and the Family.* Cambridge, MA: Harvard University Press, 1999.

Brown, Peter. *The Body and Society: Men, Women and Sexual Renunciation in Early Christianity.* New York: Columbia University, 1988.

Butler, Judith. *Bodies That Matter: On the Discursive Limits of "Sex."* New York: Routledge, 1993.

Conboy, Katie Nadia Medina, and Sarah Stanbury, eds. *Writing on the Body: Female Embodiment and Feminist Theory.* New York: Columbia University Press, 1997.

Damasio, Antonio. *Descartes' Error: Emotion, Reason and the Human Brain.* New York: G. P. Putnam's Sons, 1994.

Delemarre-van de Waal, H. A. "Environmental Factors Influencing Growth and Pubertal Development." *Environmental Health Perspectives* 101, no. 2 (1993): 39–44.

Di Vito, Robert A. "Old Testament Anthropology and the Construction of Personal Identity." *Catholic Biblical Quarterly* 61 (1999): 217–39.

Dunagan, Dianne and Danni Odom-Winn. "Crack Kids" in *School: What to Do/How to Do It.* Freeport, NY: Educational Activities, 1991.

Field, Tiffany. "Preschoolers in America are Touched Less and are More Aggressive than Preschoolers in France." *Early Childhood Development and Care* 151 (Apr. 1999): 11–17.

Field, Tiffany, Jeff Harding, Barbara Soliday, David Lasko, Nini Gonzalez, and Chad Valdeon. "Touching in Infant, Toddler and Preschool Nurseries." *Early Childhood Development and Care* 98 (1994):113–20.

Gallagher, Charles A., George A. Maloney, Mary F. Rousseau and Paul F. Wilczak. *Embodied in Love: Sacramental Spirituality and Sexual Intimacy.* New York: Crossroad, 1986.

Goleman, Daniel. "The Experience of Touch: Research Points to a Key Role in Growth." *New York Times Magazine*, 2 Feb. 1988.

Gormally, S., L. Wertheim, R. Alkawaf, N. Calinoiu, S. N. Young. "Contact and Nutrient Caregiving Effects on Newborn Pain Responses." *Developmental Medicine and Child Neurology* 43, no. 1 (Jan. 2001): 28–38.

Greenspan, Marlene. "Therapeutic Touch and Healing Meditation: A Threesome with Education." *Early Childhood Development and Care* 98 (1994): 121–29.

Gudorf, Christine. *Body, Sex and Pleasure: Reconstructing Christian Sexual Ethics.* Cleveland, Ohio: Pilgrim, 1994.

Hooker, Evelyn. "The Adjustment of the Male Overt Homosexual." *Journal of Projective Techniques* 21 (1957): 18–31.

Jones, Stanley E. "Sex Differences in Communication." *Western Journal of Speech Communication* 50, no. 3 (Summer 1986): 227–41.

Kinsey, Alfred, W. B. Pomeroy, and C. E. Martin. *Sexual Behavior in the Human Male.* Philadelphia: Saunders, 1948.

Kinsey, Alfred C., W. B. Pomeroy, C. E. Martin and P. Gebhard. *Sexual Behavior in the Human Female.* Philadelphia: Saunders, 1953.

Krugman, R., J. Bays, D. Chadwick, C. Levitt, M. McHugh, and J. Whitworth. "Guidelines for the Evaluation of Sexual Abuse of Children." *Pediatrics* 87 (1991): 254–60.

Nelson, James B. *Body Theology.* Louisville, KY: Westminster/John Knox, 1992.

Oster-Granite, M. L. and F. F. Ebner. "Developmental Processes and the Pathophysiology of Mental Retardation." *Mental Retardation and Developmental Disabilities Research Reviews* 2, no. 4 (1996): 197–208.

Porete, Marguerite. *The Mirror of Simple Souls.* Translated by Ellen K. Babinsky. New York: Paulist, 1993.

Remland, Martin S., Patricia S. Jones and Heidi Brinkman. "Interpersonal Distance, Body Orientation, and Touch: Effects of Culture, Gender and Age." *Journal of Social Psychology* 135, no. 3 (June 1995): 281–97.

Rinck, Christine M., Frank N. Willis, Jr., and Larry M. Dean. "Interpersonal Touch among Residents of Homes for the Elderly." *Journal of Communication* 30, no. 2 (Spring 1980): 44–47.

Russell, Diana E. H. *The Secret Trauma: Incest in the Lives of Girls and Women.* New York: Basic Books, 1988.

Sacred Congregation for the Doctrine of the Faith. "Declaration on Euthanasia," May 5, 1980. In *Bioethics: An Anthology,* 203-7. Edited by Helga Kuhse and Peter Singer. Oxford: Blackwell, 1999.

Salt, Robert E. "Affectionate Touch Between Fathers and Preadolescent Sons." *Journal of Marriage and Family* 53, no. 3 (Aug. 1991): 545–54.

Scarry, Elaine. *The Body in Pain: The Making and Unmaking of the World.* New York and Oxford: Oxford University Press, 1985.

Simkin, P. and M. O'Hara. "Nonpharmacologic Relief of Pain During Labor: Systematic Reviews of Five Methods." *American Journal of Obstetrics and Gynecology* 186, no. 5 (May 2002): 131–59.

Smith, D. W., P. Arnstein, K. C. Rosa, and C. Wells-Federman. "Effects of Integrating Therapeutic Touch into a Cognitive Behavioral Pain Management Program. Report of a Pilot Clinical Trial." *Journal of Holistic Nursing* 20, no. 4 (Dec. 2002): 367–87.

Taylor, Charles. *Sources of the Self: The Making of the Modern Identity.* Cambridge, MA: Harvard University Press, 1989.

Thayer, Julian F. and Bjorn H. Johnsen. "Sex Differences in Judgement of Facial Affect: A Multivariate Analysis of Recognition Errors." *Scandinavian Journal of Psychology* 41, no. 3 (Sept. 2000): 243–46.

Walker Bynum, Caroline. *Fragmentation and Redemption: Essays on Gender and the Human Body in Medieval Religion.* New York: Zone, 1992.

Wheldall, Kevin, Kate Bevan and Kath Shortall. "A Touch of Reinforcement: The Effects of Contingent Teacher Touch on the Classroom Behavior of Young Children." *Educational Review* 38, no. 3 (1986): 207–16.

Wilkinson, D.S., P.L. Knox, J.E. Chapman, T.L. Johnson, N. Barbour, Y. Miles and A. Reel. "The Clinical Effectiveness of Healing Touch." *Journal of Alternative and Complementary Medicine* 8, no. 1 (Feb. 2002): 33–47.

Willison, Beverly G. and Robert L. Masson. "The Role of Touch in Therapy: An Adjunct to Communication." *Journal of Counseling and Development* 64, no. 8 (Apr. 1996): 497–500.

Wyschograd, Edith. *Saints and Postmodernism: Revisioning Moral Philosophy* (Chicago: University of Chicago Press, 1990).

Young, L. "Sexual Abuse and the Problem of Embodiment." *Child Abuse and Neglect* 16 (1992): 89–100.

Re-visioning Eros for Asian Feminist Theologizing

Some Pointers from Tantric Philosophy

Pushpa Joseph, FMM

2

I have always been a lover of dance. As a kid my aim was to become a dancer. However, my parents were against this idea. It took me the whole of my teenage, college days, and theological career to really understand why my parents resisted this desire almost vehemently. I remember a conversation I had with my mother in this regard. She said so convincingly when I asked permission to join the dance classes in school, "Pushpa, as Christians we are different from Hindus. Dancing is not part of our Christian culture." I innocently persevered, "But mummy, didn't David dance when he was praying? Doesn't the Old Testament say that?" "Yes," my mother was quick to defend herself. "But he was a man. You are a small girl now, but very soon you will come of age and you cannot go about dancing as a young woman. You must cover your body from the gazes of men."[1] My mother, I now realize, was schooled in a theology and spirituality that understood men in terms of the Spirit and women in relation to the inferior body and matter. Rita Nakashima Brock rightly says in her book, *Casting Stones*, "Christianity split the spiritual and the body. In this theological dualism, the spirit (and the male as the spiritual principle) is always at risk from the drag of the sexual impulse (the female)."[2]

The erotic and our society's understanding of our bodies, of sexuality, and sensuality have been problematic both in Christian theology and in other dominant theologies and religions. The myth of Eve having brought sin into the world bedeviled the woman's body in Christian theology. Buttressing its customs with the story of Eden, Christianity honored the spirit above the sensual and venerated Yahweh by denying the pre-patriarchal goddesses whose sexuality and birth-giving were the major metaphors for creativity.

Friedrich Nietzsche once observed, it was "Christianity who gave Eros poison to drink; he did not die of it but degenerated into a vice."[3] St. Jerome had denounced the erotic, saying, "Regard everything as poison which bears within it the seed of sensual pleasure."[4] By the sixth century, lust and gluttony, both regarded as sins of the flesh, were listed among the seven cardinal sins.

Despite the fact that a lot of this extreme anti-body sentiment has died down, we still find vestiges of it in the Indian Church. Today Christian churches use drama, music, dance, and other forms that speak to the senses to present the Word of God through dynamic liturgies. There are many ways, however, in which the split of body and mind implicit in the religion of my childhood is still manifest in Christian theology.[5] As a result of such dualism the bodies of women continue to be subjected to violence and objectification.[6] A cursory glance at the statistics of violence on women shows us that much of the violence meted out to women is sex or body related. This violence is executed either through subjecting women's bodies to physical, verbal, and other forms of violence, or through more indirect and subtle forms like objectification of women's bodies through media and so on.[7] Jasodhara Bagchi argues that diverse attitudes and responses like objectification, denigration, or even mythologization of women's bodies exist because of the ambiguous attitude toward the body in dominant religions upheld by patriarchal censorship. "This is so," she continues, because "the erotic is very confusing for most people."[8] We immediately see eros as tied to genital sexuality, flattening out the possibilities that this term encompasses. Eros, most people assume, only aims at our love life.

In contrast feminist theologians have begun to speak of eros as the glue that binds the universe together, the allurement of one body for another, whether those bodies are human or another. They also broaden out eros to include gravity, the attraction of one physical object for another. Eros seems more useful when it can take on many more connotations than pure physical attraction. It is more appealing as a universal-bonding agent.

In the next section we will discuss the concept of eros, the manner in which Greek philosophy constructed the notion of eros, and its influences on Christian theology.

THE EROTIC IN TRADITIONAL GREEK PHILOSOPHY

The very word erotic comes from the Greek word eros, the personification of love in all aspects—born of Chaos, and personifying creative power and harmony. Mythological accounts of the god Eros go back at least to 900 B.C.E., the time of Hesiod. It is, however, with the writings of Plato that eros became a figure worthy of note.

Plato in his *Symposium* records several eulogies of eros and erotic love. For Plato eros is a reaching out of the soul to a hoped-for good. Eros is understood as the driving force of life aspiring to the absolute Good. Thus it is the motive underlying education, fine art, and philosophy. The connotation of aesthetic fascination, impersonality, and intense desire is retained in Plato's use of the term. To unite with eros, for Plato, is to find the highest manifestation of the love that controls the world in the mystic aspiration after union with eternal and super cosmic beauty. Plato's *Symposium* thus depicts Socrates as having reached the goal of union and puts the figure of Alcibiades, who has sold his spiritual birthright for the pleasures of the world, in sharp opposition to him. In this dualistic notion Socrates represents the righteous man associated with the Spirit and Alcibiades the one wedded to the world which is represented by the flesh.

Plato treats the concept of eros and the love that it implies in different levels. Firstly in its crudest form, love for a beautiful person is really a passion to achieve immortality through offspring by that person. Secondly, a more spiritual form is the aspiration to combine with a like-minded person to give birth to sound institutions and rules of life. Thirdly, and still more spiritual, is the zeal to enrich philosophy and science through noble dialogue. The insistent seeker may then suddenly discover a supreme beauty that is the cause and source of all of the beauties so far discerned. Thus the philosopher's path ends in a perception of the supreme Form of the Good, the Form that stands at the head of all others. In this regard Plato says in the Symposium, "Eros gives to us the greatest goods, for there is a certain guidance each person needs for his [sic] whole life, if he [sic] is to live well; and nothing imparts this guidance as well as Love." Eros in the Platonic understanding therefore provides guidance by acting as a motive force to self improvement and self-transcendence. Correspondingly the Platonic ideal for the human is meditation upon the immortal Forms and, ultimately, contemplative union with them by purifying the mind of material dross. Eros thus represents the longing inherent in the incarnate human being for his original source. Eros, in this sense, is a spirit *(daiuonion)* which drives us to turn away from the world of the senses to seek transcendent union. Conversely, it is concupiscent love, manifested by the many forms of lust, which binds us to the earthly realm.

From the above we realize that the Platonic understanding of eros, love and creativity was constructed on a notion of the spirit as higher and the body as lower. The primacy given to the "spirit," i.e., mind, and denigration of the body was carried through, in the Western tradition, into the modern period. In modernity, the rational independent self is the moral agent, i.e., the person who wills, chooses, acts, and hence is the site of responsibility for actions, choices, outcomes. It implies a moral recognition of what one's duty is through reason and self-determination without interference by others. The moral agent represented by the male is the one who is traditionally understood to make decisions based on spirit and reason. Simone de Beauvoir's incisive observation, "He is the Subject, he is the Absolute and she is the Other," in some respects, sums up why the self is such an important issue for feminism. To be the "other" clearly means to be the non-subject, the non-person, and the non-agent, in short the mere body. In Christian theology, women's selfhood has been systematically subordinated, diminished, and belittled. Often it has been outrightly denied. In general, women have been objectified as lesser forms of the masculine individual.

The very notion of eros in Greek philosophy has been based in dualisms, which influenced Christian theology in considerable ways. As a result of this, patriarchal theology is devoid of creativity, aesthetic affectivity, relationality, and the like.[9] Some of the male centered models of theology have emphasized a spirituality of warfare, of pilgrimage from this world to the next, of mountain climbing, of sportsmanship, of carrying one's daily cross and so on. The foundational leitmotifs of these models are achieving, arriving and conquering. The subordinate theme is effort, sacrifice and self-denial in view of achieving a final reward. In the warfare image one is expected to put up a brave fight against one's enemy including the body, which is seen as a site of temptation. These models also shun any kind of vulnerability and as a result equate women with the weak, silly, emotional and the like. The journey model emphasizes only the end of the journey dissuading the pilgrim against "pitching his tent in this wicked world below." Our theologies have taught us that assertion of worldly needs, affirmation of the body, pursuing rightful success in life, and so on is bad. Therefore we need to find viable alternatives from our own indigenous cultures. This article is an attempt to draw from the resources of Indian traditions and offer it as a case for effective theologizing in the Asian context.[10]

An equivalent to eros as creative energy is *Sakti* as seen in the Indian unorthodox tradition of Tantrism. David Gordon White says, "Tantrism is a celebration of the creative manifestation of divine energy embodied by the feminine principle Sakti. As Tantra's philosophy is never merely abstract, it states philosophic prepositions in terms of body and erotic symbolism which keeps them directly in touch with human experience."[11]

EROS AS SAKTI IN TANTRIC PHILOSOPHY

Sakti in Tantric philosophy is the creative energy inherent in and proceeding from God. It is exemplified by the female principle, the female reproductive organs, or the goddess Sakti, wife of *Shiva*. As energy, Sakti is also viewed as the merging of powers emanating from each person. In Tantric Hinduism, the goddess Sakti is associated with the lowest of the *chakras* (energy spots), lying dormant within the body as a coiled serpent (*kundalini*) that must be aroused to reach spiritual liberation by uniting with Shiva at the top of the head. The worship of the goddess Sakti is also called Saktism and is one of the major forms of unorthodox Hinduism practiced today. In popular worship Sakti has many names and some scholars consider most female deities in Hinduism to be various manifestations of her. Some of the other popular incarnations or avatars of Sakti are *Kali* and *Durga* (intimidating manifestations) and *Parvathi* (benign manifestation).[12] Sakti is worshipped and cultivated as a power that can lead to spiritual liberation. Thus Saktism is inseparably related to the system of practices for the purification of mind and body that are grouped under Tantric Hinduism. The philosophy upholding Saktism or Tantrism is called Sakta philosophy.

The Sanskrit word "tantric" has two meanings. Firstly, it means loom; a weaving machine, indicating the emphasis on relationality and connectedness. Tantrism works from the principle that the "universe we experience is nothing other than the concrete manifestation of the divine energy of the godhead that creates and maintains the universe,"[13] and therefore seeks to ritually appropriate and channel that energy, within the microcosm and macrocosm in creative and emancipatory ways. As such Tantrism teaches that all energy in the universe is an outflow of divine energy; its basic worldview is relational and the person is an embodied yet transpersonal self.

Secondly, the word "tantra" means treatise, and it is used to refer to a variety of mystical, occult, medical, and scientific works, as well as to those which we would now regard as "tantric." Most tantras were written between the 10th and 14th centuries CE. While Hinduism is typically viewed as being Vedic, the Tantras are not considered part of the orthodox Hindu/Vedic scriptures. They are said to run alongside each other, the Vedas of orthodox Hinduism on one side and the Agamas of Tantra on the other. However, Tantra has been described as the black sheep of yoga. Extolled as a short-cut to self-realization and spiritual enlightenment by some, left-hand tantric rites are often rejected as dangerous by most orthodox Hindus.

There are two "paths" in Tantra: *dakshinachara* (also known as *samayachara),* the "Right-Hand Path," and *vamachara,* the "Left-Hand Path." The latter is associated with many ritual practices that go against the grain of mainstream Hinduism. The sexual rituals in vamachara fall into two categories; culture created and natural behavior. The left-hand path of tantra yoga is also called the yoga of pleasure and power. Vamacara is the metaphysics of the feminine perspective based on the ancient realization that freedom is inclusive of one's bodily energies as well as spiritual vision. Bunker identifies Vamacara tantra as part of a broad evolutionary process in consciousness, which is moving toward an integration with the Natural World, the physical body, and the many sexual expressions of human behavior. All of Nature is then perceived as a sacred manifestation of the Divine, where there is no separation between Spirit and Nature, Mind and Body. Consequently there is not any great effort to go beyond or transcend Nature. Rather, the effort is to put one's self in accord with Nature and the physical body, and to express one's own creative potential more fully. Within this bio-spiritual context, the practice of Yoga is seen as an expression of this continuing process of inclusion and integration. It is a method and a means for moving into ever broader and deeper levels of connection and unification. Vamacara tantra does not seek to dissolve the body in a ball of light, nor does it aim at conquering physical mortality. It does not seek the spiritual at the expense of the physical, because the two are already recognized as expressions of the same underlying reality. It does not seek physical immortality by turning away from death, because it also recognizes that birth and death are the complementary sides of the same continuum.[14]

History of Tantra
Tantra as a post-Vedic Hindu Yogic movement began in North India and flourished in the middle ages before declining in the nineteenth century, partly as a result of persecution by the British and orthodox Hindus, and perhaps, because of the increasing popularity of *bhakti* yoga. Bhakti yoga is the Hindu term for the spiritual practice of fostering bhakti or loving devotion to God. Traditionally there are nine forms of bhakti yoga. Hindu movements in which bhakti yoga is the main practice are called bhakti movements. As in all of Hindu and Buddhist yogas, mantras are not only for focusing the mind but they play an important part in Tantra, often through the conduit of specific Hindu gods like Shiva, *Ma Kali* (mother Kali, another form of Sakti) and even

Ganesh, the elephant-headed god of wisdom. Similarly, *puja* will often involve concentrating on a *yantra* or mandala.[15]

Tantra, being a development of pre-Brahmanical thought, embraced the Hindu gods and goddesses, especially Shiva and Sakti. These deities may be worshipped externally (with flowers, incense etc.), but more importantly, can function as center of meditation, where the practitioner imagines himself or herself to be experiencing the *darshan* or "vision" of the deity in question. The divine love is expressed in *Shringara*[16] and Bhakti.

Concentration on the Body
Tantrics generally see the body as a microcosm; thus in the *Kaulajnana-nirnaya*, the practitioner meditates on the head as the moon, the heart as the sun, and the genitals as fire. Many groups hold that the body contains a series of energy centers, called *chakras* or wheels, which may be associated with elements, planets or occult powers (*siddhi*). Kundalini is nothing but the flow of the central *sushumna nadi*, a spiritual current, that, when moving, opens chakras, and is fundamental to the *siddhi* concept that forms a part of all tantra.

Taboo-breaking
Sexual intercourse, preferably with a low-caste partner, was one method by which traditional left-hand practice forced practitioners to confront their conditioned responses. Other methods include the eating of meat (particularly beef and pork) and drinking of alcohol. Fear has also been used as a method to break down conditioning; rites would often take place in a cremation ground amidst decomposing corpses. This, of course, also falls under the prerequisite of the practitioner's nature, in such cases demanding a *vir-* (heroic) or even *devya-* (godlike) *-bhava* (disposition of purity, self-control, suppression of pride, respect to parents and guru, and often celibacy).

The Purpose of Tantra
The implications of what is called Tantra go far beyond mere "sex." They surpass the classic *Kama Sutra*, and even sexual continence. It is true that Tantra uses sex (in fact to be more accurate, it uses sexual

energy), but this is just a means to an end. The actual aim of Tantra is ultimate spiritual freedom. Tantra believes that our spirits are of the same essence with God, pure happiness, infinite knowledge, and immortality. By achieving the state of ultimate spiritual freedom, the tantric practitioner becomes an all-powerful being. There is no limit to what she can do, but not everything is permitted. Even in ultimate spiritual freedom there are laws that must be followed—the universal laws of love, compassion and harmony. However, a spiritually liberated person enjoys a much greater freedom than other people because she or he is no longer limited by ignorance or lack of power and her or his happiness is not conditioned by anything exterior.

With its emphasis on the body, Tantric philosophy represents what seems to be the clearest and most methodical of all schools of thought on the relation between spirituality, the erotic, and the body.

Tantric philosophy also teaches that everything is to be experienced playfully, yet with awareness and a sense of sacredness in every gesture, every sensory perception, and every action. The path of Tantra thus is a spiritual one, which includes and appreciates the experience of sexuality and sensuality as a conscious meditation, as a flowing together of the physical, erotic, and cosmic energies. The spiritual part of Tantra is to use your sexual energy, not only to merge ecstatically with others especially the one you love, but also through him or her to become one with the cosmos or god.

The Feminine as the Basic Element in Sakta Philosophy

The basic foundational belief of Sakta philosophy is that there is the feminine element at the root of every creation. Hence the feminine is both the efficient and formal cause of the universe. This basic energy behind creation is ever present and is called Sakti. In addition there is neither creation nor destruction of energy, only transformations. This reality has no beginning and no end. It is eternal, self-luminous and dynamic. Sakta philosophy calls this state *Siva-Sakti Samarasya*.[17] This original state is one of unity and oneness. In this state the Siva element is inactive, neutral and just perceives everything. But the Sakti element is free and active. On the empirical level, even the element that is called Siva is also a form of Sakti. One cannot talk of Siva without Sakti. The world is grounded in oneness of Sakti and Siva. Both are independent and yet they are together. There is an implicit harmony between them. They experience two states of existence. The first state is one of intense connectedness. At the next level there exists a feeling of one's own distinctness and identity against the awareness of the other. In that level the two forms of energy start acting and reacting against one another. These two forms of energy are called fire (*agni*) and moon (*soma*).[18]

Fire produces suffering and death. Soma (moon) produces happiness and life. The function of fire is to destroy and that of the moon is to create. The whole world is the play of Siva and Sakti. It is the throbbing of energy or sakti. Sakti is non-different from Siva. When she desires to see the functioning of Siva and *Alma*, the creation of the world takes place. Tantrics believe that the whole universe is implicitly present in the womb of this great power (*Mahasaka*). The origination, growth and decay of the world is but the play of this power.

Siva is sentient and luminous, Sakti is dynamic. Sakti is free, she produces livingness, which gives rise to the awareness of one's own self. This awareness of one's self is a form of Siva, but Siva is also an inseparable part of Sakti. Siva or individual self is identical with Siva. When the self forgets its identity and becomes aware of its physical body, it develops ego and becomes proud.

It is only by the grace of the teacher that the self becomes aware of its real nature. When Bhakti, the power of worship in the self, unites with the sentience of Siva, a feeling of oneness is created. The self becomes Siva-like but not Siva himself. The worship of Siva (Bhakti) is not converted into Sakti but becomes like Sakti. In this state, there is no question of either bondage or liberation. What remains is the self-luminous, harmonious, and ever-flowing existence, par excellence. This is the perfect state of the existence of the universe.

This model of Siva-Sakti gives a new turn to feminist thought. Most philosophies presuppose a male's point of view. Central to Sakta philosophy is the thesis that the world is produced by the female element. Here woman is considered the mother of everything. She is living and intelligent. Far from being an object of enjoyment, she is an enjoyer, an agent. She helps in liberating the self. There are many beautiful names of the goddess in the Sakta philosophy, *Moksada* (the giver of liberation) is one among them. The Sakta philosophers believe that realization of self is also the result of the awakening of a power (Sakti) which is called Kundalini.[19]

Man and woman are thus seen as equal with one another. Each of them has his or her own distinguishing qualities. However, neither of them is superior or inferior. The model is suggestive of a peaceful, harmonious co-existence of man and woman. It explicitly expresses equality that is central in a feminist perspective. But, more importantly, the model supplies hints to develop a possible epistemology of feminism. Freedom, dynamism, power of creation, luminosity, the throbbing of life are some of the qualities that would be necessary for such a theory. This theory would look upon nature as a source of life.[20]

Tantric philosophy thus considers the body as a microcosm and an interplay of energies. This blending of energies embodied in the primordial energy sakti is a uniting and communitarian factor. As such it is a source of power. Moreover, tantrism underlines an egalitarian understanding of reality, thus paving the way for a society of equality. In addition by stressing embodied energy, tantrism transcends the dualism that has been so much a part of Christian theology. The erotic seen from the perspective of sakti really becomes a source of power that leads to creativity. A feminist Asian theology constructed on sakti can be called a Sakti theology.

SALIENT FEATURES OF SAKTI THEOLOGY

A feminist theology and methodology focuses on women's experience, gender assymmetry, consciousness raising, and the holistic empowerment of women. The following are some of the features and themes that characterize a Sakti theology constructed on women's experiences intersected by the variables of caste, class, gender, ethnicity, and the like. Such a theology will be empowering, embodied, agapic, context sensitive, and life generating. It will have foundational spiritual attributes that transcend the social dualisms of patriarchal theologies. Nurtured and sustained in the crucible of women's day-to-day experience, it has consciousness raising and transformation as its goal.

An Alternative to the Excessive Intellectualism of Patriarchal Theologies
In Tantrism one must rouse all the energies one can discover in one's body, emotions, and mind, and combine them into a vehicle which will carry one toward enlightenment. The moment of enlightenment is a kind of cosmic ecstasy and unbound spiritual experience, which transcends all articulation.[21]

In my visualization, the God experiences of Asian women too are unfathomable and can be equated to the depth and width of an ocean. The depth of an ocean is impenetrable, inexhaustible. Its presence is ubiquitous and encompassing. Its profundity is immeasurable. The spirituality of Asian women is characterized by a basic wholeness and intrinsic union with the creative aspects of human living. The expressions of such a Sakti spirituality will be found in the rituals, symbols and other analogical communicative acts of women. It arises from experience most especially of marginalization, silencing, and victimhood. Asian women's lives, however, are not only a collection of stories of victimization, but also of historical, religious and theological agency. A theology that starts from experience will challenge the conventional antimonies of body-soul, spirit-matter, leading to a "response of the whole person—mind and body, feelings and relationship—to the presence of whatever is held sacred, of ultimate worth."[22] A holistic theology built on a holistic spirituality ensures inner peace and harmony. Women can work better in an atmosphere conducive to growth and harmony. As such Sakti theology is an empowering theology. "Like water in a pot submerged in the sea," it empowers us to "become free, no longer separated from the ocean that is our source."[23]

An Empowering Theology
Audre Lorde, in her article "The Erotic as Power," evokes the erotic as only a great poet can. For Lorde, the erotic is not a minor power, but the basis for living fully. She says,

> Just as the Greeks shunted Eros off as a subsidiary son of Aphrodite, so we tend to see eros in restricted, sexually explicit ways. . . . [The] erotic is the life-affirming power that arises from our deepest knowing and our deepest longing. It is the creative energy that nurtures our connection to the fullness

of life, to the interdependent web of all existence, the power
that fosters our fearless capacity for joy. In the presence of the
erotic, we say "yes" to our deepest cravings.[24]

The erotic in Tantric Philosophy understood as Sakti is an assertion of
the life-force of men and women; of that creative energy empowered, the
knowledge and use of which, as Lorde says, "we are now reclaiming in our
language, our history, our dancing, our loving, our work, our lives."[25]

Authority as Nurturing Creativity

Tantrism depicts Sakti even in her intimidating avatar of Kali as "ever
gentle, nurturing and always calling to each of us." Tantrism also
constructs the relationship of Siva and Sakti on a foundational equal
anthropology that allows for each other's uniqueness. As a means of
empowerment a Sakti theology built on such egalitarian foundations
advocates "power with" and not "power over" relationships. As
such women's groups emphasize the importance of shared and
participatory leadership. Solidarity and networking are important in
their functioning. In such governance, there is much recognition of
individual contributions and initiatives and the members affirm each
other. A "power-over" relationship understands authority in terms of
the Latin *auctoritas,* which means the authority of the Lord, master,
father and so on. On the other hand, a "power with" relationship is
constructed on the notion of the Latin *augere* meaning "augmentation,
creativity, and enhancement."

What authority will Scripture have in such a Sakti theology?
Talking about the authority of Scripture in feminist theologizing,
Schüssler Fiorenza illustrates that canon can be understood either as
norma normans et non normata, a fixed norm to be obeyed, or as a
frame of meaning that gives shape to our values and beliefs. When
understood as a frame of meaning the canon functions as a democratic
and creative authority. In this line, Sakti theology will understand
the Scriptures not as tablets of stone, but as bread for sustenance on
the way.[26] Scriptures thus can become nourishment that invigorates
women in their struggle to live "the option for our women selves" in a
patriarchal society and religion.

Thus a Sakti theology cannot view Scripture in essentialist terms, but as a historically constructed terrain.[27] Scriptures have failed in different ways and have to be reconstructed, this time by a new consciousness that women have generated over the decades by their experiences. The notion of Scripture as mythical archetype is congruent with a theological view of the Bible as the "set in stone" Word of God.[28] Such a widespread theological notion restricts the nurturing power of the Word. A Sakti theology deconstructs and reconstructs the Scriptures in order to unleash its empowering aspects. This necessitates new language and new metaphors of empowerment.

Employing New Metaphors
An equally vitalizing strategy which can be employed by Sakti theology will be the project of critical and imaginative reclaiming and articulation of women's silences through new metaphors, for instance the metaphor of "Bread" with regard to Scriptures and "Not Stone." The use of metaphors from daily life and metaphors denoting movement in order to embellish the project of a feminist biblical hermeneutics is also a strategy used by feminist theology. This can be seen as a way of employing the aesthetic dimension of our existence for the purpose of authentic liberation and transformation. The use of these metaphors brings connectedness and helps overcome alienation. It creates ripples of resonance connecting the inner and outer world branching out into tributaries and ever-expanding networks of human (women) connectivity. It also facilitates a fruitful dialogic and discursive process, which is based on the "dialogical model" and not the "conduit model" of language. Schüssler Fiorenza likens the feminist engagement with the Bible to a "journey to wisdom's open house." This creates a mood for journeying into her (women's) intellectual, emotional, and erotic depths—"the rich dark depths that inspire visions for a different future of the ekklesia of women."[29] Such a "healing-movement" has the potential to create a hermeneutical and epistemological space at the borders, where delineation of identity, negotiation of meaning, and creation of radically new frameworks take place. Moreover, it reemphasizes the fluidity of margins and creates "open-ended" structures that play a considerable role in the formation of newer and ever-increasing bonds.

The movement from "power over" to "power with" in effect will have three consequences in a globalized world. First is an understanding of knowledge as a means of emancipation, second is a movement in governance from an "administered world" to subjectivity and human agency, and third, is a shift from homogenization or monoculture to accepting and welcoming differences. "Power with" also calls for an integrated inward, outward and forward or centrifugal movement. These critical movements will uncover the silencing of centuries and empower women to reclaim the sacred power of naming in order to name God, the world, and the Self.[30]

From Knowledge as Power Over
to Knowledge as Means of Emancipation
Knowledge is one of the most potent weapons for asserting power over others in the age of globalization. However, we have to ask some basic questions about the very role and purpose of knowledge. The tantric tradition sees the goal of all knowledge (*jnana*) as freedom. This tradition emphasizes the altruistic and service-oriented character of knowledge, relating knowledge and the process of knowing not with power, but with freedom. In other words, the freedom that enhancement of self brings about is for the creation of new life and new societies. Thus power redeemed through freedom leads to creative transformation. In Tantrism such a realization is true both of the inner and outer world, of the microcosm as much as the macrocosm, for both are very much intertwined.

Unfortunately in a globalized world such as ours, there has been a dissociation of knowledge from the subject of emancipation. Knowledge today is often employed for dehumanizing purposes; the number of killings, the rise in wars, rapes and so on cannot go unmentioned. Indeed, knowledge is presently used as an instrument to impose power over others. A Sakti theology on the contrary can help to redeem knowledge and orient it towards a holistic liberation especially for the poor and marginalized, most of whom are women and children. For this, Sakti theology, which is constructed on the parameters of a spiritual knowledge to freedom, is called to play a new and challenging role. As a way of ensuring this, Sakti theology will underscore the social responsibility of knowledge because Tantrism's understanding of knowledge is effectively summed up in these lines: "The education of the individual in addition to promoting her own innate abilities would attempt to develop in her a sense of responsibility for others in place of the glorification of power and successes in our present society."[31]

Even in the Christian tradition, the basic understanding of knowledge is given to us in the saying of Jesus: "The truth will make you free" (Jn 8:32). In Asian traditions the imparting of knowledge has likewise not been separated from its ethical and liberative role. George Soares-Prabhu underscores that in India, knowledge is considered as a *Brahmajijnasa* where the *mumuksu* enters into a process of transformation. This is an important aspect of all feminist theologizing too. Schüssler Fiorenza's seven-step methodology for knowledge production has the hermeneutics of experience as its starting point and the hermeneutics of transformation as its goal. A model delineated by feminist theologians for education is called the wisdom model and has the journey into the house of wisdom as its ultimate goal. Wisdom here is seen as in the book of Proverbs, as an open house with no walls and boundaries, and an open table laden with the best of foods ready for all to eat. The significance of a Sakti theology ultimately lies in its struggle to highlight the liberating role of knowledge. Knowledge in Tantric philosophy is not seen merely as a cognitive activity. Jesus too affirms "not all who call me Lord, Lord, will enter the kingdom of heaven;" instead it is those who experience freedom within and go out of themselves to free the weaker ones who will know God. Knowing in Sakti theology then is not merely a notional or cognitive enterprise.[32]

From Centralization to Participation and Agency
Today, especially in the age of globalization, both in the Church and outside, we have a mode of governance that suits the vested interests of a few. This divests people of subjectivity and agency and leads to de-politicization. Too often the inequalities and injustices are hidden under the pretext of ensuring law and good governance.

A good example is the ongoing feminization and casualization of labor that is taking place especially in Asia. In an Asian public hearing, a woman shared her experience. "I am a parent in a very poor family of seven children. My husband's low wage as a sugar-plantation worker is not enough to feed us. Hence I decided to work in the sardine factory where we work from seven in the morning until four the next." A girl laborer from another fish factory continued: "Sometimes we faint at work, since many days we sleep only two hours. We insert fish into cans, as many as 3,000 a day. We slash our fingers on the tins and fish bones, our blood sometimes dripping into the cans." Management hires women because there are more obstacles for women unionizing than for men. However, when women do get organized, of course, they get meted the same beatings as the men workers. This was glaringly evident a few years ago when hundreds of women workers of the Santa Cruz Electronics Export Processing Zone were baton-charged by the Bombay police and packed away to distant jails.

Against such a background we realize the importance of Sakti theology which would uphold the dignity and rights of women and human persons, and promote their participation in shaping the world in the political, economic, cultural and other spheres. Sakti theology with its egalitarian underpinnings can ensure the development in society and Church of governance which will affirm human persons by creating conditions for the flourishing and expression of their inherent capabilities. Sakti theology can mediate a mode of governance which allows individuals and collectivities room for self-determination; where democracy is substantial and not merely formal.[33] Civil society, as Felix Wilfred explains, "is the space where people interact and exchange views and opinions on a number of issues affecting the society."[34] In current times, however, we see civil society being exploited by the vested interests of the market. A Sakti theology constructed on the notion of responsible freedom can help the Asian Church enter into the debates as well as transform civil society. Just as we Asian women have gathered for deliberations and discussions, a Sakti theology can inspire us to create in our local contexts forums where people can interact and form public opinions.[35]

From Cultural Politics to Accepting Differences

Rajni Kothar says, "Diversity is not to be seen as a 'problem' to be managed but a resource to build upon, a basic resource emanating from the very nature of both human and natural orders. Diversity happens to be the essential 'nature of nature'; it also happens to be the essential characteristic of culture throughout human history. The same is the case with any lasting and self-sustaining polity."[36] Fostering an inclusive approach, a Sakti theology emerging from the life stories of Indian women will be contextual. It will be nourished by women's different stories of struggle. It will respect the heterogeneity of women and yet foster unity in diversity. It will lead to the embrace of a threefold movement: the inward, the outward and the forward. As Shalini Mulackal says, "The more appropriate image for women's spiritual journeys today is a spiral. For a spiral travels inward, outward and forward. These are not opposing directions, but part of a flow; a flow that moves inward to encounter the indwelling and transcendent God—the sacred in one self, outward to encounter God and the sacred in others—in human communities, and the larger community of life; and forward in conscious and active participation with God in shaping future history."[37]

An Embodied Theology which Celebrates Eros, Fertility and Life

There is an attempt of late to relate the aspects of human eros and fertility to Christian theology. By eros and fertility I imply the basic dynamo of life, integrated with its bodily expressions. Eros is a positive energy that undergirds the very personalities of deeply spiritual people who have put the world on fire with their creative genius. In a book titled *The Holy Longing—the Search for a Christian Spirituality*, the author Roland Rolheiser, considers Mother Teresa as a very "erotic woman" whose passion and fire within could never be contained and consumed. He says, "Few of us would consider Mother Teresa an erotic woman. We think of her rather as a spiritual woman. Yet she was a very erotic woman, though not necessarily in the narrow Freudian sense of that word. She was erotic because she was a dynamo of energy . . . she was a human bulldozer, an erotically driven woman."[38]

Nurturing, birthing, supporting, and other life-sustaining processes are very much part and parcel of women's lives. Women have an intimate relationship with life. They value life as a precious gift. So Sakti theology must be life affirming and creation-centered instead of being anthropocentric.

Lastly, in the true style of Tantrism, Sakti theology will emphasize the Power of the now or the resourcefulness of every moment. It will point to the transcendent dimension in every moment of human experience.

CONCLUSION

An Asian feminist theology constructed on Sakti will be empowering because it is rooted in women's experience, nourished by women's struggles, and enhanced by women's dynamic creative faculties. Moreover, in contrast to most dominant theologies, it will celebrate many aspects of bodiliness. These will lead us to sharpen our senses with the electrical charge that eros, or even more, all inclusively that Sakti offers, and to delve into our deepest cravings, our deepest longings, our most profound desires. These will heighten and sensitize our experience and strengthen our bonding as Asian Christian women, because we will have discovered our most profoundly creative source.

NOTES

[1]   Dance in the Indian tradition is seen as awakening the spiritual and physical energies of the person. In marginal communities dance is also an aesthetic activity that arouses the community's awareness and resistance to oppression. Thus dance has a communitarian significance as well. This is manifested in the circular formations of most of the dances of marginal communities and tribal groups. Dance is likewise a celebration of eros and creative power. *Therukoothu* and *swami attam* in dalit communities are specific examples. For an analysis see some of the articles in Lance Nelson, ed., *Purifying the Earthly Body of God: Religion and Ecology in Hindu India* (New York: State University of New York Press, 1998).

[2]   Rita Nakashima Brock and Susan Brooks Thistlewaite, *Casting Stones: Prostitution and Liberation in Asia and the United States* (Philadelphia: Fortress, 1996), 23.

[3]   Quoted in: "Friedrich Nietzsche," available from http://www.brainyquote.com/quotes/quotes/f/friedrichn137288.html; Internet, accessed Nov. 2004.

[4]   Quoted in "Fathers of the Church," available from http://www.Churchfatherstsads/org.html; Internet, accessed Nov. 2004.

[5]   For such an analysis especially in the Indian context see Seemanthini Niranjan, *Gender and Space: Femininity, Sexualization and the Female Body* (Delhi: Sage Publications, 2001).

[6]   It is estimated that deaths of young girls in India exceed those of young boys by over 300,000 each year, and every sixth infant death is specifically due to gender discrimination. Every 26 minutes a woman is molested. Every 34 minutes a rape takes place. Every 42 minutes a sexual harassment incident occurs. Every 43 minutes a woman is kidnapped. And every 93 minutes a woman is burnt to death over dowry. One-quarter of the reported rapes involve girls under the age of 16 but the vast majority is never reported. In India, 6,000 dowry murders are committed each year. This reality exists even though the Dowry Prohibition Act has been in existence for 33 years. Virtually nobody has been arrested under this Act.

[7]   See Evangeline Anderson-Raikumar, "Significance of the 'Body' in Feminist Theological Discourse," *Bangalore Theological Forum* 23, no. 2 (Dec. 2001): 80–98 and Pushpa Joseph, "Indian Feminist Hermeneutics: A Contextual Analysis of the Reconstructionist Model of Elisabeth Schüssler Fiorenza" (Ph. D. dissertation, University of Madras, 2002) for an analysis of the manner in which Indian women's bodies are subjected to a triple patriarchal regulation through controlling the conduct, mobility and sexuality of women.

[8]   See the collection of articles in Jasodhara Bagchi, ed., *Indian Women: Myth and Reality* (Hyderabad: Sangam Books, 1995).

[9]   Elisabeth Schüssler Fiorenza, *Wisdom Ways: Introducing Feminist Biblical Interpretation* (Maryknoll, N.Y.: Orbis, 2001), 53–57.

[10] For a similar attempt from another Indian perspective see Santanu K. Patro, "Threatening Kali and Over-Domineering Brahminisation: Indian Women's Identity and Justice in an Era of Globalization," *The Journal of Theologies and Cultures in Asia: Globalization and its Challenges to Doing Theology in Asia* 2 (2003): 42.

[11] David Gordon White, ed. *Tantra in Practice* (Princeton: Princeton University Press, 2000), 17.

[12] Susan Wadley, "Women and the Hindu Tradition," in *Women in Indian Society,* ed. Rehana Ghadially (New Delhi: Sage, 1988), 23–43.

[13] Gordon White, *Tantra in Practice*, 18.

[14] Sumanta Biswas, *Tantrism and its Practices* (Calcutta: Seagull, 2000), 116–20.

[15] Ibid., 107–13.

[16] Manu Chakravarty in his excellent article entitled "Feminism and the Indian Context" in *Beyond the Threshold: Indian Women on the Move*, ed. Yashoda Bhat and C. N. Mangala (Delhi: B. R. Publishing, 1995) speaks of the presence of the power of "aesthetic resistance" in the world of Indian dancing. He argues that the power of aesthetic resistance to subvert, to demolish dominant cultural frames is far greater than the power of the politics of resistance. To illustrate his position, he takes an example from the world of Indian dance. *Shringara* (the erotic) as a *rasa*, that is to say, the "erotic" element is not just an aesthetic element to be studied by aestheticians and those working in the area of poetics, but an active political ingredient that enables the *nayaki* (heroine) to see the *nayaka* (hero) or the beloved as an equal. The *nayaki* in her erotic gestures beckons/summons the *nayaka* as a friend. The hierarchical political/social order is thus neutralized by a certain aesthetic position that creates a "sacred space" for the impulse of the woman. The "sacred space" created for/by the human does not endorse the patriarchal order and to that extent defines its political position too. The autonomy of the self constituted the political basis of the "aesthetic" dimension. Traditionalists, mostly of the upper caste order, denounced *Shringara* (the erotic) as vulgar and profane and substituted *bhakti* (devotion) in its place, not realising that *bhakti* created a hierarchy between the *nayaka* and the *nayaki*. Their construction of the "spiritual" was steeped in the patriarchal tradition that glorified and sanctified the submission of woman to man, the *nayaki* to the *nayaka*. In doing so, they created a compartmentalisation of the erotic from the aesthetic, spiritual, rational and everyday life. Thus the political power of the aesthetic was lost.

[17] Meena A. Kelkar, "Man-Woman Relationship in Indian Philosophy," *Indian Philosophical Quarterly* 26, no. 1 (Jan. 1999): 71–87.

[18] Ibid., 76.

[19] Ibid., 77.

20 Ibid.,78

21 See the essays in Gordon White, *Tantra in Practice.*

22 James B. Nelson and Sandra P. Longfellow, *Sexuality and the Sacred: Sources for Theological Reflection* (Kentucky: Westminster/John Knox, 1994), 77.

23 Rajeswari Mazumdar, "Maa Kali," available from http://www.mypurohith.com/ Encyclopedia/enclopt.asp; Internet, accessed Nov. 2004.

24 Audre Lorde, "Uses of the Erotic: The Erotic as Power," in James B. Nelson, *Sexuality and the Sacred: Sources for Theological Reflection,* ed. Sandra P. Longfellow (Kentucky: Westminster/John Knox, 1994), 77.

25 Ibid.

26 Schüssler Fiorenza, *Wisdom Ways,* 178–79.

27 Idem, *In Memory of Her: A Feminist Theological Reconstruction of Christian Origins* (New York: Crossroad, 1983), 33.

28 Idem, *Bread Not Stone: The Challenge of Feminist Biblical Interpretation* (Boston: Beacon, 1985), 13.

29 Idem, *But She Said: Feminist Practices of Biblical Interpretation* (Boston: Beacon, 1992), 196.

30 Idem, "The Power of Naming: The Goals of Feminist Theology," paper presented at Ishvani Kendra, Pune, India, 20 Oct. 2004.

31 Felix Wilfred, "Religions Face to Face With Globalization: Some Reflections against the Asian Background," *The Journal of Theologies and Cultures in Asia: Globalization and Its Challenges to Doing Theology in Asia* 2 (2003): 40.

32 In a critique of the varied models of education, Schüssler Fiorenza identifies the prevalent models of education as the Banking model, the Master-Apprentice model, the Consumerist or Smorgasbord model and the Therapeutic model. Arguing that these models have not played their role in the formation of wholesome minds she goes on to present a fifth model called the Emancipatory Wisdom model of education. See Schüssler Fiorenza, *Wisdom Ways,* 30–32.

33 For an enlightening study of the importance of substantial democracy as against formal democracy see Neera Chaakdok, *State and Civil Society: Explorations in Political Theory* (Delhi: Sage, 1995).

34 Wilfred, "Religions Face to Face With Globalization," 42.

35 I was inspired very much by the Ayyal Kuttam project that I encountered in some of the parishes in Kerala. Ayyal Kuttam which means neighborhood gatherings are alternative spaces created by women and other ordinary men where they find time to narrate and listen to each other's stories. Some of these Ayyal Kuttams are also multi-religious.

36 Rajni Kothari, *Rethinking Development: In Search of Humane Alternatives* (Delhi: Ajanta, 1990), 224.

37 Shalini Mulackal, "Feminist Spirituality," paper presented at the CRI conference in Mysore, India, Sept. 2004.

[38] Ronald Rolheiser, *The Holy Longing—The Search for a Christian Spirituality* (New York: Doubleday), 8. Also see Gnana Patrick, "Subaltern Religions and Spirituality," paper presented at the ACPI meeting in Punjab, Oct. 2004.

BIBLIOGRAPHY

Anderson-Rajkumar, Evangeline. "Significance of the 'Body' in Feminist Theological Discourse." *Bangalore Theological Forum* 23, no. 2 (Dec. 2001): 80–98.

Bagchi, Jasodhara, ed. *Indian Women: Myth and Reality*. Hyderabad: Sangam Books, 1995.

Biswas, Sumanta. *Tantrism and its Practices*. Calcutta: Seagull, 2000.

Chaakdok, Neera. *State and Civil Society: Explorations in Political Theory*. Delhi: Sage, 1995.

Chakravarty, Manu. "Feminism and the Indian Context." In *Beyond the Threshold: Indian Women on the Move*, 84–94. Edited by Yashoda Bhat and C. N. Mangala. Delhi: B. R. Publishing, 1995.

"Fathers of the Church." Available from http://www.Churchfatherstsads/org.html; Internet, accessed Nov. 2004.

"Friedrich Nietzsche." Available from http://www.brainyquote.com/quotes/quotes/f/friedrichn137288.html; Internet, accessed Nov. 2004.

Gordon White, David, ed. *Tantra in Practice*. Princeton: Princeton University Press, 2000.

Joseph, Pushpa. "Indian Feminist Hermeneutics: A Contextual Analysis of the Reconstructionist Model of Elisabeth Schüssler Fiorenza." Ph.D. dissertation. University of Madras, 2002.

Kelkar, Meena A. "Man-Wornan Relationship in Indian Philosophy." *Indian Philosophical Quarterly* 26, no. 1 (Jan. 1999): 71–87.

Kothari, Rajni. *Rethinking Development: In Search of Humane Alternatives*. Delhi: Ajanta, 1990.

Lorde, Audre. "Uses of the Erotic: The Erotic as Power." In *Sexuality and the Sacred: Sources for Theological Reflection,* 75-79. Edited by James B. Nelson and Sandra P. Longfellow. Kentucky: Westminster/John Knox, 1994.

Mazumdar, Rajeswari. "Maa Kali." Available from http://www.mypurohith.com/Encyclopedia/enclopt.asp; Internet, accessed Nov. 2004.

Mulackal, Shalini. "Feminist Spirituality." Paper presented at the CRI conference in Mysore, India, Sept. 2004.

Nakashima Brock, Rita and Susan Brooks Thistlewaite. *Casting Stones: Prostitution and Liberation in Asia and the United States*. Philadelphia: Fortress Press, 1996.

Nelson, James B. and Sandra P. Longfellow. *Sexuality and the Sacred: Sources for Theological Reflection*. Kentucky: Westminster/John Knox, 1994.

Nelson, Lance, ed. *Purifying the Earthly Body of God: Religion and Ecology in Hindu India*. New York: State University of New York Press, 1998.

Niranjan, Seemanthini. *Gender and Space: Femininity, Sexualization and the Female Body*. Delhi: Sage Publications, 2001.

Rolheiser, Ronald. *The Holy Longing—The Search for a Christian Spirituality*. New York: Doubleday.

Patrick, Gnana. "Subaltern Religions and Spirituality." Paper presented at the ACPI meeting in Punjab, Oct. 2004.

Patro, Santanu K. "Threatening Kali and Over-Domineering Brahminisation: Indian Women's Identity and Justice in an Era of Globalization." *The Journal of Theologies and Cultures in Asia: Globalization and its Challenges to Doing Theology in Asia* 2 (2003): 113–44.

Schüssler Fiorenza, Elisabeth. *In Memory of Her: A Feminist Theological Reconstruction of Christian Origins*. New York: Crossroad, 1983.

———. *Bread Not Stone: The Challenge of Feminist Biblical Interpretation*. Boston: Beacon, 1985.

———. *But She Said: Feminist Practices of Biblical Interpretation*. Boston: Beacon, 1992.

———. *Wisdom Ways: Introducing Feminist Biblical Interpretation*. Maryknoll, N.Y.: Orbis, 2001.

———. "The Power of Naming: The Goals of Feminist Theology." Paper presented at Ishvani Kendra, Pune, India, 20 Oct. 2004.

Wadley, Susan. "Women and the Hindu Tradition." In *Women in Indian Society,* 23–43. Edited by Rehana Ghadially. New Delhi: Sage, 1988.

Wilfred, Felix. "Religions Face to Face With Globalization: Some Reflections against the Asian Background." *The Journal of Theologies and Cultures in Asia: Globalization and Its Challenges to Doing Theology in Asia* 2 (2003): 31–54.

II

Body and Sexuality:
Asian Societies/World

Em-body-ing Theology

Theological Reflections on the Experience of Filipina Domestic Workers in Hong Kong

Gemma Tulud Cruz

3

"There's so much written about the body," she groans, "but . . . in so much of it, the body dissolves into language. The body that eats, that works, that dies, that is afraid—that body just isn't there. Can't you write something for my students that would put things into a larger perspective?" I said I would try.

— Caroline Bynum[1]

The Filipina DHs in Hong Kong number more than 150,000 and account for the second largest population of Filipina domestic workers in out-migration. Based on the records of the Hong Kong Immigration Department, the earliest documented migration of Filipinas as domestic workers in this bustling city was in 1973. Driven by the economic instability in the Philippines, many of them, between the ages of twenty and forty, mostly single and educated, left the country to work as maids for expatriates in the former British colony. Most of them were young and single educated women.

When the British government liberalized the entry of female foreign domestic workers mainly from the Philippines, their number rose significantly and steadily. From the early '70s to the '90s Hong Kong has been the consistent destination of Filipina DHs in the same way as Filipina DHs have been Hong Kong employers' consistent favorite because of their relatively better facility with the English language. Today, the majority of Hong Kong's 240,000 foreign house help are Filipinas, making them the largest ethnic migrant group.

But despite all the seeming advantages, life for Hong Kong's modern-day "amah" is in itself a saga riddled with drama. It is a saga born in the constricting mold of gendered Filipino socialization, forged in the gendered economy of globalization,[2] and sealed by the anti-migrant domestic worker policies of Hong Kong.[3]

GENDERED BODIES, GENDERED IDENTITIES

It is no secret that women's bodies have often been sacrificed not just in the home but also in the workplace. With globalization, women as both consumer and consumed end up being sacrificed even more at the altar of greed on a daily basis. For domestic workers, particularly migrant domestic workers, this happens not just daily but with a certain kind of severity both in public and in private, locally and internationally, by their host and home country, by their communities and even by their own families. This is so as they often take on or are made to take on gendered bodies and identities.

Gendered Migration
In many ways, the migration of the Filipina DHs in Hong Kong is gendered. The stereotyping of women with domestic work alone reflects how the politics of gender is at play, first of all, in the global economy. There is a discernible international division of labor as women continue to be segregated in jobs associated with the service sector or care work. Globally, the gendering of the process of (Filipino) migration[4] can also be seen in the way the global economy creates and manipulates a job market where the jobs available for foreign women of color are mainly

those that are traditionally associated with women, e.g., domestic work, nursing, and "sex work."

Aside from the economy, the decision to migrate, which is often a family strategy for upward social mobility, is also gendered. Gender stereotypes play a major role in singling out the womenfolk to be the one to leave and work abroad. With domestic work as the available job in Hong Kong,[5] sexual division of labor comes into play. Filipino families think it is but "natural" for the daughter, sister, or wife to apply for the job because it entails woman's work.

For single women, families often capitalize on the imposed and popular notion of the language of care among women as nurturance in all aspects, e.g. emotional, physical etc., for them to acquiesce to leave to work as DH. Parents especially tap into the highly ingrained sense of responsibility among women in choosing them to be the one to migrate.

Gendered Transitions

The Filipina DHs also undergo gendered transitions as (Filipino and single/unmarried) women when they work and live in Hong Kong. Married DHs feel a lot of guilt at their being "absentee mothers." At the root of their guilt is what they perceive as their transgression of a "good" Christian woman's proper place and role, which is at home with her husband and children. This perception of their sojourn in Hong Kong as a betrayal of their primary duty and responsibility then becomes like a millstone hanging around the neck. Such is this perception that some do not even say goodbye to their children or immediately tell the truth as to where they are going. Some even ask someone else, for instance, the husband, to reveal and explain the truth about their departure.

Most married DHs also feel guilty about leaving their children with others to care for children not their own. They worry about the emotional needs and guidance of their children whom they think will suffer terribly because the *ilaw ng tahanan* (light of the house) is gone. They are guilty and anxious too that the husband, the *haligi ng tahanan* (foundation of the house) will not be able to take good and proper care of the house and the children since it is not his responsibility to do so. Many DHs therefore find a *tagasalo*, another woman, e.g. their mother, a sister, female cousin, or even their eldest daughter, to whom they pass on their direct nurturing responsibility. Some hire the services of a poorer Filipina to be the family's domestic helper. The DHs, however, still try to make up for their absence by doing transnational mothering. Among migrant women, these are often known as "cell phone mothers" since they try to do their responsibilities as mothers via the cell phone. Some even help their children with homework via the mobile phone. Nevertheless, homilies and entreaties that they prioritize their family and return home, add to their guilt. Ray Corpus of the Philippine Mission, for instance, urges them to make their families a priority and return home.[6] This places them in a moral dilemma because in the first place, they left for their family's sake.

Single DHs, in the meantime, have difficulties "finding a good man to be a husband." According to *Romance and Resistance: The Experience of the Filipina Domestic Workers in Hong Kong,*[7] single DHs prioritize the "white, middle-class male" thinking that marrying one would mean higher social class, more "freedom" and rights. But of course, this does not happen because of cultural differences exacerbated by the low social regard for them. For others who do get involved with foreigners, particularly Chinese, not being taken seriously remains a problem. As a result, many unmarried DHs end up preferring Filipino men. But since there are also very few Filipino men in Hong Kong and class boundaries within the Filipino migrant community are very much in place, the "field" for the single DHs becomes all the more limited.

For single DHs socialized to believe that marriage is the be-all and end-all of a woman's existence, the severe limitation of "husband material" often becomes a problem. This is especially so because most of them are in the so-called marrying age or older.[8]

Indeed, their sexuality often puts the DHs in problematic situations. Single or married, some get involved in casual relationships or even trysts because of loneliness or when the husband cheats on them. Pregnancy from extramarital affairs causes problems and many women end up ruining their marriage. The emergence and increase in relationships with tomboys or lesbians among them is an indicator of the intensity of the problems posed by the women's emotional, psychological, and sexual needs.

Marilen Abesamis talks about this in the conclusions she gave for the reasons Filipina DHs in Hong Kong engage in "tomboy love." She deduced that they do it because "a tomboy relationship is a 'safe' way of expressing one's sexuality without getting pregnant," considered a work hazard. She also points out that "this is simply a response to the need for pleasure and intimacy." As tomboys are perceived, especially by women with failed marriages, to be "sensitive" and "caring" these normally heterosexual women enter into what they call the "For Hong Kong only" affair[9]—a relationship that is usually a well-kept secret from their families. The problem is, they are often unable to get out of it unscathed even after they end it and return to the Philippines. Most feel guilty because Filipino religious culture frowns upon same-sex relationships.

Despite the disadvantages, many DHs enter into intimate relationships—heterosexual and homosexual, because these serve as a form of daily resistance—their assertion as female subjects against the oppressive forces that reduce them to servant objects. Making their sexuality a means of resistance, they prove that they remain persons, not objects reduced to a role.[10] But on a larger scale, sexuality is also a contentious issue for and among the DHs. As Kimberly Chang and Julian McAllister Groves in their fieldwork-based article "Neither 'Saints' Nor 'Prostitutes': Sexual Discourse in the Filipina Domestic Worker Community in Hong Kong" point out, the Filipina DHs' sexuality is the subject of considerable social commentary and control in Hong Kong due to their image as "prostitute." While some, indeed, resort to prostitution for economic reasons, the image has been significantly associated with Filipinas collectively. Most DHs respond by constructing an "ethic of service" within their own communities to counter the negative image.[11]

Gendered Violence

Gendered violence economically, physically and sexually also plagues the Filipina DHs. To ease Hong Kong's economic slowdown, the government cut down the wages of domestic workers. With domestic work (a woman-dominated job) as the lowest paid employment in Hong Kong, singling this out for further reduction of wages is "making the poor even poorer."

The Hong Kong government reinforced institutionalized gendered violence with the proposal to remove maternity protection for foreign domestic helpers (FDH). Concocted to offer "flexibility" to employers wishing to terminate their FDH on the basis of "mutual agreement," the proposal, according to a letter by the Asian Migrant Coordinating Body, is "discriminatory, as it is applicable only to those in the category of foreign domestic helpers . . . and racist as it seeks to exclude workers of certain nationalities from enjoying a right available to local workers and those of other nationalities." The proposal is also "sexist as it targets women for oppression" by considering "pregnancy and maternity as a 'hindrance' to more effective and productive labour." The letter goes on to say that the proposal, "brings us back to the age of slavery when the right to bear children was considered a threat to productivity[12]—a violation of the DH's reproductive rights which is a hard-won right of women workers around the world.

The scourge of the Filipina DHs as women is not only the H.K. government but also their employers and recruiters. For instance, because of the popular perception and fear in Hong Kong that foreign domestic workers will go to great lengths to snag rich or economically stable men like their male employers, the DH's physical appearance is usually controlled mostly by women employers. The maid's uniform is imposed as a dress code. Others are required to wear jeans and T-shirts or other "harmless" and gender-neutral clothes. Body control and discipline as women[13] are important adjustments the DH has to make right at the start. Recruiters, upon the desires of prospective employers, "transform" the DH's body and appearance by dictating her weight, length of hair, facial appearance (no make-up), kind of shoes to wear. When the external fits the prescribed ideal DH's body appearance, the internal is the next one the recruiters tinker with. Aside from being subjected to the X-ray machine and the weighing scale, the DH's body is exposed to numerous tests as part of the application process. These include tests for hepatitis, syphilis, herpes, and even a pregnancy test. When the DH passes the "body quality control" she is photographed with her "signature" clothes: the standard pastel pink or blue-striped maid's uniform. This "perfect maid" look is then photographed twice: a close-up of the face and a "full body" shot. All in all, the ideal DH must be neat and tidy but not so attractive.

Employers, especially women employers, do not go for pretty domestic workers. If she has what mainstream society considers as physical imperfections like acne, scars, birthmarks, and a slightly dark complexion, the more likely is she to be employed. Skin color is a factor that Chinese employers value. Many of them shun women with darker skin because a woman with dark color allegedly scares the children. They also go for those who are more Chinese looking. As a result, there are quite a number of what DHs call "from airport to airport." These are women whose contracts were terminated the moment their employer laid eyes on them at the airport and saw "how beautiful" or "how dark" they were.

Various forms of physical abuse, in the meantime, plague those who actually get to work. These include slapping on the face or hands or any part of the body, spitting, kicking, being hit with or having objects thrown at them, beating, etc. Others, like Lilia Dangco were treated more atrociously:

> Six days later (after arriving in Hong Kong), her employer burned her left forearm with a flat iron after she failed to follow her employer's instruction to put a handkerchief on top of a black long skirt that she was ironing. She was confined at the Queen Mary Hospital. She said her employer warned her not to tell the incident to anybody or her face would be the next target . . .[14]

In terms of sexual abuse, kissing, touching, and sexual advances are the most common forms of abuse for Filipina DHs. This is closely followed by the employer displaying himself naked or asking the DH to touch him. Other complaints include employers peeping while the DH is bathing or changing, videotaping the DH in the bathroom or bedroom, and touching the DH while she is sleeping.[15] Male employers also tend to regard their DH as an in-house masseuse who is available for 24 hours. Some make "substitute wives" out of their DH especially if the wife seems unable to provide adequate "sexual services." There are even DHs who were turned into virtual sex slaves.

Unjust Working Conditions

Unjust working conditions account for most of the body-negating experiences of the Filipina DHs. Many employers provide poor accommodations. DHs are made to sleep on the kitchen or living room floor, near the bathroom and under the table where they have no privacy.[16] As a result, some sleep for 3-4 hours only because they cannot sleep until everyone leaves the living room or stops going to the kitchen. The situation becomes all the more difficult when employers entertain guests or the DHs have to serve refreshments at *mahjong* parties which could take place several nights a week.

DHs also encounter problems with their employers when it comes to food. The employers determine not only what the DH eats but also where, when, and how much she eats. Meals can be irregular, late, or inadequate. One respondent in a study by Rita Ybanez complained of being fed just a piece of bread and coffee in the morning though the next meal was at 3 or 4 in the afternoon. Other respondents revealed that they were given only porridge, noodles, or a hamburger as their food for the whole day.[17]

DHs' bodies suffer as they are turned into workhorses. A study done by the Asian Migrant Center pointed out that possibly more than 5,000 of the then existing number of Filipino DHs suffer from virtual slavery (0–1 day off per month).[18] Aside from their "official" job, some are actually made to work outside their employer's homes either as secretaries, nurses, waitresses, dishwashers, medical technicians, cooks, salespersons, messengers, hawkers, factory workers, and researchers.

Recruiters contribute to this objectification of the DH with the practice of a three-month "product" warranty. Products are "packaged" and advertised even in cyberspace as far superior, better trained and more "obedient." Some recruitment agencies offer as much as three free replacements if the employer is not satisfied with the "product." An agency, at one time, even put them on "sale" with a "15% discount" price tag because it was celebrating its fifteenth anniversary.[19] The DH then becomes like goods in a store where one has the ultimate freedom to choose which to buy and if the "goods" is "damaged" to return her, free of charge. Employers have been known not only for unreasonably terminating their maid's employment, but also for callously discarding her by dumping her on the doorstep as easily as they throw out the day's garbage.

Geraldine Pratt narrates another form of commodification where "a domestic worker's body and function as servant is further objectified by building an equivalence between her and the household décor." The employer made Cora, the Filipina maid, wear a uniform "coordinated with her employer's dishes." Cora was even "asked to wear her black uniform when the black dishes were in use."[20] Nothing beats, however, the names "my Filipino[a]" which means "my maid" and *banmui*[21] which are used to refer to Filipina DHs in Hong Kong. These do not just inscribe domestic work in women's bodies, but racialize it.

THEOLOGICAL CHALLENGES AND PERSPECTIVES

DHs. Its inscription in the bodies of the Filipina reveals not only the identification of domestic work with women but also that it is, under the gendered global economy, specifically for poor women of color, particularly the Filipina.

The challenge is: How can Christian theology promote the dignity especially of the bodies of domestic workers?[22] As physicality and embodiedness is basic in all social encounters, the body is an active witness to the passage of life. Doing theology therefore must begin and be constantly grounded in our experience of embodiment. As Chung Hyun Kyung further asserts, the text of God's revelation was, is, and will be written in our bodies and in people's everyday struggle for survival and liberation.[23] Hence, for the Word of God to be really made flesh, the body must be a primary theological category.

One very important theological framework for an embodied theology that has not been deeply explored in Christian theology is the Incarnation.[24] Theological reflections on it often focus and/or end in the idea of God's love without taking into account the concrete act and form of that love: taking on human flesh in the person of the historical Jesus. "Central to re-claiming the dignity and power of women over their bodies is a radical understanding of incarnation that places the divine solidly in the world and challenges any notions of dualism."[25] How much more dignified can the flesh get than with the Divine inhabiting it?

The Incarnation, indeed, gives the body a sense of integrity that is yet to be deeply articulated in Christian theology. To talk about bodily integrity, for instance, would mean making biological or body processes holy.[26] It would also mean critiquing and shattering the patriarchal global capitalism that commodifies women. Lastly, it would mean cutting right through the issue of violence against women, not just in its glaring physical forms, e.g. rape, but also in its subtle forms, e.g. the "violence of un-rest."[27] Domestic workers cry out to the Lord of the Sabbath not just for the much-needed justice but also for often-denied physical rest.

To talk about bodily integrity is to articulate a theology of daily reality. It is important to subject to scrutiny this gendered disembodiment that happens everyday. Christian theology should take into account the seemingly mundane, boring, or routinary activities, e.g., cooking and cleaning, that the body does, as part of the em-body-ing of theology. There is a need to reflect on manual work, especially domestic work to enable theology to unmask the body-based mechanisms employed to oppress women. Such a reflection can also serve as a springboard to talk about bodily integrity in a way that celebrates the body.

Our bodies also resist and heal. They do not just suffer. The problem is that much of Christian theology overemphasizes the suffering body. Fixation with the cross and the crucified Jesus accounts for domestic helpers' romanticizing and glorification of suffering. This, of course, is lamentable as it is incomplete. The Jesus event did not end with his death but in the resurrection, hence, the Christian's final experience is life and not death. In the end, our theology must be on what saves and not so much on what enslaves.

EM-BODY-ING THEOLOGY: A CONCLUSION

In the light of the experiences of Filipina domestic workers, em-body-ing theology or redeeming and celebrating the body in theology is therefore a crucial task for Christian theology. The body, particularly the female body, has to be liberated from the multiple layers of suppression and denigration it has been subjected to in society and in the Church. Em-body-ing Christian theology does not only mean according the female body the beauty and integrity that have been denied it. For Christian theology to be an authentically embodied theology it must also take into account the differences between and among women based on race or ethnicity, class, religion, etc. Lastly, em-body-ing Christian theology entails removing emphasis from that which enslaves and stressing that which saves. Em-body-ing Christian theology must insist that in God's great economy of salvation, love, and life, not suffering and death, are the Christian's final experience.

NOTES

1. Caroline Walker Bynum, "Why all the Fuss about the Body?: A Medievalist's Perspective," *Critical Inquiry* 22 (Autumn 1995): 1, cited by Geraldine Pratt, "Inscribing Domestic Work on Filipina Bodies," in *Places Through the Body*, ed. Heidi J. Nast and Steve Pile (London: Routledge, 1998), 283.

2. See, for example, Kimberly Chang and L. H. Ling, "Globalization and its Intimate Other: Filipina Domestic Workers in Hong Kong," in *Gender and Global Structuring: Sightings, Sites, and Resistances*, ed. Marianne H. Marchand and Anne Sisson Runyan (London: Routledge, 2003), 27–43.

3. For an example on this, see Melville Boase, "The Two Weeks Rule in the Context of the Legal Position of Foreign Domestic Helpers (FDHs)" in Christian Conference of Asia, *Serving One Another: The Report of the Consultation on the Mission and Ministry to Filipino Migrant Workers in Hong Kong, April 28 to May 1, 1991, Kowloon, Hong Kong* (Hong Kong: CCA Urban Rural Mission, 1991).

4. Rhacel Salazar Parreñas, *Servants of Globalization: Women, Migration and Domestic Work* (Stanford, CA: Stanford University, 2001; Quezon City: Ateneo de Manila University Press, 2003) gives a substantial discussion and examples on this based on her study of Filipina domestic workers in Rome and Los Angeles.

5. In the case of Hong Kong, its economic expansion increased the demand for labor in service-oriented infrastructure like hotels and hospitals as well as for more lucrative positions, luring local workers engaged in the demeaned service jobs. The tremendous job opportunities and the consequent financial strain due to the increase in the standard of living also took the local women away from their home thereby creating the demand for foreign domestic workers.

6. Anil Stephen, "Maid in Hong Kong: The City's Churches are Helping Exploited Migrant Workers," available from http://www.christianitytoday.com/ct/2000/011/19.26.html; Internet, accessed 23 Aug. 2003.

7. Marilen Abesamis, *Romance and Resistance: The Experience of the Filipina Domestic Workers in Hong Kong*, cited by Ma. Ceres P. Doyo, "Tomboy Love," in Inter-Press Service, *Risks and Rewards: Stories from the Philippine Migration Trail*, 39–43 (Bangkok: IPS Asia-Pacific, 2002).

8. In mainstream Philippine standard the ideal marrying age is around 25. In rural areas the usual marrying age even tends to be earlier.

9. Abesamis, *Romance and Resistance*, cited by Ma. Ceres P. Doyo, "Tomboy Love," 41.

10. Ibid., 39–40.

11. Kimberly Chang and Julian McAllister Groves explicitly point at international developments, e.g. global economy, migration policies, the conditions of domestic work, and Hong Kong's popular culture as factors that drive DHs to prostitution. See Kimberly Chang and Julian McAllister Groves, "Neither 'Saints' Nor 'Prostitutes': Sexual Discourse in the Filipina Domestic Worker

Community in Hong Kong," *Women's Studies International Forum* 23, no. 1 (2000): 73–87.

12 See related report "Maternity Benefits for Maids Opposed," *Philippine Daily Inquirer,* 4 July 1997, 3. Nick Constable and Nicole Constable, *Maid to Order in Hong Kong: Stories of Filipina Workers* (Ithaca, N.Y.: Cornell University Press, 1997), 72 cites a similar violation of the DHs' reproductive right whereby the DH was given an abortion without her knowledge when her employer brought her for physical exam and pregnancy test.

13 Constable, *Maid to Order in Hong Kong,* 60–82 provides a more comprehensive discussion on this.

14 "MRV Case Profiles: Lilia Bernardino Dangco," available from http://www. asian migrants.org/mrvcases/999433070427.php; Internet, accessed 2 Feb. 2003. Cases of abuses are considerable enough to warrant the establishment of Bethune House, a Filipino-run shelter for DHs in distress.

15 Roseanne Calamaan, for instance, was forced by her employers to watch them have sex and was also asked to watch the couple's "private videos." See "Maid 'Forced to Watch Sex,'" *Asia Migrant Bulletin* 11, nos. 3 and 4 (July-Dec. 1994): 4.

16 There are also complaints from DHs who are made to sleep in cupboards, cardboard carton cubicles, in the toilets, under tables, and on top of washing machines because of the small house of their employers. See "No More Sleeping in the Bathroom," *TNT Hong Kong* 2, no. 2 (Feb. 1996): 28 and Julian Lee, "Filipino Maids' Act of Resistance,"available from http://info.anu.edu.au/ mac/Newsletters_an_Journals/ANU_Reporter/_pdf/vol_29_no._07; Internet, accessed 3 Nov. 2003.

17 Riza Faith Ybanez, "Conditions in Labor Migration that Contribute to the HIV Vulnerability of Migrant Domestic Workers: A Case Study of Filipino Domestic Workers in Hong Kong," available from http://caramasia.gn.apc.org/ Ritchie_HK_cdtn.htm; Internet, accessed 22 Jan. 2003.

18 Asian Migrant Center, *Baseline Research on Racial and Gender Discrimination Towards Filipino, Indonesian and Thai Domestic Helpers in Hong Kong* (Hong Kong: AMC, 2001), 29.

19 Constable, *Maid to Order in Hong Kong,* 61.

20 Pratt, "Inscribing Domestic Work on Filipina Bodies," 289.

21 *Ban* is the final syllable of the Cantonese term for "Philippines" and *mui* is from "*muijai*" the lowest servant in the history of the Chinese slaveholding population. See Constable, *Maid to Order in Hong Kong,* 15, 47, 77 for a deeper analysis on how this name reflects the denigration of the Filipina DHs.

22 We shall no longer tackle in this paper how the body, especially women's body, has been denigrated in the history of Christianity since this has already been developed substantially in many other publications.

23 Ibid., 22–52.

24 The Incarnation seen as God taking on human form to dialogue with humanity also presents the body in a relational way. As John A. T. Robinson points out: "The body . . . is the symbol, not of individuality, but of solidarity. It is that which binds every individual, divinely unique . . . , in inescapable relatedness with the whole of nature and history and the totality of the cosmic order. It is the bond of continuity and unity between [human beings] and [their] environment, between individual and community, between generation and generation." John A. T. Robinson, *In the End, God . . .: A Study of the Christian Doctrine of the Last Things* (London: James Clarke and Co., 1950), 86–87 cited by Melanie May, *A Body Knows: A Theopoetics of Death and Resurrection* (New York: Continuum, 1995), 103.

25 Lisa Isherwood and Elizabeth Stuart, *Introducing Body Theology* (Sheffield: Sheffield Academic Press, 1998), 132.

26 Elizabeth Stuart, "Bodiliness," in *An A-Z of Feminist Theology* (Sheffield: Sheffield Academic Press, 1996), 24.

27 I have talked about this in Gemma Tulud Cruz, "Our Bodies, Ourselves: Towards an Embodied Spirituality for Women," *In God's Image* 22, no. 2 (June 2003): 3–6.

BIBLIOGRAPHY

Abesamis, Marilen. *Romance and Resistance: The Experience of the Filipina Domestic Workers in Hong Kong.* Cited by Ma. Ceres P. Doyo, "Tomboy Love." In Inter-Press Service, *Risks and Rewards: Stories from the Philippine Migration Trail*, 39–43. Bangkok: IPS Asia-Pacific, 2002.

Asian Migrant Center. *Baseline Research on Racial and Gender Discrimination Towards Filipino, Indonesian and Thai Domestic Helpers in Hong Kong.* Hong Kong: AMC, 2001.

Boase, Melville. "The Two Weeks Rule in the Context of the Legal Position of Foreign Domestic Helpers (FDHs)." In Christian Conference of Asia. *Serving One Another: The Report of the Consultation on the Mission and Ministry to Filipino Migrant Workers in Hong Kong, April 28-May 1, 1991 Kowloon, Hong Kong*, 85–94. Hong Kong: CCA Urban Rural Mission, 1991.

Chang, Kimberly and L. H. Ling. "Globalization and its Intimate Other: Filipina Domestic Workers in Hong Kong." In *Gender and Global Structuring: Sightings, Sites, and Resistances*, 27–43. Edited by Marianne H. Marchand and Anne Sisson Runyan. London: Routledge, 2003.

Chang, Kimberly and Julian McAllister Groves. "Neither 'Saints' Nor 'Prostitutes': Sexual Discourse in the Filipina Domestic Worker Community in Hong Kong." *Women's Studies International Forum* 23, no. 1 (2000): 73–87.

Constable, Nick and Nicole Constable. *Maid to Order in Hong Kong: Stories of Filipina Workers*. Ithaca, N.Y.: Cornell University Press, 1997.

Isherwood, Lisa and Elizabeth Stuart. *Introducing Body Theology*. Sheffield: Sheffield Academic Press, 1998.

Lee, Julian. "Filipino Maids' Act of Resistance."Available from http://info.anu. edu.au/mac/Newsletters_an_Journals/ANU_Reporter/_pdf/vol_29_no._07; Internet, accessed 3 Nov. 2003.

"Maternity Benefits for Maids Opposed." *Philippine Daily Inquirer,* 4 July 1997, 3.

"Maid 'Forced to Watch Sex.'" *Asia Migrant Bulletin* 11, nos. 3 and 4 (July-Dec. 1994): 4.

May, Melanie. *A Body Knows: A Theopoetics of Death and Resurrection*. New York: Continuum, 1995.

"MRV Case Profiles: Lilia Bernardino Dangco." Available from http://www.asian migrants.org/mrvcases/999433070427.php; Internet, accessed 2 Feb. 2003.

"No More Sleeping in the Bathroom." *TNT Hong Kong*. 2, no. 2 (Feb. 1996): 28.

Pratt, Geraldine. "Inscribing Domestic Work on Filipina Bodies." In *Places Through the Body*, 283–304. Edited by Heidi J. Nast and Steve Pile. London: Routledge, 1998.

Salazar Parreñas, Rhacel. *Servants of Globalization: Women, Migration and Domestic Work*. Stanford, CA: Stanford University, 2001.

Stephen, Anil. "Maid in Hong Kong: The City's Churches are Helping Exploited Migrant Workers." Available from http://www.christianitytoday.com/ ct/2000/011/19.26.html; Internet, accessed 23 Aug. 2003.

Stuart, Elizabeth. "Bodiliness." In *An A-Z of Feminist Theology*. Sheffield: Sheffield Academic Press, 1996.

Tulud Cruz, Gemma. "Our Bodies, Ourselves: Towards an Embodied Spirituality for Women." *In God's Image* 22, no. 2 (June 2003): 3–6.

Ybanez, Riza Faith. "Conditions in Labor Migration that Contribute to the HIV Vulnerability of Migrant Domestic Workers: A Case Study of Filipino Domestic Workers in Hong Kong." Available from http://caramasia.gn.apc.org/Ritchie_ HK_cdtn.htm; Internet, accessed 22 Jan. 2003.

Theological Reflection on Sex Work

Theresa Yih-Lan Tsou, SSS

4

In 1997 when the Taipei City government attempted to close places of prostitution, the licensed prostitutes did not simply disappear or go underground as illegal "private prostitutes" (私娼). Instead, with heads covered by a hat connected to a working scarf, they appeared in public for the first time to protest the "clean up." Women's groups as well as human rights groups began to intervene. They wanted to help but had different perspectives as to the best course of action. Strong protests that prostitution is against human dignity was heard from Christian social service agencies that helped rescue teen prostitutes from trafficking. There was tension between two courses of action that the prostitutes could take: to stop work immediately or ask for a two-year provision for transition to some other work. The former sounded too difficult but the latter was harder for the older women.

In May 1999, supporters of the prostitute movement and sex workers established COSWAS—Collective Of Sex Workers And Supporters (日日春) to advocate for "prostitute rights as human rights." On 24 November 1999 the Executive Yuan Committee for the Promotion of Women's Right began an interdisciplinary research group to study how to manage the sex industry effectively. By 2001 when licensed prostitution was formally ended, COSWAS had already organized both a cooperative to sell simple things and a choir composed of former prostitutes. The members worked together to develop a prostitute culture and challenge society's traditional way of thinking about social seclusion and the moral scandal of sexual activities. At the same time they strove to decriminalize prostitution. In 2002 they organized a three-day forum on policy making, social work, and prostitute culture for professionals and interested citizens of Taipei city. The main speaker was the German prostitute rights activist Maya Czajka, foundress of Madonna. Madonna is an organization which advocates quality improvement and development of prostitution, and provides assistance for those who either want to find other jobs or start a private practice in prostitution.

Government studies were done in preparation for new legislation to legalize sex work but no public, formal Catholic voice was heard. A small ecumenical group of women theologians, two Sprout[1] members and three Presbyterians, researched various literatures but were not able to find Christian material relevant to the current issue. I wrote this article in order to clarify my understanding of the issues and respond to the needs of the times in this particular place.

THE PROSTITUTE AS PERSON AND HER WORK

Among the different voices, the reasons given in defense of "adult voluntary prostitution" were totally new for us. It seemed that the arguments previously used by Christians to protest against prostitution were irrelevant in this discussion. How do we respond to the needs of adult voluntary prostitutes? How do we extend our hands to these women in the margins of society? Even with the diversity of opinions there was general agreement that the old laws governing sexually related work were strongly biased against women and needed to be revised. What can we contribute to the legislative process in the light of our Christian heritage?

When we look at Jesus, we find that many times he ate with sinners including prostitutes. This scandalous behavior created tension among his kinsmen since a good Jew would never do such a prohibited thing! (Mt 9:10). He invited prostitutes and tax collectors to be his followers

(Mt 21:31–32; Mk 2:15–16). He let himself be touched by a woman sinner—by her tears, hair, kisses, and hands anointing him with oil. His heart was moved by her sincere expression of contrition (Lk 7:36–50). What was it like when Jesus, prostitutes, and tax collectors shared a meal together? Did he preach to them or did he listen to their stories with compassion, enabling them to experience a profound conversion and to regain their dignity? Have we ever listened to prostitutes' perceptions, experiences and reasoning?

"Sex Workers" as Persons

Who are the sex workers? Are they "special types of people," "very different" from the rest of society? On 26 May 2001, during the conference "Gender, Psychology, and Culture—the Development of Native Feminism," the presentation on "Licensed-Prostitute Event and Women's Movement" was followed by a heated and energetic discussion. Licensed prostitutes were carefully referred to as "licensed prostitute sisters" (公娼姊妹), said perhaps with a slight sense of guilt. The woman next to me, a former prostitute and now vice-president of their new organization, stood up and expressed the pain of being illiterate. This was the first time I was side by side with a woman who had been called different names, referred to as "they," and discussed by others as an "object." Others too easily say to them, "Do something else," without first walking in their shoes to see how many options they really have. In my earlier work to improve the condition of disadvantaged women, the exposure part of many conferences only allowed an opportunity to "look at them" from a short distance. Here she was one of "us."

The next presentation was given by Professor Hwang Shu-Ling on "Exploring the Erotic Policy of Taiwan: Research, Movement, and Feminism." She shared some of the findings from her doctoral thesis that included interviews with over 100 teenage and adult women prostitutes in Taiwan from 1991–1992.[2] In another article she categorized these women into three: adult women who resort to prostitution as temporary work, teenagers sold into these jobs, and teenagers who ran away from home and became sex workers for curiosity and to get money quickly.[3]

Since then, more women have committed themselves to be with those who for various reasons engage in sex-related work, and to understand their real life experience. One example is Jih Huey-Wen who did her 1998 master's thesis on the life experiences of twelve women in the sex industry and published a book.[4] Another is Chang Kuei-Ying who spent two to three years of field study with prostitutes and related personnel then completed her master's thesis in 2004.[5]

What about Church people? Do we stay away from "them"? Or do we try to "rescue them," "save them from sin," "reform them," "back into a mainstream, normal life style"? Despite all the good will, these responses fail to regard prostitutes as human beings and equals, treating them more as "objects," as if they do not know what they are doing and that we know better.

Sex Work

So far I have intermingled sex work and prostitution but have not given a definition for "sex work." From the studies of Hwang, Jih, and Chang, as well as from the daily newspapers, there is a spectrum of sexually related work which is called "service work" (服務業). This includes being a maid companion to "warm up" the atmosphere with chatting, joking, singing for fun, pouring alcoholic beverages, and drinking to enhance the above "fun"; then various degrees of touching, holding, caressing, and joking about body parts. Women may be asked to be scantily clad or to be naked to perform the above tasks though extra pay is given to take a particular woman out for sexual intercourse. These activities (花酒 erotic drinking) are usually part of business deals, rewards, bribes, or relaxation after a hard day of work. Young women may be called "princess of public relations" (公關公主). They are required to enter the room kneeling and to continue kneeling as they move forward if the activity is in a Japanese-style room with a wooden floor. They are to play a lower, weaker, feminine role in order to give men an inflated feeling of masculinity and a sense of brotherhood especially when it is necessary to connect opposing business partners.[6] Therefore women's body and sexuality are used and abused on many different levels and in many different ways.

ARGUMENTS REGARDING SEX WORK AND RIGHTS

There is a general understanding that teen prostitution is exploitation and the damage done interferes with her development into mature personhood. The trafficking of teenage girls is not acceptable and these young women ought to be protected.[7] The argument for the right to sex work exists mainly for adult women who voluntarily choose to be prostitutes. For example, during the early years of Madonna, Czajka worked again as a prostitute for a few years to raise funds for the running of this organization.[8]

Western feminists are not necessarily advocates of prostitution.[9] In fact, they are quite divided. While some see prostitution as symbolic of the degradation and domination of women, and the prostitute as a victim of patriarchy, others see prostitution as unconventional and demeaning but work that one should be allowed to choose, just like other women in marginal, sexist, and low-status work.[10] In terms of social relations, sexual romanticists tend to see commercial sexuality as corrupt and dehumanizing; while sexual libertarians tend to see it as one of many legitimate forms of sexual expression.[11] Various organizations that advocate prostitution have very different viewpoints. WHISPER (Women Hurt in Systems of Prostitution Engaged in Revolt), which comes from the sexual romanticist side, maintains that prostitutes' right groups make prostitution sound like a profitable and happy choice despite the fact that women are under coercion. On the other hand, Margo St. James, founder of C.O.Y.O.T.E. (Call Off Your Old Tired Ethics), an organization for prostitutes' rights, affirms from the libertarian side the value of sexual expression and economic freedom for women.[12]

What can be said about Church teachings regarding human work? John Paul II's document "Laborem Exercens—On Human Work" states:

> we must concentrate our attention on *work in the subjective sense*, much more than we did on the objective significance ... In fact there is no doubt that human work has an ethical value of its own, which clearly and directly remain linked to the fact that the one who carries it out is a person, a conscious and free

subject, that is to say a subject that decides about himself. (no. 6, emphasis mine)

If we take this seriously we need to listen to what women in prostitution say about their work, not just what others—whether they be legislators, philosophers, pastoral workers, or feminists, etc.—say *about* them.

Some of the arguments for prostitution include:

1. Where there is demand so there is supply. When the need is larger than the supply, the law will not stop the "selling of sex."
2. Sex work is no different from selling goods in a department store or doing continuous massage work.[13]
3. What is the difference between selling one's mind and selling one's body? There are other jobs that sell various parts of the body.
4. Sex is a positive, nurturing act.
5. It is a service and gives the other pleasure while there are activities that give people pain.
6. It gives psychological satisfaction.[14]
7. It is not degrading so long as the one who is engaged in it sees its importance.[15]
8. Prostitution has a bad name and is connected with drugs and Mafia, police bribery, and a high criminal rate because it is illegal. In parts of Germany where prostitution is legalized, these problems have been eliminated.[16]

Advocates of voluntary prostitution continue to challenge people who are hypocritical about the "purchase of sex." Gifts bought, activities paid for, even affectionate words used in the dating game, are also for the purpose of having sex with a person.[17] As for the "selling the body," there are other jobs, such as manual labor and athletics, which sell different services of the body. When society pretends to have a certain moral standard and prohibits prostitution, prostitution becomes invisible and more difficult to manage. The promoters of sex work say: We need to descandalize prostitution, and recognize it as a form of work, a formal profession. They also express that it is not immoral, degrading, or abusive, if others would not treat prostitutes with misunderstanding.[18] The next step after the descandalization of prostitution is to decriminalize it. The way to decriminalize is to legalize prostitution.

If the sex industry is not legalized, several problems need to be addressed. First, the human rights aspect of sex work which includes: 1) law enforcers' lack of respect for the human rights of prostitutes; 2) exploitation from customers; 3) exploitation by employers and other middle persons; 4) exploitation by other "protectors" including legislators. Second, there are public-related problems like: 1) public health and the prevention of venereal disease; 2) public order and abuse of power; 3) public safety. The police may spend more time arresting prostitutes than dangerous criminals; 4) trafficking of persons and drugs.[19]

If prostitution is legalized, it will be seen as a regular occupation instead of a deviation from the norm. Rules and regulations can be set with specific requirements for a license which would then be under government control. Sex workers will have rights and will be protected under contract, their health insurance, retirement insurance, and unemployment insurance provided for. They would also be able to organize unions to deal with customers who do not pay. Some prostitutes want to pay taxes which would give them a sense of their dignity and responsibility as citizens.[20] The income tax collected from them for any given country would be a good sum.

What do prostitutes think and feel about their bodies? During "Prostitute Culture festivals" feminist scholars and lawyers are invited to follow international prostitutes in a dance. How well prostitutes know their bodies and are comfortable with their bodies contrasted with the stiff, awkward movements of well-educated intellectual women. Some prostitutes express that they do appreciate their bodies and take good care of them.[21] A medical doctor's daughter, a university student in London, England, feels that she gained self-confidence after becoming a lap dancer; she now has power and is not exploited.[22] Above all, those who voluntarily choose prostitution view themselves as active agents of their own lives instead of passive victims.

REFLECTION ON SEX AS WORK

The above arguments to promote sex work and sex workers' rights involve areas from the personal to the national level. While issues about work usually concerns working conditions, in the case of prostitution the discussion even asks if it can be considered real work. The root of the issue has to do with attitudes and myths about sex. Yet, there are other types of work that also involve sale of the body with sexual implications, for example modeling, gymnastics, ballet, etc.[23] Though these are seen as high-class, artistic professions, the long-term strenuous exercises and/or extreme weight reduction programs required have harmed the bodies of many women.

The dictionary definition of "work" includes, among other things, "the occupation for which you are paid." We hear arguments from prostitutes like, "I am paid for the service I provide. I receive the money through work, not through stealing or robbery."

In the 1990 US Catholic Bishops document, human sexuality was defined as "a fundamental component of personality in and through which we, as male or female, experience our relatedness to self, others, the world and even God."[24] Ideally, from our faith tradition, we see that the sexual union of two persons affects every level of their lives and therefore it belongs to two people who have an exclusive relationship in the committed form of marriage. In reality, the sexual drive as an instinct can be so strong that it may overwhelm a person to act on it before he/she is prepared on other levels. Ideally, casual sex is not acceptable. In reality, sexual activities fulfill different needs for people on various levels therefore money is used to exchange for it.

IS WOMAN'S BODY AND SEXUALITY A "PROBLEM"?

Illusion serves to shield a person from the pain and fear of reality. Our familiar Church teachings usually warn men about the dangers or evil that comes from women. These teachings come out of great fear. Women's beauty is connected to sexuality. Beauty is one kind of power because it makes men willing to do anything to possess it. Historically, kings and generals fought wars for the sake of women and nations were lost for beautiful women. Women were therefore the sinners to be blamed for what happens to a whole country. Instead of dealing with men's fear and trying to appreciate the woman as a person, women's beauty has been objectified by the focus on the size and shape of different parts of her body, especially those parts which are specifically related to sexuality, e.g. breasts, waist, and buttocks. Women are mocked for their ugliness and blamed for their beauty.

Not only have we been conditioned to think that women's value is determined by the size of their sexual body parts, the so-called "feminine" style refers to the woman's capacity to satisfy the male ego, even to the point of pretending orgasm to help him feel his potency. Responsibility for giving birth to a child, especially a son, is put on women, who, when they fail, undergo complicated and uncomfortable physical examinations to determine what is wrong with them. Meanwhile the men do not need to submit to simpler tests. A woman's body is not hers until she is sick, especially with illness related to her reproductive organs, breast cancer and uterine tumor, for instance. With these illnesses she further loses her value.

Frequently heard problems between mother-in-law and daughter-in-law in families from the Han culture actually have something to do with the man "in between," a man who is grown up externally but remains "mother's little boy" inside. Marriage, therefore, is not the union of two equal partners as stated in definitions of the Sacrament of Matrimony. Rather, many women experienced that as a wife she is always seen as an outsider, invader, and competitor of the woman of the house. When women ask for marriage based on sharing, mutuality, and equal partnership, many men refrain from regular marriage and seek out a foreign bride with a lower educational and socio-economic status so that he can feel a sense of importance and is in charge at home. The wife's asking for a satisfactory sexual life is even more threatening. In that case, visits to a prostitute or engaging in other sexually oriented recreation becomes a way out. Many of the rules and regulations regarding morality or tight family values are in fact also an illusion since they hide immoral or unjust systems which have come down to us through the ages.

While men's premarital sexual experiences, multiple partners, extramarital affairs, mistresses, visits to prostitutes, sex tours, erotic drinking, etc. are to be "understood" and "forgiven," a higher standard is required of women to keep them "pure." Sexually independent women are given derogatory labels. Adult women who voluntarily choose prostitution for a living are too threatening to the "normal" way of thinking for both men and women. But what can we say about a starving woman refugee on a boat when she exchanges sex for a piece of bread, vs. a prostitute exchanging sex for the daily meals of her family, vs. women in "normal" marriages who exchange sex (and house work) for life? This question recalls a common expression that to find a husband is to find a "long-term meal ticket" (長期飯票). Not all marriages are this way, but many who were married in the past cannot deny that this understanding of marriage exists.

INSPIRATION FROM SCRIPTURE

It is difficult to find theological readings relating to this topic. What comes to mind is the story of Tamar, Judah's daughter-in-law (Genesis 38).

Tamar was widowed when her husband Er died after he "offended Yahweh greatly." Er's younger brother Onan was obliged to have relations with her so she could bear the older brother an heir. Onan, however, ejaculated on the ground offending Yahweh and causing Onan's death. Tamar was sent back to her family of origin as Judah was afraid his youngest son Shelah would also die if he had a relationship with her. Although his two sons had been killed by God for their own sins to Yahweh, Tamar was at fault.

What could Tamar do? What options did she have? If she continued living the role assigned to her, she would remain a childless widow with no social status, no future, and no way to survive after her father's death.

Tamar pretended to be a temple prostitute and waited for Judah. She knew too well that when she became pregnant, she might be burned alive for misconduct but by showing proof that Judah was the father, the critical moment would also be the life giving moment. Of course she also risked Judah's recognizing her while they were having sexual contact. Had that happened, Judah would have thought she prostituted herself regularly and the outcome would have been worse.

She was not blamed for initiating intercourse with her father-in-law, a violation of cultural taboo. Because as a Canaanite—a pagan woman—she was faithfully trying to comply with the Law and fulfilling the obligations prescribed by the patriarchal system. Her own feelings and sexual needs are not mentioned in the passage. Her basic function was for reproduction.

Caught between a slow death as a childless widow and a quick death by burning for adultery, Tamar opted for life by becoming a one-time-only prostitute. By going beyond the prescribed possibilities, she was able to choose her time, place, person, and method to obtain what she needed for survival.

We see a parallel between the story of Tamar and women prostitutes today. How can we blame women who choose undesirable work to fulfill family obligations when they have no other choice?

RESPONSE TO THE NEEDS AND
CHALLENGES TO BE FACED

No matter how many positive reasons are given for voluntary prostitution, i.e., a consensual act which is not coerced, we come back to the reality of ordinary life. The truth is, only a small number of women really love to be prostitutes.[25] Some of the positive reasons listed earlier were stated by only one person as in McWilliams[26] or Hong Kong case.[27] Most adult women prostitutes voluntarily chose this work because there were not many options open to them during that time in their lives when a choice had to be made. When the women have a goal in mind, rationalizing that the work is temporary helps them maintain a sense of integrity. The goal is to raise enough money for whatever will help them achieve a better career, pay their husband's debts, put children through school, etc. Once they have solved the problem at hand, they know they can move on to something else.[28]

It is easy for others who have job opportunities to say, "Why don't you do something else?" or "Try something else!" The women from COSWAS did. They made crafts to sell during the conferences and other public occasions. Many people looked at the items but very few were sold. This is a difficult and unreliable way to make a living. Several years have passed. The group of ex-prostitutes who struggled to "get back to normal life" still is having a hard time. In their early life their families could not afford or did not allow them to go to school even when education was mandatory and not so costly. Lack of education limits one's options in life. Gender made the difference: even when they did better in school than their brothers, girls were to work to earn money so their brothers could get further education. Poverty is not only lack of money; poverty is lack of choice!

The question is this: If it is not moral to sell sex, then who pushes the situation to the extent where a woman has no other options? When men control most of the resources, why are they willing to pay big amounts of money for sex, but hesitate, if not refuse, to give better wages and provide better work opportunities for women? "Laborem Exercens—On Human Work" states: "[I]n every case, a just wage is the concrete means of *verifying the justice* of the whole socioeconomic system and, in any case, of checking that it is functioning justly." (no. 19; emphasis mine) Is prostitution a moral issue or in actuality, a justice issue?

NOTES

1   Sprout: Taiwan Catholic Sprout Women-Concerns Association was established to promote the rights, dignity, and equal partnership of women as well as participation in other justice actions based on feminist theological reflection.

2   黃淑玲　(2001.5)　〈思索台灣色情政策：研究、運動與女性主義〉。Hwang, Shu-Ling, "Exploring the Erotic Policy of Taiwan: Research, Movement, and Feminism," paper presented at the conference "Gender, Psychology, and Culture—the Development of Native Feminism," Taipei, May 2001.

3   黃淑玲　(1996)　〈台灣特種行業婦女：受害者？行動者？偏差者?〉，《台灣社會研究季刊》，第22期，1996年4月，頁103-152。Idem, "Women in Sex Industries: Victims, Agents, or Deviants?," *A Radical Quarterly in Social Studies* (1996): 103–52.

4   紀慧文(1998)《12個上班小姐的生涯故事》，唐山。Jih, Huey-Wen, *The Career Stories of Twelve Call Girls* (Taipei, Tonsam, 1998); available from http://sex. ncu.edu.tw/activities/1998/19980313a.htm; Internet, accessed Nov. 2004.

5   張貴英(2004)《高雄市公娼制度的歷史脈絡與存廢之社會歷程》，國立高雄師範大學性別教育研究所論文。Chang, Kuei-Ying Cindy, *The History of Legal Prostitution System and Social Impact in Kaoshiung City* (National Kaoshiung Normal University, 2004).

6   黃淑玲(2001.12)〈台灣男性集體喝花酒的文化意涵：餽贈女人、社會交換、男性氣概〉，『台灣少女、色情市場、男性買色客』之研究 – 運動、法律、社工、心理、文化的觀點，【研究報告論文】，婦女救援基金會。Hwang,　Shu-Ling, "The Cultural Implications of Group Erotic Drinking of Taiwanese Men: Giving Women, Social Exchange, and Masculinity," paper presented at the conference "Gender, Psychology, and Culture – the Development of Native Feminism," Taipei, May 2001.

7   Kathleen Peratis, "Q: Should the U.N. Treat Voluntary Prostitution as a Form of Women's Labor? Yes: Sex Workers are Entitled to Dignity and to Respect for their Human Right," Insight on the News, available from http://www.insightmag.com/.../Q.Should.The U.N.Treat.Voluntary.Prostitution.As A.Form.Of.Womens.Labor-210658.shtml; Internet, accessed Oct. 2004.

8   探討一個進步的公共政策 – 從務實合法的德國看掃黃的台灣，2002台北市第三屆亞洲NGO會議：性工作、人權、社會變革系列論壇，「性產業政策」國際研討會。"Dialogue with Maya Czajka: Toward a Progressive Sex Work Public Policy – From Germany to Taiwan," handout from Third Asian NGO Meeting, Taipei, 2002.

9   Laurie Shrage, *Moral Dilemmas of Feminism: Prostitution, Adultery, and Abortion* (New York, London: Routledge, 1994), preface.

10 Ibid., 82.

11 Ibid., 88.

12 Ibid., x, 89; see also Hwang, *Women in Sex Industries,* 103–52.

13   "Dialogue with Maya Czajka"; Peter McWilliams, *Ain't Nobody's Business If You Do—Part III: A Closer Look at the Consensual Crimes—Prostitution*, available from www.mcwilliams.com/books/aint/306.htm; Internet accessed Oct. 2004.

14   Ibid.

15   Margo St. James, cited by McWilliams, *Ain't Nobody's Business If You Do*;〈爭取平權是我最大的願望一個性工作者的自白〉,《香港天主教正義和平委員會通訊》4.2004: 6–7 "*To Fight for Equal Rights Is My Greatest Desire—Self Disclosure of a Sex Worker,*" Justice and Peace Newsletter —Justice & Peace Commission of the Hong Kong Catholic Diocese, Apr. 2004, 6–7.

16   "Dialogue with Maya Czajka."

17   See McWilliams, *Ain't Nobody's Business If You Do.*

18   Margo St. James, cited by ibid.; Jean Almodovar, *Cop to Call Girl: Why I Left the LAPD to Make an Honest Living as a Beverly Hills Prostitute*, quoted in McWilliams, *Ain't Nobody's Business If You Do.*

19   王芳萍《台灣掃黃下性工作者人權問題》2002台北市第三屆亞洲NGO會議：性工作、人權、社會變革系列論壇,「性產業政策」國際研討會,頁2及口頭報告。Wang, Fang Ping, cited by Kathleen Peratis, Q: Should the U.N. Treat Voluntary Prostitution as a Form of Women's Labor?"

20   Hong Kong case, see "Dialogue with Maya Czajka."

21   Ibid.

22   "Daughter of M.D. becomes a Lap Dancer," *United Daily News*, 15 Feb. 2004.

23   If it is not clear why there are sexual implications, even the title of the following book tells something. Judith Lynne Hanna, *Dance, Sex, and Gender—Signs of Identity, Dominance, Defiance, and Desire* (Chicago: University of Chicago Press, 1988).

24   1990 U.S. Catholic Bishops, *Human Sexuality: A Catholic Perspective for Education and Lifelong Learning*, quoted in *Youth Update Glossary*, St. Anthony Messenger, 2002, available from http://www.americancatholic.org/Messenger/Oct2005/; Internet accessed Oct. 2004.

25   Peratis, "Q: Should the U.N. Treat Voluntary Prostitution as a Form of Women's Labor?"

26   See McWilliams, *Ain't Nobody's Business If You Do.*

27   "Dialogue with Maya Czajka."

28   Hwang, *Exploring the Erotic Policy of Taiwan*; also in Peratis, "Q: Should the U.N. Treat Voluntary Prostitution as a Form of Women's Labor?" and from personal sharing of experiences.

BIBLIOGRAPHY

Almodovar, Jean. *Cop to Call Girl: Why I Left the LAPD to Make an Honest Living as a Beverly Hills Prostitute.* Quoted in McWilliams, *Ain't Nobody's Business If You Do.*

Chang, Kuei-Ying Cindy. *The History of Legal Prostitution System and Social Impact in Kaoshiung City.* National Kaoshiung Normal University, 2004.

"Daughter of M.D. becomes a Lap Dancer." *United Daily News,* 15 Feb. 2004.

"Dialogue with Maya Czajka: Toward a Progressive Sex Work Public Policy—From Germany to Taiwan." Handout from Third Asian NGO Meeting, Taipei, 2002.

Hanna, Judith Lynne. *Dance, Sex, and Gender—Signs of Identity, Dominance, Defiance, and Desire.* Chicago: University of Chicago Press, 1988.

Hwang, Shu-Ling. "Exploring the Erotic Policy of Taiwan: Research, Movement, and Feminism." Paper presented at the conference "Gender, Psychology, and Culture—the Development of Native Feminism." Taipei, May 2001.

———. "The Cultural Implications of Group Erotic Drinking of Taiwanese Men: Giving Women, Social Exchange, and Masculinity." Paper presented at the conference "Gender, Psychology, and Culture—the Development of Native Feminism." Taipei, May 2001.

———. "Women in Sex Industries: Victims, Agents, or Deviants?" *A Radical Quarterly in Social Studies* (1996): 103–52.

Jih, Huey-Wen. *The Career Stories of Twelve Call Girls.* Taipei, Tonsam, 1998. Available from http://sex.ncu.edu.tw/activities/1998/19980313a.htm; Internet, accessed Nov. 2004.

McWilliams, Peter. *Ain't Nobody's Business If You Do—Part III: A Closer Look at the Consensual Crimes—Prostitution.* Available from www.mcwilliams.com/books/aint/306.htm; Internet, accessed Oct. 2004.

Peratis, Kathleen. "Q: Should the U.N. Treat Voluntary Prostitution as a Form of Women's Labor? Yes: Sex Workers are Entitled to Dignity and to Respect for their Human Right." Insight on the News. Available from http://www.insightmag.com/ . . . /Q.Should.The U.N.Treat.Voluntary.Prostitution.As A.Form.Of.Womens.Labor-210658.shtml; Internet, accessed Oct. 2004.

Shrage, Laurie. *Moral Dilemmas of Feminism: Prostitution, Adultery, and Abortion.* New York, London: Routledge, 1994.

"*To Fight for Equal Rights Is My Greatest Desire—Self Disclosure of a Sex Worker.*" Justice and Peace Newsletter—Justice & Peace Commission of the Hong Kong Catholic Diocese. Apr. 2004, 6–7.

1990 U.S. Catholic Bishops. *Human Sexuality: A Catholic Perspective for Education and Lifelong Learning.* Quoted in *Youth Update Glossary.* St. Anthony Messenger, 2002. Available from http://www.americancatholic.org/Messenger/Oct2005/; Internet accessed Oct. 2004.

Ecological Approach Towards Redefining the Sexuality of Women

Dzintra Ilishko

Ecological and cultural crises in the western world provide clear signs everywhere that both communism in Eastern Europe and Western capitalism have failed. The two worlds built on the thought of Galileo, Descartes, Newton, Marx, and Smith are in ruins.[1] Their worldviews reduce the Universe to atomistic terms where phenomena is perceived only in isolation from each other. The two systems are not sustainable in either human or ecological terms.

The Western world has been built on interpretation of Newtonian physics, described by Arthur Peacock in the following way:

> By the end of the 19th century the absolutes of space, time, object, and determinism were apparently securely enthroned in an unmysterious, mechanistically determined world, basically simple in structure at the atomic level and, unchanging in form—for even geological and biological transformations operated under fixed laws.[2]

This philosophy has found expression in disastrous practices—pollution (e.g. the widespread use of biocides, the long-term containment of highly toxic chemicals and nuclear waste, the release of genetically engineered organisms into the environment), the degradation of fisheries, and forests, and the destruction of wilderness. The universe is so mechanically determined and simple that clear distinctions may be drawn and a hierarchy established between spirit and body, human and nonhuman, objective and subjective, reason and passion, bodies, especially women's bodies, become subjects to be used and abused. This all leads to deep ecological crisis which theologians and educators can try to overcome by developing a new ecological sensitivity towards a human being, its body, the other and the world. We have to learn a new way of thinking in terms of interdependence, relationality, harmony and reciprocity. Therefore, a holistic sensibility needs to be developed; our way of perceiving ourselves and our place in the world should be re-evaluated.

The new view can better be expressed through the principle of population ecology: the interdependence of each living organism with other living organisms and components of its environment.

Now people all over the world are faced with the tremendous task of rebuilding for a more sustainable world. This transition requires creativity, moral leadership, foresight, wisdom, and openness to other cultural and religious traditions. We must move from a mechanistic to a more holistic and ecological perspective where the world is seen to be made up of interconnected parts and systems. All phenomena can only be understood in relation to each other and in relation to the larger system or whole where the human is an implicit part of the natural world. Historical insights might be helpful in understanding the roots of the ecological crisis and the negative view of sexuality.

HISTORICAL INSIGHTS DEFINING WOMEN'S SEXUALITY

If we look into the pages of history of Asia, Eastern and Western Europe, women most often were identified with nature. On the psychological level the woman's body was considered to be closer to nature, while the man's sphere was associated more with culture. The woman's body was designed to produce and nurture children. Man's role was to carry on social and political tasks integral to culture. Platonic thought has also left a tremendous influence on Christianity by sharply separating matter from the spirit, and body from the flesh. Mind was considered primal, and eternal; body as secondary, derivative, and the source of evil. As Rosemary Ruether argues the Greek worldview not only established a cosmic hierarchy, it also fostered alienation from the human body.[3]

In medieval times, the exploitation of nature was restrained by the association of nature with demonic powers and by an organic view of nature as both female and alive. Nature and women were held in some awe and fear because of their association with demons, witchcraft, and many superstitions. Because productive activity was still largely based in the home and women were valued as partners, the respect due to them as mothers also carried over into an attitude of respect towards nature, which was viewed as a powerful mother.

The rise of science led to a change in attitudes towards both women and nature. As science progressed during the seventeenth and eighteenth centuries, extreme formulations of spirit/matter dualism developed in philosophical thought and nature came to be regarded by many as "dead matter" to be analyzed and manipulated. With nature so objectified, the bodies of women also became objects to be abused, an attitude reflected in widespread prostitution and the various forms of torture of women's bodies. With the onset of industrial capitalist culture, women, being identified with nature, increasingly became commodified as well.

It is necessary to stress that the disenchantments of nature was brought about by the scientific revolution of the seventeenth and eighteenth centuries, and the industrial capitalist cultures as well. The medieval organic vision of nature was replaced by a mechanistic worldview that saw the natural world as dead and passive. This period marks "the death of nature."

The Enlightenment meant increasing confidence in the power of man's rational mind to master and manipulate the natural world. It was a period of indisputable advances in science, advances that may be considered both cause and effect of a shift in the balance of power in favor of humans against nature.

In summary, it may be said that dominance is the principle of the industrial-capitalist worldview which has molded our understanding of ourselves and our place in the world. The anthropocentric worldview concomitant to industrial capitalism sees nature as made for man's use. Therefore, today's theological challenge is to reevaluate the dominant destructive ways of being in the world, and to develop positive ecological attitudes and approaches towards women and nature

KEY CHALLENGES OF THE ECOFEMINIST MOVEMENT

Break Down Patriarchal Structures

According to ecofeminist thinkers, the connections between the oppression of women and the destruction of nature are embedded in a patriarchal conceptual framework and reflect the logic of domination that justifies and maintains the subordination of both women and nature. Patriarchy in its wider definition is a male pyramid of graded subordination and exploitation based on class, race, ethnicity, and religion. Like women, certain races, class, ethnicities are viewed as closer to nature and therefore inferior. A patriarchal conceptual mindset explains, justifies and maintains the subordination of an "inferior" group over a "superior" group.[4]

Challenge Dualistic Thinking

Hierarchical thinking also generates normative dualisms; thinking in which disjunctive terms are seen as exclusive rather than inclusive, and oppositions conflicting rather than complementary. Feminist theologians believe that this sort of logic, as we have noted, has justified humans' domination of fellow humans and nature. It also justifies the domination of nature. An example of dualistic thinking is reflected in traditional theological anthropologies (e.g., the two-nature anthropologies of Augustine and Thomas) that fostered body/spirit dualism, and defined women by their procreative abilities. By defining women primarily in terms of their physiology, the other potentialities of women were ignored. Furthermore, dualistic anthropologies have led to an easy acceptance of patriarchy, "the rule of powerful men over less powerful men and women, as natural, as the way the world should be, as ordained by God."[5] Many feminist theologians call for rejection of traditional dualism and the liberation of women to full participation in the life of the human species.

Feminist theologians also challenged how the notion of femininity has been constructed in history. Ecofeminist thinkers do not support any glorification of the feminine. The affirmation of women's nature and sexuality should be seen as compatible with agency and independence. The identification of females with inferior bodies and nature, identification of males with superior reason and spirit, are social constructs that have reinforced negative stereotyping of women.

The extremes represented by radical and liberal feminism, however, have not served women well. As Valerie Saivings explains, by denying women's bodily reality, early radical feminism fostered patriarchal alienation from body.[6] Early radical feminists located the root of women's oppression in their biology (i.e., their potentiality to become mothers, their capacity to lactate thus making them primarily responsible for child care, etc.). The rejection of motherhood and lesbianism (which has been forced on some women) were regarded as among the ways by which women can be liberated. Liberal feminism, on the other hand, appropriated liberal philosophy's superior regard for rationality and intellectual labor, thus rejecting the association of women with nature. For the early radical and liberal feminists, therefore, women's liberation required rejection of women's biology, considered the source of their inequality and oppression. Later radical feminists on the other hand moved from seeing women's biology as the problem to women's biology as the solution. Because of women's potentialities to become mothers, they are closer to nature, less dualistic, more caring and peace-loving.

Ecofeminist theologians see the danger in early radical and liberal feminists' rejection of the importance of embodiment. In contrast, they reclaim women's bodies and their biologically linked roles. Ecofeminists hold that bodies are sacred and have their intrinsic value, and that the denial of women's bodies has implications on the denial of the bodies of all marginalized and the body of the Universe. This denial of the body leads to a utilitarian attitude towards both, nature and body. Thus, liberation of women rests upon redefining women's body.

Ecofeminist theologians draw heavily upon the thinker Whitehead who expands the notion of body by denoting how the living human person organically relates to the body and also transcends it. The difference between women and men's bodies cannot be ignored for these can affect our being, but at the same time, there is also the possibility of transcending this embodiment. Whitehead's conceptualization of self and its relation to body is very helpful to achieve the goal of avoiding alienation from the body and identification with it. His philosophy of organism does not identify the person with the body, although it affirms the relation of a person to his/her body and dissolves other traditional dualisms, such as activity/passivity, self/other, subject/object, body/mind by his "rhythm of process."[7]

Re-evaluate Dominant Metaphors

One of the ways towards a sustainable future is a change of consciousness. New ecological sensibility requires us to see ourselves not as rulers of the Earth but as gardeners, caretakers, mothers, fathers, stewards, trustees, lovers, co-creators, and friends of a world. Educators need to reflect critically on dominant metaphors which support dualistic, unchanging, atomistic, anthropocentric ways of being in the world and relating to our bodies.

Therefore, one of the tasks is re-evaluating dominant assumptions and prejudices, which Jack Mezirow calls "meaning schemas."[8] He defines these meaning schemas as sets of habitual expectations, cause-effect or event sequences. Mezirow discusses how epistemic, sociocultural and psychic distortions are acquired through the process of the uncritical acceptance of another's values. Epistemic distortions are "distorted presuppositions" that every problem has a correct solution made up by the only expert.[9] Sociocultural distortions involve "taking for granted belief systems that pertain to power and social relationships, especially those currently prevailing, legitimized and enforced by institution or other individuals."[10] For example, in Europe, there are negative perceptions of colored women and those from other religions. Psychic distortions are "presuppositions generating unwarranted anxiety that impedes taking action."[11] Mezirow's insights are very helpful in understanding how the knower and the known are situated in "a social matrix of interconnected relations." Thus, knowledge of the epistemic, sociocultural, and psychic distortions is an essential task for the ecofeminist thinkers in deconstructing patriarchal mindset.

Develop a Feminist Epistemology
Ecofeminist theologians work to uncover how patriarchy has permeated knowledge. For them the starting point is a new epistemology that: 1) challenges dualisms of subject-object, mind-body, and inner-outer that are abstract, incomplete, and not adequately grounded in human experience; 2) incorporates women's experience which has been excluded from the realm of the known, and of the rational; 3) thinks in relational and contextual ways, and 4) redefines the concept of human being and their place in the Universe. Ecofeminist theologians suggest a transformation of knowledge adequate to human beings, which points beyond present distorted forms of a great whole and: "opens us up to the possibility of multiple ways of knowing what is to be known, of appealing to the diversity of cognitive capacities we have within us."[12] This holistic perspective affects theology, inviting it to broaden its horizon beyond monotheistic discourse about God, and beyond a dogma that can become authoritarian. It also opens possibilities to the many-sided human experience of relating to the values that give meaning to human existence. Inclusive epistemology welcomes the great multiplicity of all religious experience as "different expressions of a single breath, a single pursuit of oneness."[13]

Medieval historian Lynn White suggests that an ecological perspective implies the abandonment of anthropocentric views. Anthropocentrism is an exaggerated sense of the importance of the human in relation to all other species. White views Christianity as having promoted the deepest and most persistent assumption of all dominant Western philosophical, social, and political traditions since classical Greece—the assumption that humans are the crowning glory of creation, the source of all value, the measure of all things.

Expand One's Ecological Self

Thomas Berry maintains today that the survival of humankind must involve a journey back into intimacy with the Universe. While the journey of the person from the West has generally led into estrangement from the other and the self,[14] Matthew Fox suggests expanding the self beyond "the limits of one's egoistic, biographical or personal sense of self to "something which is more inclusive than individual self."[15] Dewey's notion of an expanded self includes such attitudes as straightforwardness, open-mindedness, breath of outlook, integrity of purpose, and responsibility towards the different other. Such qualities characterize a person who is extending and deepening an interest in learning from all his or her contacts in the world. Dewey's notion of self reaches beyond such terms as self-interest, personal preference, and the like. Conceptualizing the self as an ecosystem existing within a larger ecosystem can facilitate the shift from thinking of self as a separate, independent entity to recognizing its complete interdependence.

Treat the World as a Body of God

Sallie McFague underlines the importance of envisioning theology as metaphorical. Metaphorical theology experiments and tests and imagines possibilities that are novel in their nature.[16] Images provide lenses through which one views reality. Gibson Winter calls these images "comprehensive metaphors."[17] They "furnish the coherence of one's world and impose a fundamental pattern on one's existence."[18]

McFague's metaphor of "the world as God's body"[19] helps us humans to understand better how humans can treat bodies more responsibly. McFague's image brings together immanence and transcendence and the dignity of both creation and Creator. This image speaks of an embodiment of God that gives sacred dimension to matter and the world.

When the body earth is viewed as alive and sacred, not as functioning like a machine, then human actions are less likely to be manipulative of nature and more likely to be sensitive. Treating the world as God's body can elicit a contemplative response towards nature, where the beauty of nature is appreciated not simply as pointing to the Divine but for its intrinsic value and sacredness.[20]

Where the body is concerned, ecofeminist theologians critique the glorification of different kinds of universalism that underscore sameness, not difference. They invite a change in the dominant perspective, from a narrow focus on the one ideal, human (male) body as the base of the model to a cosmic focus, which underscores differences and values every body. These differences lead to the ideal of union, convergence, and mutuality,[21] an understanding that aligns with the biblical presentation: "and God created humanity in God's own image, male and female God created them" (Gn 1:27). Not only does God transcend human sexuality and yet embrace both male and female reality, the future can be realized only in productive union, a unity that embraces sexual differentiation and does not impose the superiority of one sex over the other.

The reclaiming of body extends to all earth bodies that are being used, abused, and oppressed. An ecological perspective implies consideration of the planetary agenda, thinking inclusively and globally, and acting locally. Embodied living means: (a) validating the value of different earth bodies; (b) supporting diversity of women's embodied experiences; (c) unmasking the androcentric and Eurocentric process of constructing and validating knowledge claims; and (d) legitimating embodied knowledge claims.

Develop Eco-Spirituality

Another sign of an ecological and cultural crisis is young people's alienation from traditional religious traditions in Eastern and Western Europe and their search for alternative spirituality in Buddhism, Yoga and other Eastern religions. More often people reject spirituality in its confessional or traditional understanding because of its association with institutionalized religion and its non-ecological, non-relational view of existence. In contrast, ecological spirituality aims to create consciousness of the interdependence of all things, and the need to live in harmony with the environment.[22] It promotes a sense of kinship with others, and also with the non-human world, the denizens of which are viewed as having their own experiences, values, and purposes.[23] Ecological spirituality develops a new sensibility in humans towards nature and the body. It fosters personal integrity that means taking body and spirit seriously. Ecological spirituality can also be called incarnate because it celebrates bodyliness as a normal and natural part of created order. Incarnation spirituality affirms the goodness of matter and regards the person as embodied spirit. Ecofeminist theologians encourage the adoption of practices that nurture the integration of body/spirit, emotion/intellect, sexuality/spirituality. Eco-spirituality is concerned about the whole person. The integration of bodily reality into spiritual life is a challenge in a situation of ecological and cultural crisis. The affirmation of body and sexuality leads to integrative ways of living.

Another very significant aspect of ecological spirituality is its communal aspect. Traditional Western spirituality is focused on inwardness. Ecological spirituality begins in intense inwardness but is not opposed to extensive outwardness. Although it is deeply personal, it is not necessarily individualistic because relationship with God, touches everything: one's relationships with others, community and the World. Eco-spirituality can be described as holistic. It insists on building right relationships with God, others and nature.

CONCLUSION

The cultural and ecological crisis in Eastern and Western Europe demands the development of an ecologically sustainable global community, that rejects materialistic philosophy and acknowledges Otherness and Bodyliness. The reality of our multicultural and multireligious world challenges us to think creatively of alternative ways of thinking, living and doing. Ecofeminism, in underlining the connection between the subordination of women, the destruction of nature, and other forms of oppression (class, racial ethnic, etc.) offers a holistic response to the issue.

NOTES

1 David Orr, *Ecological Literacy: Education in Transition to a Postmodern World* (New York: State University of New York Press, 1991).

2 Arthur Peacocke, *Creation and the World of Science* (Oxford: Clarendon, 1979), 54.

3 Rosemary Radford Ruether, *Women Healing Earth: Third World Women on Ecology and Religion* (New York: Orbis Books, 1996).

4 Karen Warren, "The Power and Promise of Ecological Feminism," in *Readings in Ecology and Feminist Theology*, ed. M. MacKinnon and M. McIntyre (Kansas City: Sheed and Ward, 1995), 172–96.

5 Regina Coll, *Christianity and Feminism in Conversation* (Mystic, CT Connecticut: Twenty Third Publication, 1994), 76.

6 Valerie Saivings, "The Human Situation: A Feminine View," in *Woman Spirit Rising: A Feminist Reader in Religion*, ed. Carol Christ and Judith Plaskow (New York: Harper and Row Books, 1979), 19–32.

7 Alfred Whitehead, *Adventure of Ideas* (New York: Free Press, 1966), 9.

8 Jack Mezirow, "How Critical Reflection Triggers Transformative Theory," in *Fostering Critical Reflection in Adulthood*, ed. Jack Mezirow (San Francisco: Jossey Bass, 1991), 1–19.

9 Ibid., 15.

10 Ibid., 16.

11 Ibid.

12 Ivone Gebara, *Longing for Running Water* (Minneapolis, MN : Fortress Press, 1999), 62.

13 Ibid., 65.

14 Dietrich Hansen, "Dewey's Conception of An Environment for Teaching and Learning," *Curriculum Enquiry* 32, no. 3 (2002): 268–80.

15 Ibid., 199.

16 Sallie McFague, *Super, Natural Christians: How We Should Love Nature* (Minneapolis, MN: Fortress Press, 1997).

17 Gibson Winter, *Liberating Creation* (New York: Crossroad, 1981), 1.

18 Ibid., 28.

19 Sallie McFague, *The Body of God: An Ecological Theology* (Minneapolis MN: Fortress Press, 1993), 64.

20 Elizabeth Johnson, "God's Beloved Creation," *America* 10 (Apr. 2001): 13.

21 McFague, *The Body of God*, 76.

22 David Ray Griffin, *Spirituality and Society: Postmodern Visions* (New York: State University Press, 1988).

23 Ibid., 45.

BIBLIOGRAPHY

Coll, Regina. *Christianity and Feminism in Conversation.* Mystic, CT Connecticut: Twenty Third Publication, 1994.

Gebara, Ivone. *Longing for Running Water.* Minneapolis, MN: Fortress Press, 1999.

Griffin, David Ray. *Spirituality and Society: Postmodern Visions.* New York: State University Press, 1988.

Hansen, Dietrich. "Dewey's Conception of An Environment for Teaching and Learning." *Curriculum Enquiry* 32, no. 3 (2002): 268–80.

Johnson, Elizabeth. "God's Beloved Creation." *America* 10 (Apr. 2001): 8–13.

McFague, Sallie. *Super, Natural Christians: How We Should Love Nature.* Minneapolis, MN: Fortress Press, 1997.

McFague, Sallie. *The Body of God: An Ecological Theology.* Minneapolis MN: Fortress Press, 1993.

Mezirow, Jack. "How Critical Reflection Triggers Transformative Theory." In *Fostering Critical Reflection in Adulthood,* 1–19. Edited by Jack Mezirow. San Francisco: Jossey Bass, 1991.

Orr, David. *Ecological Literacy: Education in Transition to a Postmodern World.* New York: State University of New York Press, 1991.

Peacocke, Arthur. *Creation and the World of Science.* Oxford: Clarendon, 1979.

Radford Ruether, Rosemary. *Women Healing Earth: Third World Women on Ecology and Religion.* Maryknoll, New York: Orbis Books, 1996.

Saivings, Valerie. "The Human Situation: A Feminine View." In *Woman Spirit Rising. A Feminist Reader in Religion,* 19–32. Edited by Carol Christ and Judith Plaskow. New York: Harper and Row Books, 1979.

Warren, Karen. "The Power and Promise of Ecological Feminism." In *Readings in Ecology and Feminist Theology,* 172–96. Edited by M. MacKinnon and M. McIntyre. Kansas City: Sheed and Ward, 1995.

Whitehead, Alfred. *Adventure of Ideas.* New York: Free Press, 1966.

Winter, Gibson. *Liberating Creation.* New York: Crossroad, 1981.

III

Body and Scriptures

Gender Identity and Ezekiel 16

Julia Ong Siu Yin, IJS

6

The verses about the metaphorical "woman" in the marriage imagery in Ezekiel constitute the most lengthy, detailed, coherent, and explicit description in the prophetic books in the Old Testament. A unique piece of work that is useful for the study of the marriage imagery, the metaphor in chapter 16 provokes reactions that cannot be ignored. For instance, there are readers who found the nymphomaniac harlot[1] or the notions of an abused or raped woman with its pornographic descriptions far too insulting to be appropriate for the message it is supposed to convey.[2] Without doubt, the chapter has the power to disturb and to cause conflict within and among readers. Certainly, it is a rare reader who can remain indifferent to its images.

This essay explores the differences in the conflict that both metaphor and marriage imagery evoke in the context of the sexuality of male and female readers. The journey begins with the historical background of the text then proceeds towards the spiritual, social, political and cultural context of today. Subsequently it investigates whether gender identity has an effect on the response of readers. The thread that runs through this journey is the constant questioning of the relevance of the message and the usefulness of the metaphor and the marriage imagery.

CONTEXT AND LIMITATIONS

The Community

Ezekiel 16 was presented during the season of Lent 2003, to a faith community of mostly young adult men and women belonging to a church group in Singapore. The members who participated in this research were six men and twenty-six women, singles and married, of Chinese and Indian ethnicity.[3]

The chapter was presented in English, over three lectures with cell group discussions before each presentation. The total of six sessions lasted six weeks and personal reflection was required. Before the closing lecture was given, individuals were asked to answer the following questions anonymously in writing, but stating whether the answer came from a male or female:

In what way do you identify yourself with the characters in Ezekiel chapter sixteen? How do you appreciate the association? What are the feelings that were evoked in you? How did the text affect you as a male or female reader? Write a paragraph about how you have experienced God in your life.

The recommendations and conclusion of this article are derived from the contribution of this community which openly and generously struggled through the metaphor and imagery for their journey of growth during Lent.

GENDER IDENTITY AND SEXUAL ORIENTATION

The sexuality of a person depends on the interrelated factors of his or her sexual identity, sexual behavior, gender identity, and sexual orientation.[4] This article does not focus on sexual identity, which is the biological character of the reader; neither does it focus on the sexual behavior of the person. Rather it takes into consideration the gender identity of the reader, that is, the person's sense of maleness or femaleness. This sense is the context in which the reader interacts with the metaphor of the woman in the text. This work also considers the sexual orientation of the reader as he/she interacts with the marriage imagery presented by Ezekiel.[5]

THE HISTORICAL CONTEXT

The Text

Ezekiel 16 today has sixty-three verses including verses forty-four to sixty-three, probably a redacted addition that does not include the vocabulary of the marriage imagery. Verses one to forty-three offer a chiastic structure with defilement as the core message; the entire sixty-three verses have a concentric structure with shame as the center of the chapter and the compassion of YHWH circumscribing it.[6] While the metaphor of the woman and the marriage imagery remained intact in the chapter, because of the redacted addition, the whole meaning and emphasis of the message took a turn which we cannot afford to ignore.

The chiastic structure of verses 1 – 43:

vv. 1 – 5 (A)	Death, nakedness, blood and rejection
vv. 6 – 8 (B)	YHWH passes by, enters into a relationship with Jerusalem
vv. 9 – 14 (C)	YHWH washes, cleans and clothes Jerusalem
vv. 15 –22 (C)	Jerusalem clothes men and sacrifices children
vv. 23 – 34 (B)	Men pass by, Jerusalem enters into a relationship with them
vv. 35 – 43 (A)	Death, nakedness, blood and rejection

This shorter chapter records the priestly tradition's view that the defilement of the temple sanctuary was an irreversible disaster.[7] The theme of this chapter falls into the first section of the book that had intended to warn the Israelites of Jerusalem's approaching fall.[8] The context was war. The marriage imagery was not only defilement in terms of adultery, penalized with death by stoning (Lev 20:10) it included the violence that women suffer from rape as a weapon of war.[9] The metaphor says that Jerusalem, the woman, brought these upon herself because she entered into foreign alliances and idolatry. The language of idolatry and paying tribute to foreign powers is intertwined.

In its historical context, the purpose of stripping the woman is to shame her[10] and remove from her all property, including her clothes, which belonged to her husband. Perception of female sexuality as being good only under the possession and control of the male was a cultural reality.[11] But the point is that the religious, cultural, political, and economic realities of the Israelites of Ezekiel's time were all woven into the personification of the adulterous woman and the violence was indeed necessarily real.[12]

As we read Ezekiel 16 today, we feel for women who suffer abuse and are sexually exploited. We empathize with women who are voiceless, are used as mere objects of pleasure, and are blamed unfairly for bringing about their own fate. We feel their anger and are often moved to protest against how these women are often stripped of their dignity. However, we also realize that the context in which Ezekiel 16 was written does reflect the historical mindset that Jerusalem did bring on the destruction of the city herself. Accordingly, this destruction has been interpreted as an expression of God's uncompromising wrath.

But that was not the end of the chapter! With the redaction, we need not read the text and be immobilized by the blame and the wrath. The concentric structure of the sixty-three verses offers us the compassion of God.

The concentric structure of verses 1 – 63:

vv. 1 – 14 (A)	YHWH's compassion
vv. 15 – 34 (B)	Jerusalem's infidelity
vv. 35 – 43 (C)	Jerusalem's shame　　*
vv. 44 – 52 (B)	Jerusalem's infidelity
vv. 53 – 63 (A)	YHWH's compassion

The central theme of the chapter is the shamed Jerusalem; her infidelity causes her shame and the milieu that contains both her infidelity and shame is YHWH's compassion.

With this redaction, restoration of Jerusalem is possible. What was irreversible in the shorter chapter is now possible because YHWH is compassion and mercy.

RELEVANCE OF THE MESSAGE

Now we need to dislodge ourselves from the metaphor and the marriage imagery to hear the message that Ezekiel is speaking to us. With the destruction of the temple, Ezekiel began to preach a message of hope. As cleansing and sacrifice for restoration of grace are no longer possible without the temple, the individual must now take up the responsibility for her/his personal inner renewal.[13] "Cast away from you all the transgressions which you have committed against me, and get yourselves a new heart and a new spirit! Why will you die, O house of Israel? For I have no pleasure in the death of any one, says the Lord God; so turn and live" (Ez 18:31).[14] Besides being responsible for our personal renewal, we have to be responsible for our neighbor, especially when we are prophets or leaders of our communities. "So . . . I have made a watchman for the house of Israel; whenever you hear a word from my mouth, you shall give them warning from me. If . . . you do not speak to warn the wicked to turn from his way, that wicked man shall die in his iniquity, but his blood I will require at your hand. But if you warn the wicked to turn from his way, and he does not . . . you will have saved your life" (Ez 33: 7–9). The message that remains relevant for us is that in our relationship with God, we need to take responsibility for both personal and communal renewal.

IN THE CONTEXT OF TODAY

Reading the text today, we need to re-enter into the metaphor of the woman and the marriage imagery. We begin by recalling our initial conversion or relationship with God. Then we shall contextualize the infidelity of Jerusalem and see how we sin today (see table 1).

The redacted chapter of Ezekiel 16 allows us to structure it in a way that shows how Jerusalem betrayed her relationship with YHWH and

Table 1. The Relevance of the Message Today

POLITICS (vv. 26–28)	ECONOMICS (vv. 29,49)	RELIGION (vv. 15–25)	SOCIAL/MORAL (vv. 48)
Love Tenderly (Vow of Chastity)	Act Justly (Vow of Poverty)	Walk Humbly (Vow of Obedience)	Consequences
Alliance, coalition, "friends," boundaries, enmeshment and disengagement	Globalization, unfair trade agreements.	Idols, Ideologies, Power, addictions, domination, slavery.	We define ourselves by whom or what we base our security on.
Call to building non-possessive and respectable relationships	Call for simple lifestyle, sustainable economy and justice.	Call for building communities of faith.	Call for social ethics that would hear the cry of those who suffer.
Historical setting:	Historical setting:	Historical setting:	Historical setting:
1020 – 930: David's Reign 930 –722: Split of the kingdom 722 – 586: Exile/ Temple destroyed. (598: Ezekiel prophecy)	Surfeit of food and prosperous ease, but did not aid the poor and needy.	Canaanite fertility cult: worship of phallic symbol. Practice of burning children as offering to idols and even to YHWH.	Genesis 18–19 Story of Sodom and Gomorrah. Sexual disorder as a symptom of social and moral decay.

by doing so, traded in her dignity. Through the following structure, we see the equivalence of our sins today.

Repetition

vv. 3 – 25 Idolatry   (religious)
vv. 26 – 43 Foreign Alliance (social/political)
vv. 44 – 52 Injustice   (economic)

+

vv. 53 – 63 Restoration   (covenant)

As a country, as a family and as individuals, do we enter into political alliances that deprive ourselves of freedom because we are enslaved to certain dependencies and benefits? Do we establish clear and healthy boundaries in our family, at our work place, and in our faith community so that we may respect the dignity of each person?

Are we concerned about the negative effects of globalization? Are we supporting unfair trade agreements? What is just in our relationship with the migrant workers in our country, especially the domestic worker in our home? How much do we care to protect our ecology?

What are the national ideologies, social trends, and personal philosophies that overrule the law of God's love in my life? Where is my loyalty? Who am I?

RELEVANCE OF EZEKIEL'S PEDAGOGY

The dynamics of shame and forgiveness in Ezekiel 16 is what I call "Ezekiel's pedagogy." Ezekiel exposed sins to shame the woman. What are our answers to the questions that were posed? Are we adulterous like Jerusalem? How do we get a new heart and a new spirit?

Perhaps Ignatian Spirituality might help us with this aspect. The objective of the first week of Ignatius' spiritual exercises is to bring about shame and confusion for our personal sin. "The end and object . . . is principally the attainment of the knowledge that we have gone astray from the path which should lead us to the end for which we are created. Consequently, it also involves sorrow . . . of such magnitude, and the kindling of an intense desire to return to that path and to persevere in it forever."[15] The first rule for the first week of the "Discernment of Spirits" is to observe that the good spirit may prick the conscience through the process of reason,[16] thereby bringing about a shame, which turns to God for forgiveness.

Entering into the metaphor and the imagery of Ezekiel 16 allows us to go through a similar contemplation of sins and experience shame for our state so that we may turn to God for a new heart and a new spirit. The shame we end with in v. 63 is a shame that is *qualitatively different* from the shame in all the preceding verses. This shame is a shame before the ultimate goodness, a shame that is the outcome of our compunction and not a scrupulous guilt of what we have or have not done. It carries a sense of awe and wonder before a God whose mercy is completely beyond our expectation and comprehension.

THE READER AND THE IMAGE

Ezekiel's pedagogy, understood better in the context of Ignatian Spirituality, was the process that the faith community journeyed through during Lent in 2003. At the end of the journey the community was asked how the metaphor and the marriage imagery affected them.

Female Readers

Out of the twenty-six female participants, twenty-one of them could identify with Jerusalem, the woman. They did feel insulted by the metaphor. They described their feelings with words such as: intimidated, cheap, guilty, frightened, condemned, filthy, dignity lost, modesty stripped away, shame exposed, polluted self, resentment towards God, embarrassed, appalled, angry, punished, and sluttish.

But they did not remain with these initial feelings. They managed to "dislodge" the metaphor when the sins were contextualised. In the process, shame gradually grew into contrition. Eleven of them said that they were ashamed of their sins. "How could I have sold my dignity just to gain acceptance and recognition from others?" "I am aware of my excessive materialism." "I have taken God for granted and my husband has been a god to me."

The God-images were mainly positive. Their God-images seem to have been built from their childhood or since they developed a notion of God. Some participants recorded more than one God-image. Thirteen females described God as love; there were 13 descriptions of God as forgiving; five wrote about compassion; and five on faithfulness. There were nine descriptions of God as redeemer, and the other descriptions were about God as lover, parent, trainer, friend, refuge, consolation, and comfort. Three had God as father and one as mother. There were two negative descriptions of God: a punisher who watches every moment to mete out judgment and God as traffic police, intense and jealous.

A female reader could not identify with a male God and found the nagging nature of God more like a mother. Another could not see the "harlot" in herself but insisted that fits someone she was angry with.

Two females distanced themselves from the metaphor and saw it as a concept that spoke of God's love and a call to repentance. Those distancing themselves might seem to have the right concept but they had difficulty entering into the process affectively and therefore felt little or no shame and no contrition. One female did not identify herself with Jerusalem but placed herself in the position of God and confessed that if she were in God's place she would not have forgiven her husband; only God would forgive that way.

Male Readers

All six male readers could not identify with the woman in the text. They also could not enter into the marriage imagery. They were more at ease with the Father and Son imagery. One felt that he could identify better with God than with the woman, two were conscious of their refusal to enter into the state of shame, two remained as distant observers, and one said it was as if he was reading a story in the papers. One did not think it was necessary to seek further forgiveness as God had already forgiven.

Of these six males, two felt sorry for Jerusalem, one thought that she deserved it and that she should have known better. One wondered why the woman had to stoop so low when she was punished and rejected. One acknowledged his self-righteousness and another confessed that he was simply agitated as he was trying very hard to hide the truth that he had been taking God for granted.

Their God-images were also mainly positive images. Four said that God is love, and there were four descriptions of God as mercy; God is father, giver of courage and strength against temptations, God is always there; is a comforter and a guide. After reading the text, one male reader was convinced of what he had believed God to be all his life: God is a judge. This reader is always wary of God's punishment. He believes that his misfortune is retribution for his sins and that God's wrath can have almost immediate effect sometimes.

Summary
Although the female readers felt insulted by the metaphor of the woman, on the whole they were the ones who could enter into the analogy and the process of "Ezekiel's pedagogy" and benefit from it. The male readers had more difficulty identifying with the metaphor and some in fact resisted the identification.

During the last lecture, the male readers were asked where the man in the text was. No one saw how much God's character from verses 3–43 was a strong projection of a man in the exilic period. In that sense, God was the metaphor of man as the woman was the metaphor of Jerusalem. Men, not God, treated women as their possessions. Men, not God, executed the law of stoning the adulterous. Men were the ones who stripped their women to shame them but would tolerate no shame for themselves. Men projected their jealousy onto God.

Where was God in the text then? The closest image we have of God was in the last two verses, verses 62 and 63, the God who loves faithfully and forgives unconditionally.

REDEEMING THE IMAGE

The Man in the Text
It was only when "God" in verses 3–61 was discussed as a projection of and therefore a metaphor of man that the male readers in the group could be "shamed." These verses record the deeds and emotions of

a husband enraged by his unfaithful wife and God as the husband demanding that justice be done according to the Law of Moses. God is described as a man. With this understanding, both male and female readers could enter into the metaphor of a self-righteous person who, because of jealousy, blames, condemns, and judges others. We see here the man who has made an idol out of his own pride and becomes god to himself! Then we may invite both male and female readers to identify with the sins of the man and be ashamed.

vv 37	"I will gather all your lovers . . . will uncover your nakedness to them, that they may see all your nakedness."
vv 38	"And I will judge you as women who break wedlock and shed blood are judged, and bring upon you the blood of wrath and jealousy."
vv 39	"And I will give you into the hand of your lovers, . . . they shall strip you of your clothes . . . leave you naked and bare."
vv 42	"So will I satisfy my fury on you, and my jealousy shall depart from you; I will be calm, and will no more be angry."

Reading the Text as a Community

A Christian community includes persons of different gender identities and sexual orientations. In the community that we studied, female readers identified with the harlot more readily than did the males. Those who had experienced betrayal by their husbands were able to identify with the pain of God. Some females who had difficulty relating with a male God could experience intimacy with God only when they imaged God as female. One female could only relate with God as mother. A homosexual friend expressed her personal opinion that she needs a female image of God to enter into the intimacy of the marriage imagery.

Elizabeth Johnson, in *She Who Is*,[17] wrote about the necessity of freeing our stereotyped image of God of its literary prison and directing the symbols towards meaning. Thus an emancipatory speech about God may contain multi-images of male, female, mother, father, a wisdom figure, etc. Ezekiel 16 not only offers a metaphor of a woman for Jerusalem, it ties the metaphor to the marriage imagery as well. Because it does so, both gender identity and sexual orientation come into play in encountering the story of the text.

It is not easy to free the images from the text and from our personal limited flexibility in order to enter into one metaphor, dislodge ourselves from it, and then enter into another. It is also not easy to read the text from the perspective of another gender identity. Therefore we need to read and share the text in a faith community with members of different gender identity and sexual orientation. In this way we allow ourselves to be challenged by the different gender roles and be helped to remove the fixation of one meaning for any image.

Reading Old Testament Images with Jesus

We may also allow Jesus to redeem us from any fossilized images of the past. Ezekiel 16 may be read with John 8:2–11. Jesus did not condemn the woman who was caught in the act of adultery; he forgave her and freed her from her public shame. "Teacher, this woman has been caught in the act of adultery. . . . What do you say about her? . . . Woman. . . . Has no one condemned you? . . . . Neither do I condemn you; go, and do not sin again." Jesus did not condemn the condemning Pharisees either; he challenged their self-righteousness and at the same time gave them the opportunity to walk away without being shamed. "Let him who is without sin among you be the first to throw a stone at her." In one breath, Jesus freed the stereotyped images of both the condemning male and condemned female.

Women, why do we need to remain as victim and engrave shame into our identity?

BEYOND IMAGE

Images and metaphors are powerful means of bringing across messages. Images can hurt and images also have the power to heal. While we may hold on to beautiful and meaningful images and discard unhelpful ones, images remain as a means of communication. Images are not the original thing. We look for the best way to speak about God and very often the best way comes from our best experience of being loved by a human person or from the ideal we have created out of our desire. Whatever image we choose, God remains as an ultimate other who is beyond all images.

The Muslim tradition provides us with a meaningful way of contemplating this reality. Muslims pray a litany of the ninety-nine names of God: The King, the Protector, the Creator, the Destroyer, the Watcher, the Raiser of the Dead, the One, the Hidden, the *Nourisher*, the Compassionate . . . and the one hundredth name is SILENCE . . .

CONCLUSION

This article was presented for validation to three representatives of the faith community involved. The female representative thought that the brothers in her community should be able to understand the application of the sins of Ezekiel 16 in the context of today. The male representative affirmed how "wrong images" damaged his relationship with God when he was younger. He said that this study has helped him to understand the sisters in the community better. The male leader of the community likewise appreciated it and validated it as being representative of his community, especially in terms of the experiences of the male members. This work helped him to deal with the imageries and metaphors used in scriptures.

The gender identity of the reader of Ezekiel 16 does matter for we are sexual beings and we read text through the eyes of our sexuality. Therefore our sexuality is one of the contexts in which we do theology. It is a context we cannot afford to ignore. As a faith community, we read text while standing together on the common ground of our human dignity. We read it together with others who are different, exchanging views that are rooted in our own specific gender identity and sexual orientation. We read celebrating the gift of our sexuality, we read respecting diversity.

We read scripture by entering into the historical context with our identity and then distance from history to carry its relevant message with us and enter into the context of our reality today. Next, we detach ourselves from the image and allow it to interact with the different images of the others in our faith community. We read the collective meaning with Jesus, who is the perfect image of God. We bring the multiple images before God, and allow them to dissolve as we worship God who is beyond all images. We face God as we are, we come face to face with God who is the ultimate Other.

NOTES

[1]   Moshe Greenberg, *Ezekiel 1-20: A New Translation with Introduction and Commentary*, 22: *The Anchor Bible* (New York: Doubleday & Company, Inc., 1983), 293.

[2]   Jessica Richard, "Misnamed Female Experiences: Reflections on Some Passages in Ezekiel," *In God's Image: Journal of Asian Women's Resource Centre for Culture and Theology* 20, no. 2 (June 2001): 21.

[3]   Traditionally many Chinese and Indian families prefer the male child to the female child. No survey was done to identify to what extent that the prejudice was the conscious or the subconscious preference of this group of adults. There were two mixed marriages between the two races in the group, giving the impression that the community may not be stereotyped.

[4]   Harold I. Kaplan, Benjamin J. Sadock and Jack A. Grebb, "Human Sexuality," in *Synopsis of Psychiatry: Behavioural Sciences, Clinical Psychiatry*, 7th ed. (Baltimore: Williams and Wilkins, 1994), 653.

[5]   The sexual orientation of the participants was not asked.

[6]   Gerlinde Baumann, *Love and Violence: Marriage as Metaphor for the Relationship between YHWH and Israel in the Prophetic Books* (Collegeville, Minnesota: Liturgical Press, 2003), 138.

[7]   Ibid., 153.

[8]   John W. Miller, *Meet the Prophets: A Beginner's Guide to the Books of the Biblical Prophets* (New York: Paulist, 1987), 199 and 201.

[9]   A recent article in the *Straits Times,* "Myanmar Using Rape to Subdue Ethnic Minorities," reported that Myanmar's army has continued the widespread use of state-sanctioned rape against women to intimidate ethnic minorities that are opposing the military regime (*Straits Times, Singapore [A 4]*, 10 Sept. 2004).

[10] Baumann, *Love and Violence*, 155.

[11] Ibid., 160.

[12] Ibid., 228.

[13] Miller, *Meet the Prophets*, 199.

[14] Quotations of Biblical texts are from the Revised Standard Version.

[15] W. W. Meissner, *To the Greater Glory: A Psychological Study of Ignatian Spirituality* (Boston: Marquette University Press, 1999), 145–46.

[16] Ibid., 251.

[17] Elizabeth Johnson, *She Who Is: Mystery of God in Feminist Theological Discourse* (New York: Crossroad, 1992), 56–57.

BIBLIOGRAPHY

Baumann, Gerlinde. *Love and Violence: Marriage as Metaphor for the Relationship between YHWH and Israel in the Prophetic Books.* Collegeville, Minnesota: Liturgical Press, 2003.

Greenberg, Moshe. *Ezekiel 1–20: A New Translation with Introduction and Commentary.* Vol. 22: *The Anchor Bible.* New York: Doubleday & Company, Inc., 1983.

Johnson, Elizabeth. *She Who Is: Mystery of God in Feminist Theological Discourse.* New York: Crossroad, 1992.

Kaplan, Harold I., Benjamin J. Sadock and Jack A. Grebb. "Human Sexuality." In *Synopsis of Psychiatry: Behavioural Sciences, Clinical Psychiatry.* 7th ed. Baltimore: Williams and Wilkins, 1994.

Meissner, W. W. *To the Greater Glory: A Psychological Study of Ignatian Spirituality.* Boston: Marquette University Press, 1999.

Miller, John W. *Meet the Prophets: A Beginner's Guide to the Books of the Biblical Prophets.* New York: Paulist, 1987.

"Myanmar Using Rape to Subdue Ethnic Minorities." *Straits Times, Singapore (A 4),* 10 Sept., 2004.

Richard, Jessica. "Misnamed Female Experiences: Reflections on Some Passages in Ezekiel." *In God's Image: Journal of Asian Women's Resource Centre for Culture and Theology* 20, no. 2 (June 2001): 17–21.

Pauline Body in 1 Corinthians

A Metaphor of Whole Human Being and of Christian Community

Nozomi Miura, RSCJ

7

THE STRUCTURE OF 1 CORINTHIANS

The First Epistle to the Corinthians is mainly composed of Paul's reaction and answers to an oral report brought by "Chloe's people" (1:10–6:20) and a written report (7:1–16:24).[1] The first deals with the division in the Corinthian community (1:10–4:21), and the importance of body (5:1–6:20). The second touches a series of issues, marriage (7:1–40), idol meat (8:1–11:1), liturgical assemblies (11:2–14:40), the resurrection (15:1–58), the collection (16:1–4), and Apollo (16:5–24). The structure of the letter may be summarized as follows:[2]

The Structure of 1 Corinthians	The body imagery in the letter
1. Introduction (1:1–9)	1. 3:16–17......(a)
2. Part I: Division in the Community (1:10–4:21)	2. 6:12–20......(b)
3. Part II: The Importance of the Body (5:1–6:20)	
4. Part III: Responses to Corinthian Questions (7:1–14:40)	

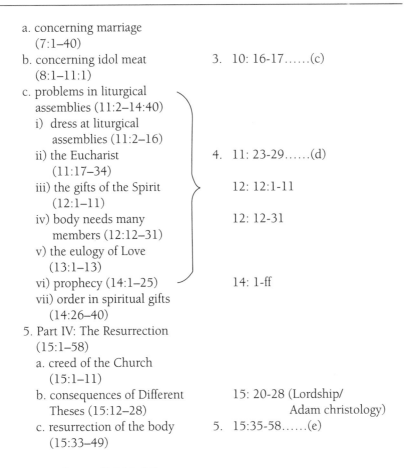

a. concerning marriage
   (7:1–40)
b. concerning idol meat   3. 10: 16-17......(c)
   (8:1–11:1)
c. problems in liturgical
   assemblies (11:2–14:40)
   i) dress at liturgical
       assemblies (11:2–16)
   ii) the Eucharist   4. 11: 23-29......(d)
       (11:17–34)
   iii) the gifts of the Spirit   12: 12:1-11
        (12:1–11)
   iv) body needs many   12: 12-31
       members (12:12–31)
   v) the eulogy of Love
       (13:1–13)
   vi) prophecy (14:1–25)   14: 1-ff
   vii) order in spiritual gifts
        (14:26–40)
5. Part IV: The Resurrection
   (15:1–58)
   a. creed of the Church
      (15:1–11)
   b. consequences of Different   15: 20-28 (Lordship/
      Theses (15:12–28)   Adam christology)
   c. resurrection of the body 5. 15:35-58......(e)
      (15:33–49)

6. Conclusion (16:13–24)

Evident from the structure is the body imagery that runs through the letter. The sections which include the body imagery are shown in the right column of the structure above. The references to body imagery are the five different sections, which are related and cumulated into a composite imagery of Body, especially in chapters 11 to 14. In this short article, therefore, I would like to focus on the function of body imagery in the letter, and Pauline understanding of body.

THE BODY IMAGERY RUNNING THROUGH THE LETTER

The Response to the Oral Report: Chapters 1–6

It is difficult to reconstruct the original questions for which Parts I and II are intended to be a response, however, the consistent element that threads through all the arguments is Paul's theology of the role of the apostle in light of the Gospel. In this sense, the passage in 3:6, "I [Paul] planted, Apollo watered, but God gave the growth," functions as a leitmotif all through chapters 1 to 4, holding the fragmented discussion together. Now, the issue raised in this section is the factions within the community (1:10–17), with each group maintaining some special relation to and pride in a particular apostle who baptized them—Paul, Apollo, Cephas, or even Christ (1:12). Such factionalism—which indicates the immaturity of the community, treating the apostle like a popular philosopher who formed a clique, and making much of the preaching itself and the appeal it made to them[3]—is a rather serious problem, for the distinctive feature of a Christian community is its "unity" in Christ.[4] Thus, focusing on the gravity of the Christ-event (the cross), Paul explains and emphasizes the centrality of God and the Gospel, differentiating essentials that merit attention (namely, Christ and the Gospel) from the apostles who were "sent" by God to preach the gospel. By so doing, Paul emphasizes the unity of the community under One God and Gospel.

The metaphors Paul employs in this section are very interesting. The first is the image of farming; all believers are "field" (3:9), the apostles are "co-workers" planting and watering this field (3:6–9), and God is the one who sustains all growth (3:6–7). The second is the image of building; all believers are "building of God" ($\theta\epsilon o\hat{u}$ $o\mathrm{i}\kappa o\delta o\mu\dot{\eta}$, 3:9), the apostles are "skilled master builders" ($o\phi\grave{o}\varsigma$ $\dot{\alpha}\rho\chi\iota\tau\acute{\epsilon}\kappa\tau\omega\nu$:10) laying the foundation. The third is the image of temple; all believers are "God's temple" ($\nu\alpha\grave{o}\varsigma$ $\theta\epsilon o\hat{u}$/, 3:16–17) and in it, both the individual and community level, the Spirit dwells. What is underlined here is the unitary image of the community under God or in Christ. These images, especially that of building and temple, are elaborated toward the end of the letter (chapters 11 to 14). Accordingly, the proper attitude toward the apostles becomes self-evident. Since the co-workers (for example, Paul and Apollo) are for building unity, it is nonsense for believers to be divided among co-workers.[5] Paul even contends that one who destroys this temple of God, who brings division to the community, destroys God. Believers are to be united under one God.

In chapters 5 and 6, the issues turn to the importance of body. The images of "building" and "temple" serve as a nexus from the preceding sections; also, the body image continues, either physically or figuratively, providing a kind of coherent imagery throughout the letter.

This section (5:1–6:20) deals with: a. the case of incest, marriage with one's stepmother (5:1–8), b. clearing up a misunderstanding about contact with "immoral people" (5:9–13), c. lawsuits among Christians (6:1–11), and d. casual sex with a prostitute (6:12–20). From this section onward, the underlying problem in the Corinthian community becomes more manifest. The Corinthians had a syncretic tendency to interpret Christianity in the light of popular Greek philosophical/religious modes of thought. Early gnosticism's emphasis on the attainment of special knowledge (***gnosis***) for salvation and a dualistic anthropological view (Spirit/soul/good vs. physical/body/evil), therefore seems to have had a strong impact on their understanding of Christianity.

The moral implications of this dualistic anthropological view are all the more problematic because of its two extreme positions, antinomianism and asceticism. Antinomians presupposed that Christ has freed Christians from Law and from the power of sin (identified with "the world"), and that spiritual reality is totally independent of physical reality, which has nothing to do with salvation. In other words, salvation had already been granted to Christians. It is well known that the slogan-like passage in 6:12, "All things are lawful for me," was their catchword for advocating "sexual libertinism,"[6] claiming that they do not need to be concerned about morality so far as their spiritual salvation is assured by "special knowledge." In addition, it is generally admitted that in the first century world, "Greek males, . . . whether married or single, had sexual relationships with more than one woman."[7]

On the other hand, asceticism, which shares a similar anthropological view as antinomianism, underlined that spirituality is attained through renunciation of physical pleasures and personal desires. "[A] strong emphasis on ascetic piety was already in place of Hellenistic religion by the first century."[8] This asceticism proceeds to the gnostic or Cynico-

Stoic assumption that the physical body is "evil" and the ultimate cause of sin; therefore, ascetics underscore "spiritualism," despising and abdicating physical reality.[9] Accordingly, behind the case of incest (5:1–8) and that of casual sex with a prostitute (6:12–20), there lies the problem of antinomians.

Paul answers these erroneous conceptions of the moral irrelevance of the body, by presenting his own anthropological view that the body of a Christian is the "temple" in which the Holy Spirit dwells (6:19). It is intriguing to note the parallel structure of the sentences between 3:16 and 6:19:

3:16 Οὐκ οἴδατε ὅτι ναὸς θεοῦ ἐστε καὶ τὸ πνεῦμα τοῦ θεοῦ οἰκεῖ ἐν ὑμῖν;
6:19 ἢ οὐκ οἴδατε ὅτι τὸ σῶμα ὑμῶν ναὸς τοῦ ἐν ὑμῖν ἁγίου πνεύματός ἐστιν

From these parallel sentences, it is plain that "you" (*pl*, 3:16) is equated to "your body" (6:19), both of which are "God's temple" (ναὸς θεοῦ) and "temple of holy spirit" (αὸς τοῦ ... ἁγίου πνεύματός). Paul's logic is simple here; he stresses that the human body is God's holy temple where God's spirit dwells. Since God raised Christ from the dead (presumes the resurrection of the body), the body is the object of divine action and salvation (6:14), hence is also the locus that "glorifies God" (6:20). Here we see Paul endeavoring to justify the nobility of the body. In addition, while the "spiritual" Corinthians stressed the glorified Christ, Paul repeatedly points out that the heart of the Gospel is not Christ glorified but rather Christ crucified.

The Response to the Written Report: Chapters 7–16

Part III and Part IV, mainly chapters 7–15, contain Paul's response to the written report, and reveals more definitely the problems caused by these extremists, the antinomians and ascetics.[10] When we read the series of social and practical problems in the Corinthian community, it is important to keep in mind that Paul was responding to these questions within a particular context, the eschatological "imminence" of the end-time (Paul believed that the end of the world was close at hand), and the dilemma of Christians living in the strongly syncretic religious and cultural milieu of Corinthian society. Furthermore, what Paul writes here is a "response" to questions specifically posed by the community; Paul is not giving his general idea on moral theology. His attitude is basically pastoral, taking into consideration the social reality of the Corinthians.

Chapter 7 deals with marriage (7:1–9), whether believers, be they married, widowed, unmarried, should refrain from sexual intercourse. The problem here derives from the extreme asceticism that denies sexual intercourse in the marital relationship. As I mentioned earlier, behind this tendency, was a "strong emphasis on ascetic piety"[11] with regard to the human body and sexuality. Paul, in attempting to moderate their ascetic drive, explains that nothing is morally wrong with sexual relations within marriage (7:1–7). Instead, he insists on mutual responsibility in matters of sex (7:3–4), underscoring that the body never hinders one's salvation, that sex is a meaningful part of marriage, and that it is not for the purpose of exploiting one's spouse. Although he admits some cases for abstinence, these are rather "exceptions" (7:5–6).[12]

Paul's fundamental position, "let each of you lead the life that the Lord assigned, to which God called you" (7:17; also, 7:20, 24), presupposes the imminence of the end-time. Moreover, his way of speaking is never a "command," but pastoral care and advice on the assumption that the authority of the Church should not function in an imperative manner.[13] Paul's pastoral advice is "concession," a technical term from his rabbinic training, meaning "a position that owes more to an understanding of the real possibilities open to humanity in its concrete historical situation than to a theoretical ideal."[14] In other words, different circumstances require different measures and Paul deals with each case quite flexibly in order to "promote good order and unhindered devotion to the Lord" (7:35).[15] Therefore, the same attitude is applied to the following issues: marriage and divorce (7:10–16), one's social status (slave or free) (7:17–24), and change in one's status (7:25–40). While Paul appears to recommend celibacy in these passages, he only seeks "practicality" in the situation of eschatological imminence; at least, he never claims the "spiritual superiority" of celibacy.

The problems that follow in Chapters 8 to 11 exemplify the particular social and cultural context of Corinth, where contacts with various pagan religious elements were unavoidable. While springing from very practical matter, such as the appropriateness of eating meat offered to idols (8:1–13) or the worship of idols (10:14–22), the intra-community problems embrace some essential questions: the nature of Christian freedom, the location of the believer in a pagan world, and conscience.[16] All through these discussions, Paul underscores that Christian liberty should be subordinated to love. In fact, Paul himself shares the view of "the strong," but he stands on the side of "the weak" for the sake of love, showing his heartwarming pastoral care for the issues. For Paul, the ultimate concern is the "community," not the "individual": the unity of the community precedes individual insistence on freedom. Therefore, love "that builds up" (ἀγάπη οἰκοδομεῖ, 8:1) the community must have priority over individual freedom.[17] The motivation and norm of love are given precedence (8:1, 3). Needless to say, the underlying theme is the unity. Moreover, the image of "building-up-the-community" links to the previous sections (chapters 1–6); at the same time, it is a precursor to the culminating image of building-up the "Body of Christ" in chapters 12 to 14. Indeed, here again the images of "body," "building," "temple," and "Body of Christ" function to unify diverse issues. Interestingly enough, the short reference to bread (10:16) is also connected to "body of Christ" (v.10) in the sense of both "eucharistic bread" and "Church," making a nexus to the succeeding section.

The section that follows deals with three abuses in the liturgical assembly (11:2–14:40): a. dress of both men and women when they "pray and prophesy" (11:2–16), b. Lord's supper (11:17–34), and c. spiritual gift/*charismata* (12:1–14:40).

Although Paul appears to lose a focal point of the arguments, these issues have "the hidden agenda."[18] The point Paul wants to make is that "women should be women, and men should be men, and the difference should be obvious."[19] Here, Paul treats both women and men fairly on equal footing; "[t]he man and woman mutually have each other's body, a Stoic idea opposed to the widespread patriarchal assumption that man owns the woman, not vice versa."[20] The reason he is emphatic on this "difference of sex" (not "discrimination of sex") is deeply related, above all, to divine intention expressed in Creation (Gn 2:18–23; 1 Cor 11; 8–9; 11–12). This difference of sex reminds us that God is the Creator of the universe a truth that resonates with "But God gave the growth" (3:6). God creates the world, and sustains life and growth in it. This section also prepares for the image to be elaborated in Chapter 12, which focuses on diversity (of believers) in unity (in Christ) or unity in diversity. As God made distinction between male and female in Creation and they became "one body" (Gn 2:24), so "the Spirit" bestows difference in charismata among believers, who then build up (οἰκοδομειν) the one "Body of Christ" (σῶμα Χριστοῦ, 12:27). Taking into consideration that the Christ-event opened up the "New Creation," I think these two "Creation" images are parallel.[21]

It is, therefore, no wonder that the installation (or regulation) of the Lord's Supper (11:17–34) is placed in the middle of dress of men and women and spiritual gift, since the "body of Christ" or the eucharistic bread is the core of both the liturgy and the Christian community, also the way in which believers "remember" (εἰς τὴν ἐμὴν ἀνάμνησιν, lit. for my memory, 11:24, 25) Christ's death and "proclaim" (11:26) it. "Christ remains incarnationally present in and to the world through the community that is his Body."[22] Through the "body of Christ," the eucharistic bread, we also become the "Body of Christ," the Christian community. Indeed, it is amazing how carefully Paul prepares his arguments to lead into more important themes, such as that of eucharist (11:17–34), the gifts of the Spirit (12:1–11), and the eulogy of Love (13:1–13), so that his own thesis—Lordship/Adam christology—in 15:20–28 would also become very convincing.

The last section (12:1–14:40) sees the further elaboration of the image of "body" and "building-up." In fact, the word, "to build up" (οἰκοδομειν, is repeated in chapter 14.[23] At the same time, Paul gets to the heart of the Corinthians' problems, the issues surrounding spiritual gifts or charismata (χαρισματα) especially, of "*glossolalia*" or speaking in tongues (λαλειν γλωσσαι). Enumerating various "gifts" (12:8–10) and intentionally listing the gift of *glossolalia* and its interpretation as the lowest ones,[24] Paul emphasizes that all these "gifts" are "freely given" by the Holy Spirit. They are not natural human qualities, but "free gifts" from the Holy Spirit in the New Creation, in order to "build up" community. "The value of the spiritual gifts is thus strictly derived from their usefulness in solidifying and 'building' the group. . . . The highest of all gifts is accordingly other-regarding love (ch. 13)."[25] It is, therefore, an outrageous abuse to regard the gifts as intrinsic to individuals, much less, a subject of boasting. They are given for a "communal" purpose. "To each is given a manifestation of the Spirit for the common good" (12:7).

Paul then shifts from the charismata to the analogy of the body (12:12–31); the same image of "organic unity" as a body continues with the multiplicity of members constituting a single body (12:12). For Paul, within the unity of the community—under One God, One Lord (8:6), and One Spirit (12:9), the diversity of each member is very important to enrich this community. Finally, his argument comes to a climax in the "eulogy of love" (13:1–13). In this contextual flow, love is the indispensable element (gift) for "building-up" the community, for enlivening this organic unity. Paul's ravishing description is simultaneously incisive to the Corinthians who, though gifted in various ways, lacked the most essential thing for a Christian community, love.[26] Whatever spiritual gifts they may have, these are meaningless unless these gifts are integrated into love and contribute to community formation. Thus, Paul returns full circle to the unity of the community, after dexterously building up his arguments and removing the possibility that the Corinthians would understand "Spirit" in a totally different way.

Chapter 15 concerns the resurrection of Christ (15:1–34), and the resurrection of the bodies of believers (15:35–58). It is, however, obvious that this also pertains to the "body" problem. Paul, re-stating the basic *kerygma* (15:3ff, plus, his own witness story, vv. 8–10), tries to correct Corinthians' devastating misunderstanding that they have been freed from the restraint of the body by the Christ-event—devastating, because rejecting the resurrection of Christ nullifies the whole edifice of Christianity and the Gospel. The resurrection of Christ is the prototype of our transformation of body, i.e., the resurrection of Christians' *somatic* selves.[27] The logical consequence of the Corinthians' erroneous thesis, no resurrection of Christ (15:13, 16) means that Paul's preaching was in vain (v. 14) and even false testimony (v. 15); also that there will not be any hope for the deceased (v. 18).[28] Here, the thematic parallel between 1 Cor 15 and Rom 5, notably the Adam-Christ typology, is prominent. The letter to the Romans develops this typology more fully: the first person, Adam, is the progenitor of death, whereas the second person (15:47), Christ, is the prototype of life.

PAUL'S PURPOSE IN EMPLOYING BODY IMAGERY—
BODY IN PAULINE THEOLOGY

Throughout the argument above, it is obvious that the basic problem of the Corinthian community was the Greek philosophical/religious context that caused the misunderstandings and deviations from genuine Christianity. The Corinthian community was tremendously influenced by the soil of Greek philosophical/ religious speculations, "traditional Greek metaphysical dualism which (later) gnosticism intensified."[29] In this sense, the Corinthian community was strongly on the way of "gnosticising" the Gospel. The problem in chapter 15 typically exemplifies this predicament. And the two extreme positions, antinomianism and asceticism, also derive from these dualistic anthropological/soteriological assumptions that the human body has nothing to do with salvation.

Paul's persistent assertion of the importance of body, both on practical and metaphorical levels, can be his counterbalance for the Corinthians' extreme views of spiritualism; what is more, the series of "body" images demonstrate "the *incarnational* character of Christianity."[30] While the use of human body as a metaphor for community was commonplace in ancient rhetoric, Paul's originality is that "so often the phrase 'the body of Christ' or its equivalent is used with a concrete allusion to the human body of Jesus, crucified and raised from the dead."[31] Whereas the Corinthians underscored the glorified Christ and the deification of human existence through liberation from bodily existence, Paul emphasized the crucified Christ who came into the world, lived and died as a human being, and the meaningfulness of our whole being. His theses on Lordship christology (15:24–28) and Adam christology (15:20–23, 45–49) evince his prime focus on the historical, therefore, bodily existence of Jesus of Nazareth.

Paul offsets Corinthian devaluation of body and their anthropological view, by stressing the psychosomatic unity of human reality. Thus, 1 Corinthians exhibits Paul's body ethics, along with his theology of the Spirit. Body (σῶμα) is one of the important Pauline terms in his anthropological and soteriological understanding and this epistle uses the term intensively. For a post-Cartesian mind-set, the word "body" may signify "physical and material organism or corpus"[32]; however, Paul's own usage has a wide spectrum of meaning, and "physicality" is one end of the spectrum. It is more than a human body.[33] For Paul, "the central meaning of 'body' is the actual self, what we might call the psychosomatic entity that I am."[34] Therefore, salvation is not only for the soul as the Corinthian extremists thought, but for this actual (or *somatic* self, the whole being, as understood in the traditional Jewish anthropological view. Different from the term "flesh" (σαρξ) which Paul mostly uses with negative connotations, *sōma* (σῶμα) is the embodiment of the person and it is soma that enables individuals to relate to a particular environment and interact and cooperate with each other.

Body, therefore, is an indispensable dimension for relatedness, especially for community formation, and therefore for salvation. Because of this, Paul is strict about whose body one unites with: if one's body fuses with a prostitute, then one becomes the same as the prostitute (1 Cor 6:15–16). But if the body is one with Christ, then unity with Christ is attained. Our being is therefore shaped and formed by that to which we commit ourselves, however, the reality is, our body is "from God" (6:19). Sōma (σῶμα) expresses the character of the human as God's created being. The view that God never created the human body as "unredeemable" (1 Cor 1:30; 6:20) is quite different from the gnostic speculation that the body is "evil" and imprisons the divine soul. Paul, on the contrary, refers to the Creation story to accentuate the benevolence of the divine plan for human embodiment. Accordingly, the two extreme ethical views on human body, libertinism and spiritualism, are utter deviations from the Body ethics of Christianity. For Paul, the body is an essential part of our humanity, which is to be transformed, through the power of the Spirit and in the unity of Christ, into an "immortal" and "heavenly" body (1 Cor 15:42–55). It is through the body that one participates in the New Creation and functions as an active part thereof.

INSIGHT FROM AN ASIAN CONTEXT FOR PAULINE UNDERSTANDING OF BODY[35]

The Pauline sense of "body" (σῶμα) was lost relatively quickly in the process of Christian theologizing. In Ephesians and Colossians, the deutero-Pauline writers changed the focus of Paul's "Body of Christ," and instead, brought to the fore, the absolute, comprehensive term "the church."[36] In 2 Corinthians 5:14 and Romans 5, Paul contends that "Christ has died for all"; however, Ephesians 5:25 states that "Christ loved the church and gave himself up for her." Thus, the goal of Christ's life and death was shifted from each member to the church.[37] Simultaneously, the holiness of this church came to be underlined; "the letters have given an almost divine character to the church."[38] It is ironical that in this process, each member of the community had to become a spiritual/holy being, getting rid of the sinful body in order to participate in the church. Further, as christological speculation shifted from *low* christology, typically expressed in Paul's Lordship christology or Adam christology, to *high* christology, the significance of the historical Jesus and the importance of his bodily existence began to fade out.[39] "[T]he historical Jesus, his humanity and especially his body, was of prime importance to the early church. The resurrection in particular focuses on the body of Jesus and says in essence that the man Jesus, not just his spirit, lives again."[40] Unfortunately, this understanding of body in the Semitic anthropological view was virtually distorted and lost. It is, therefore, undeniable that there is a breach between the Pauline understanding of body and that of the deutero-Pauline writers and the first theologians.

It is on this point that our Asian sense of body can contribute to recover or rediscover Paul's original understanding of body, there being striking similarities between the Asian understanding of body and Paul's sōma ($\sigma\hat{\omega}\mu\alpha$). In the Asian cultural context, body is an essential part of our whole being, indissolubly integrated or interwoven with spirit (even though the modern Asian mind may be very much influenced by the influence of post-Cartesian speculation of body-and-soul dichotomy in a sense *globalized* in the post-modern mentality). Asians naturally have an experiential awareness of the psychic and somatic unity; body and soul are one for us. Yasuo Yuasa, a Japanese Jungian psychologist, postulates that in the Asian cultural context the basic cosmological speculation based on animism and naturalism typically promotes a sense of sympathetic continuation with nature and the world enabling us to have this sense of the psycho-somatic unity of human existence.[41] Assuredly, it is true that the Pauline cosmological view, a typical Hellenistic-Jewish one, is also very similar to the Asian animistic view.[42]

In addition, it is characteristically Asiatic to regard the human body as *sacred and holy*. The antithesis between Nature and human being in the Occidental tradition is quite alien to the Asian mind. Nature is sacred. It is the place primarily filled with sacredness and human beings are a part of this sacred nature. The sense of sympathetic continuation with nature makes it possible to experience Paul's metaphor that the human body is God's temple, the dwelling of the holy Spirit as very natural and self-evident to our Asian mind. Furthermore, most religions of the world recognize the correspondence between the human body and the building (temple)—or between the human body and the cosmos.[43] For example, in Buddhist traditions, the human body is often understood as a microcosm of the macrocosm. Figure 1 (see next page) shows the structure of a *stupa* (*chaitya*), which corresponds to a human body.[44] Similar examples would be too many to enumerate.[45] In the Christian tradition, the church structure is also coordinated to a human body (cf. Figure 2, see next page).[46] However, while it is not difficult to find the correspondence between human body and cosmos, or between human body and temple (church) in various cultural contexts, in the Christian tradition, the correspondence does not express a regard of the human body as *sacred and holy* in itself. When the theologized Christianity, along with the Hellenistic philosophical/religious views that gnosticized Christianity began to underscore the superiority of spirit, contrasted with or even opposed to body, the underestimation of the bodily aspect of being human started. The biblical conception of the human being's fundamental unity was therefore not inherited by the Occidental tradition in the way it should have. In contrast, Paul did regard human body (sōma) as sacred, denoting it as "God's temple," and reflecting the Semitic and biblical anthropological view that the human being is "God's image and likeness."

Therefore, I wonder if it is too much to say that the Asian sense could provide insight for a dimension of the biblical understanding of human body. Indeed, Asian perspectives can contribute to a fuller realization of biblical truth and the actualization of true catholicism in this multicultural modern world of today.

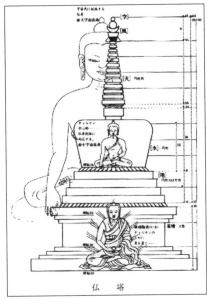

Figure 1: Stupa and human body

Figure 2: Church and human body

NOTES

[1]   Jerome Murphy-O'Connor, "The First Letter to the Corinthians," in *New Jerome Biblical Commentary*, ed. R. E. Brown, et al. (New Jersey: Prentice Hall, 1990), 799; Earl Richard, *Jesus: One and Many The Christological Concept of New Testament Authors* (Wilmington, Delaware: Michael Glazier, 1988), 283–84; Calvin J. Roetzel, *The Letters of Paul: Conversations in Context*, 4th ed. (Louisville, London, Leiden: Westminster John Knox, 1998), 86–87; Maurice L. Soards, *The Apostle Paul: An Introduction to His Writing and Teaching* (New York: Paulist, 1987), 73.

[2]   Murphy-O'Connor, "The First Letter to the Corinthians," 799; Roetzel, *The Letters of Paul*, 94–95.

[3]   Underlying motifs in chapters 1–4 are based on Hellenistic-Jewish wisdom traditions, which were popular among the first-century Diaspora Jews. Paul's own speculation, however, is quite critical of the Hellenistic-Jewish wisdom tradition, and is based on the Hellenistic-Jewish apocalyptic tradition. Cf. Briger A. Pearson, "Hellenistic-Jewish Wisdom Speculation and Paul," in *Aspects of Wisdom in Judaism and Early Christianity*, ed. Robert Louis Wilken (Notre Dame: University of Notre Dame, 1975), 43–66.

[4]   Jerome Murphy-O'Connor, *1 Corinthians*, Doubleday Bible Commentary (New York: Doubleday, 1998), 9.

[5]   Murphy-O'Connor, "The First Letter to the Corinthians," 802.

[6]   Idem, *1 Corinthians*, 51; Idem, "The First Letter to the Corinthians," 804; Calvin J. Roetzel, *Paul: The Man and the Myth* (Minneapolis: Fortress, 1999), 135–45; Carolyn Osiek and David L. Balch, *Families in the New Testament World: Households and House Churches* (Louisville, Kentucky: Westminster John Knox, 1997), 103–25; Wayne A. Meeks, *The First Urban Christians: the Social World of the Apostle Paul*, 2nd ed. (New Haven: Yale University, 2003), 122–23.

[7]   Osiek and Balch, *Families*, 112.

[8]   Roetzel, *Paul*, 138–39. It is quite interesting to note that "sexual abstinence became foundational for a single-minded commitment to philosophical ideas, and sexual passion was described as the enemy of the holy, the good, and the rational. Interestingly, anthropological dualism thrived in a period when confidence in civic institutions was on the wane and intellectuals were increasingly cynical about or skeptical of ancestral religious traditions." Ibid., 138. Also, see Osiek and Balch, *Families*, 103–15.

[9]   Murphy-O'Connor, *1 Corinthians*, 39–54; V.P. Furnish, *The Moral Teaching of Paul* (Nashville: Abington, 1979), 30–33; James D. G. Dunn, *Unity and Diversity in the New Testament: An Inquiry into the Character of Earliest Christianity* (Philadelphia: The Westminster, 1977), 275–79; Leander E. Keck, *Paul and His Letters* (Philadelphia: Fortress, 1973), 95–102.

10 Richard, *Jesus*, 290; Murphy-O'Connor, *1 Corinthians*, 77. Structurally, the A-B-A pattern provides a coherence of whole sections, tying all the issues together (cf. chapters 5–6; 7; 8–11; 11:17–34; 12:1–14:40).

11 Roetzel, *Paul*, 139.

12 Furnish, *The Moral Teaching of Paul*, 33–36. Sexual abstinence can be practiced in certain cases on the condition that it is "temporal," with "mutual agreement," and "for prayer."

13 Murphy-O'Connor, *1 Corinthians*, 58.

14 Ibid, 61.

15 Furnish, *The Moral Teaching of Paul*, 46–50.

16 Murphy-O'Connor, *1 Corinthians*, 77. Cf. James D.G. Dunn, *The Theology of Paul the Apostle* (Grand Rapids, Michigan: Eerdmans, 1998), 701–4. Both in 1 Corinthians and Romans, "weak" and "strong" are used in relation to "food," referring to the issues of Christian liberty and desirability for Christians to maintain social involvement. However, the differences are: (1) Romans pertains to "unclean" food, while 1 Corinthians deals with "idol" food; (2) Romans pertains to the purely "internal" problem of the community, whereas 1 Corinthians has the "internal" but also "external" problem (contact with surrounding society); (3) in Romans, "faith" is the appropriate criterion for an internal issue, while in 1 Corinthians, "conscience" is the proper criterion for a more general court of appeal in a mixed society. "The weak" are probably those who shared more conservative and traditional Jewish scruples; the problem might involve some social class tension, "the weak" belonging to rather lower strata of society. And "the strong" are those who, possessing a more liberal understanding ("knowledge" 8:1, 4, 7, 10, and 11), are free from traditional Jewish scruples, implying that they belong to a higher social status, that sometimes obliges them to share table with pagans (and their food). Dunn, *The Theology of Paul the Apostle*, 701; Murphy-O'Connor, *1 Corinthians*, 78–82; Richard, *Jesus*, 289.

17 Dunn, *The Theology of Paul the Apostle*, 705–6; Murphy-O'Connor, *1 Corinthians*, 81–82.

18 Murphy-O'Connor, *1 Corinthians*, 106.

19 Ibid, 106; Richard, *Jesus*, 289–90.

20 Osiek and Balch, *Families in the New Testament World*, 115. In this relation, I agree with the position that 1 Corinthians 14:33b–36 is an interpolation, which rather evinces a reinterpretation of the Deutero-Pauline literature. Cf. Murphy-O'Connor, "The First Letter to the Corinthians," in *New Jerome Biblical Commentary*, 811. As is often pointed out, 1 Corinthians 14:34–35 has some textual problem. Bruce M. Metzger, *A Textual Commentary on the Greek New Testament*, 2nd ed. (Stuttgart and New York: Deutsche Bibelgellschaft/United Bible Societies, 2002), 499–500.

[21]   For me, the antithesis of the First Adam and the Second Adam (=Christ) also seems to echo this parallel image between Old Creation and New Creation.

[22]   Murphy-O'Connor, 1 Corinthians, 115.

[23]   The words, "to build up" (οἰκοδομεῖν are found in 1 Corinthians 8:1,10; 10:23; 14:4,17; also, the word "building" (οἰκοδομή is in 3:9; 14: 3, 5, 12, 26.

[24]   Paul regards "prophecy" as higher than "glossolalia" since prophecy is more intelligible and useful for building up the community (Cf. 14:1–25, particularly, v.4).

[25]   Meeks, The First Urban Christians, 123.

[26]   Murphy-O'Connor, 1 Corinthians, 126–31; Richard, Jesus, 290.

[27]   Keck, Paul and His Letters, 46–48.

[28]   Murphy-O'Connor, 1 Corinthians, 140; idem, "The First Letter to the Corinthians," 812.

[29]   Keck, Paul and His Letters, 96.

[30]   Murphy-O'Connor, 1 Corinthians, 137.

[31]   Meeks, The First Urban Christians, 89.

[32]   This sense may be closer to the early Greek usage, however.

[33]   Dunn, The Theology of Paul the Apostle, 55–56.

[34]   Keck, Paul and His Letters, 103.

[35]   By "an Asian context," I mean mainly the East Asian cultural context, where Buddhism in its various forms is at the base of culture. Specifically, I have Sino-Korean-Japanese cultural orbit in mind.

[36]   Raymond E. Brown, The Churches The Apostles Left Behind (New York: Paulist, 1984), 49.

[37]   Ibid, 51. Also, it is well known that in Colossians/Ephesians Christ became the head of this Body due to their ecclesiastical emphasis (Eph 1:22–23; 5:23; Col 1:18, 24).

[38]   Ibid., 53.

[39]   Of course, this process was not "linear" from low to high, as was supposed in the past. Cf. John P. Meier, A Marginal Jew: Rethinking the Historical Jesus, vol. 2: Mentor, Message, and Miracles (New York: Doubleday, 1991), 923; Larry W. Hurtado, One God and One Lord: Early Christian Devotion and Ancient Jewish Monotheism, 2nd ed. (New York: T&T Clark, 1998), 93–124.

[40]   George Howard, "Phil 2:6–11 and the Human Christ," Catholic Biblical Quarterly 40 (1978): 381.

[41]   Yasuo Yuasa, Shintai-ron—Tōyō-teki Shinsin-ron to Gendai [Body: Toward an Eastern Mind-Body Theory] (Tokyo: Kodansha Gakujutsu Bunko, 1990), 152–61; idem, Shintai no Uchu-sei [Cosmological Dimension of Body] (Tokyo: Iwanami Shoten, 1994), 262. Yuasa also remarks that the Asian sense of body-and-soul unity is well evinced in the religious practice of meditation, such as zazen (meditation practice) in Zen Buddhism. Also, knowing in the Asian

sense is primarily experiential, presupposing our bodily existence; thus, it approximates the Hebrew *yadda'*.

[42] Because of the limits of this article, I cannot go into detail, but Paul's cosmological view is typical of the Hellenistic-Jewish—a kind of combination of Hellenistic animism/pantheism (=the world is filled with "elementary spirits" [=stoiceia]) and Jewish apocalyptic (two-aeon theory). Cf. James D. G. Dunn, *Christology in the Making: the New Testament Inquiry into the Origins of the Doctrine of the Incarnation* (Philadelphia: The Westminster, 1980), 154–55.

[43] Mircea Eliade, *Cosmos and History: The Myth of the Eternal Return*, trans. W. Trask (New Jersey: Princeton University, 1964); idem, *Sacred and Profane: the Nature of Religion*, trans. W. Trask (New York: Harcourt, 1959).

[44] Hiroshi Ichikawa, *Shintai-ron Shūsei [The Collection of Body Theories]*, ed. Yūjirō Nakamura (Tokyo: Iwanami Gendai Bunko, 2001), 212.

[45] Actually, it is well known that the precincts of a Zen Buddhist temple are planned analogously to a human body. Cf. Heinrich Dumoulin, *Zen Buddhism: A History*, vol. 2. *Japan* (New York: Macmillan, 1990).

[46] Ichikawa, *Shintai-ron Shūsei*, 215.

BIBLIOGRAPHY

Brown, Raymond E. *The Churches The Apostles Left Behind*. New York: Paulist, 1984.

Dumoulin, Heinrich. *Zen Buddhism: A History*. Vol. 2. *Japan*. New York: Macmillan, 1990.

Dunn, James D. G. *Christology in the Making: the New Testament Inquiry into the Origins of the Doctrine of the Incarnation*. Philadelphia: The Westminster, 1980.

Dunn, James D. G. *Unity and Diversity in the New Testament: An Inquiry into the Character of Earliest Christianity*. Philadelphia: The Westminster, 1977.

Dunn, James D. G. *The Theology of Paul the Apostle*. Grand Rapids, Michigan: Eerdmans, 1998.

Eliade, Mircea. *Cosmos and History: The Myth of the Eternal Return*. Translated by W. Trask. New Jersey: Princeton University, 1964.

Eliade, Mircea. *Sacred and Profane: the Nature of Religion*. Translated by W. Trask. New York: Harcourt, 1959.

Furnish, V. P. *The Moral Teaching of Paul*. Nashville: Abington, 1979.

Howard, George. "Phil 2:6-11 and the Human Christ." *Catholic Biblical Quarterly* 40 (1978): 368-87.

Hurtado, Larry W. *One God and One Lord: Early Christian Devotion and Ancient Jewish Monotheism*. 2nd ed. New York: T&T Clark, 1998.

Ichikawa, Hiroshi. *Shintai-ron Shūsei* [*The Collection of Body Theories*]. Edited by Yūjirō Nakamura. Tokyo: Iwanami Gendai Bunko, 2001.

Leander E. Keck. *Paul and His Letter*. Philadelphia: Fortress Press, 1973.

Meeks, Wayne A. *The First Urban Christians: The Social World of the Apostle Paul*. 2nd ed. New Haven: Yale University, 2003.

Meier, John P. *A Marginal Jew: Rethinking the Historical Jesus*. Vol. 2: *Mentor, Message, and Miracles*. New York: Doubleday, 1991.

Murphy-O'Connor, Jerome. *1 Corinthians*, Doubleday Bible Commentary. New York: Doubleday, 1998.

Murphy-O'Connor, Jerome. "The First Letter to the Corinthians." In *New Jerome Biblical Commentary*, 798–815. Edited by Raymond E. Brown, Joseph A. Fitzmyer and Roland E. Murphy. New Jersey: Prentice Hall, 1990.

Osiek, Carolyn and David L. Balch. *Families in the New Testament World: Households and House Churches*. Louisville, Kentucky: Westminster John Knox, 1997.

Pearson, Briger A. "Hellenistic-Jewish Wisdom Speculation and Paul." In *Aspects of Wisdom in Judaism and Early Christianity*, 43–66. Edited by Robert Louis Wilken. Notre Dame: University of Notre Dame, 1975.

Richard, Earl. *Jesus: One and Many. The Christological Concept of New Testament Authors*. Wilmington, Delaware: Michael Glazier, 1988.

Roetzel, Calvin J. *The Letter of Paul: Conversations in Context*. 4th ed. Louisville, London, Leiden: Westminster John Knox, 1998.

Roetzel, Calvin J. *Paul: The Man and the Myth*. Minneapolis, MN: Fortress Press, 1999.

Soards, Maurice L. *The Apostle Paul: An Introduction to His Writing and Teaching*. New York: Paulist, 1987.

Yasuo Yuasa. *Shintai-ron—Tōyō-teki Shinsin-ron to Gendai* [*Body: Toward an Eastern Mind-Body Theory*]. Tokyo: Kodansha Gakujutsu Bunko, 1990.

Yasuo Yuasa. *Shintai no Uchu-sei* [*Cosmological Dimension of Body*]. Tokyo: Iwanami Shoten, 1994.

Re-imaging Woman and Reshaping her Destiny

An Indian Feminist Reading of the Bent Body
(Lk 13:10–17)

Evelyn Monteiro, SCC

8

This article analyses the position of women in India in the light of the story of the bent woman. The first part deals with the situation of women within the framework of religion, culture, social traditions and economic development. The second part is an attempt to re-read the story of the bent woman in Luke 13:10–17 from an Indian feminist perspective with the aim of discovering elements that would be insightful to re-image the Indian woman and straighten her bent status in the Indian society.

THE BENT BODY OF INDIAN WOMEN

The Polity of Domination-Dependency
One cannot deny that in postmodern India, women's position and consciousness have altered significantly. The efforts of Indian women themselves in initiating and mobilizing support for change must be recognized. However, one must also accept the reality that the powerful and complex system of Indian patriarchy continues to subject women

to multiple bends: by the social caste system, by the religious laws and structures, by cultural traditions, by the political system, by the caste ridden Christian community and hierarchical Church.

Sylvia Walby, a feminist sociologist, defines patriarchy as a system of social structures and practices in which men dominate, oppress and exploit women. Patriarchy as it exists in India is a system of total domination since the denial of liberation to women is embedded in the Hindu/Indian philosophy as a matter of religious doctrine. The polity of domination-dependency, the catch phrase of patriarchy is prevalent in various ways. There is the affective domination, as it exists in the master-slave relationship. All throughout her life, the woman lives in subjugation as she is not fit for independence: "In childhood, a female must be subject to her father, in youth to her husband, in widowhood to her sons" (*Manusmriti*[1] 5:148, 9:3).

The Fallacy of Economic Ethics

The economic domination-dependency pattern as it exists in the class system, in a system of landlords and landless bonded laborers or industrialists and workers is another form of patriarchal control. In such a system, male-female economic discrimination is particularly evident in the practice of unequal wages and unjust property rights.

With regard to property rights, men can acquire wealth through seven ways: inheritance, profit, purchase, conquering, investing, working and gifts (*Manusmriti* 10:115) whereas a woman's property is traditionally regarded as of six sorts: what was given in front of the marriage fire, on the bridal procession, or as a token of affection, and what she received from her father, mother, or brother as dowry (*Manusmriti* 9:194). In addition, she should not accumulate wealth without her husband's permission (9:199) and any gift and whatever her husband might give her should become the property of her children when she dies, (even) during her husband's lifetime (9:195). In the urban set-up, women are not only homemakers, they substantially and even equally contribute as wage earners. A rapidly growing culture of professionally educated and working women with independent bank savings, which goes against the economic ethos of the traditional Indian home as determined by *Manusmriti,* is creating dents in husband-wife relationships and family life.

Furthermore, within the global capitalist order, Indian women of every class stratum fall prey to the consumer culture that "promotes not only a Western brand of consumption and lifestyle, but also projects an image of women which is discriminatory, oppressive and male-oriented."[2]

Interplay of Religion and Culture
Contrary to popular belief and misconception, there is no Scriptural sanction in Hinduism for the oppression of women. Hindu philosophy treats men and women as essentially the ever-pure, ever-free, ever-illumined *Atman,* the genderless Self. This *Atman* becomes conditioned as male and female when associated with the mind and body. The Vedanta teaches us that divinity is innate in every human being. It promotes the "Self" that is present in every person, whether male or female. In fact, the *Brihadaranyaka* Upanishad (1.4.3) assigns equal status to men and women "The Divine person parted one's very body into two; from that came husband and wife. Therefore this body of husband or wife is one half of oneself, like one of the two halves of a split pea." In fact Swami Vivekananda often appealed to the people to respect the rights of women saying that they were living images of the supreme power, *Shakti.*

It is only the later tradition of Hindu Scriptures as edited by various schools of Hindu philosophy that gradually resulted in discrimination against women as impure, untouchable, evil, and of lower birth. Religious sanctions coupled with cultural gender-biased code of conduct (dress, food, education, career . . .) denied women their rightful place and space, subjecting them to multiple discriminations: as woman (biological status), as female (sociocultural construct), as daughter/wife/mother/widow (family/marital status), as Indian (caste system), as Hindu/Muslim/Christian (religious structure).

Let me explain this system of multiple discriminations that VICTIMIZES Indian women. The woman's biological status determines her primary purpose of life, she "was created only for procreation" (*prajana, Manusmriti* 9:96). Her reproductive system reduces her to a mere medium for the production of sons. Her womb becomes an active but non-recognized means of wealth production and continuity of family heritage. In addition, the laws of purity in the Book of Manu (3:239, 4:40) and *Vyasa Samhita* (2:37–40) and the *Atr-smriti* (5:49–66) sanction the belief that a menstruating woman is like "candela" (despised caste). She must remain in an isolated place in shame and destitution.

An ancient Indian adage that reads "the wife is a friend, the daughter a misery, the son is for the father light in the highest heaven" explains the place of the daughter in the family. A daughter is a misfortune for the family and a son-less mother can be cast off according to the Hindu law books. And as wife, the woman owes her husband absolute obedience. Her primary duty is to please and serve him. Such a wife becomes a *pativrata*, one who worships her lord, and is considered a paragon of womanhood in Hinduism.

Hindu literature glorifies motherhood, or rather being the mother of sons. This "apotheosis of the mother," Maria Mies explains, "is the direct consequence of the requirements of a patriarchal social system" since the male offspring was the primary concern of married life.[3] Absolute monogamy for women is manifest in the prohibition of widow marriage. The widow is stigmatized as impure or an omen. Her polluted state excludes her from ancestor worship, temples and family rituals. Prohibition of widow marriage has socioeconomic implications. It excludes her from succession and inheritance.[4]

In sum, the Indian social history confirms the hypothesis that the stereotyped role of daughter-wife-mother-widow for the woman is the creation of the Brahmanic lawgivers. This was to perpetuate the male dominance-female dependency system to ensure the continuity of the economic benefits of the upper castes.

Culture of Violence

Finally, women are caught in the mesh of domination through violence. Violence against women has a cultural, psychological, economic and sociological base. Madhu Bhushan states:

A complex interplay of the forces of an unequal socio-economic system and the institution of patriarchy generates an ideology and value system which seeks to propagate itself through an invidious process of socialization and structural forms of violence in institutions such as the law, media and family, which reinforce social and economic relations and roles. Personal violence against women, like rape and dowry deaths, therefore only reflect the systematic violence of our society that creates conditions which are in themselves destructive.[5]

Dalit women, for instance, are victims of the Devadasi system by which the women are forced into prostitution for the pleasure of Hindu priests and other powerful people. Quite often when Dalits breach tradition by entering spaces like the temple and wells reserved for the upper castes, women become easy targets of vengeance. They are either raped or paraded naked before the entire village. A little Dalit school girl was blinded because she touched the drinking water jar for caste children in a school in Salem, Tamilnadu. In another case at Delhi a Dalit girl was severely beaten up for greeting *namaskar* (Good morning) to her Brahmin teacher.

Women in the Indian Church
While in Christianity, the dharma of Jesus, can be acclaimed for elevating the position of women, the Church can boast little in its treatment of women. The Hindu perception of the place of women in religion and society as well as the Hindu conception of purity and pollution are, in subtle ways, present in the Church. Several gender-biased beliefs, discriminatory practices, and customs observed at different stages in an Indian girl's life continue in Christian homes.

Today we may not have overt laws and taboos that confine women to a bent status within the Church, but we have their equivalents. Women are barred, marginalized and considered inappropriate for certain places and pursuits in the Church. In fact, Leonard Swidler and others are of the opinion that "taboo was the basis for the Catholic Church in not allowing a woman in the sanctuary during Mass, for she might be menstruating and hence is unclean."[6] Today women may be given token recognition and representation in the Church, but they are still excluded from decision-making and given a peripheral place in the church's system of governance. This exclusion and subjugation are partially based on the traditional association of women's status with sexuality, sin and reproduction, and cultural myths that label women as polluted, as temptress, as weak and inferior.

AN INDIAN FEMINIST RE-READING OF LUKE 13:10–17

Women's experiences of marginalization and oppression as well as their struggles for legitimate freedom in all spheres of life are central to Indian feminist consciousness and hermeneutics. Women's bodies are bent and disfigured. Who are responsible for the wounds inflicted on them? The powerful words of Jesus "You hypocrites" when he addressed and challenged the Scribes and Pharisees for their unjust and inhuman practices ring loud and clear today.

Rooted in the sufferings, struggles, resistance and hopes of the invisible and silenced women in all strata of Indian society, our hermeneutical method of re-reading the episode is an attempt to question and challenge the Indian patriarchal society.

The episode, at first glance seems to be an interesting narration of the story of the bent woman. Most exegetes have tagged it as a healing incident or a Sabbath controversy thus limiting its meaning to a mere Sabbath healing episode. A close reading of the text also reveals a liberative significance for the women-theophilus of today. The passage poses a few questions for consideration:

- What is the significance of the insertion of the controversy in vv 15 and 16 and of the summary verse 17 in the story?
- What message does it have for the "Theophilus" of today?

Call to Repentance: A Sign Value of the Reign of God
When viewed within the immediate context of 12:49–13:35, a teaching section in the Lucan travel narrative which states that a necessary condition for the coming of God's Reign is repentance, the insertion of the episode which is special only to Luke seems to have a purposeful

aim. The unit of vv 1–9 is a renewed call to repentance to the people (Pharisees) already addressed in 12:54–59. Jesus insists that these Jewish leaders have a distorted conception of God's reign. He exhorts them to repent, change their mindset and lay aside resistance to "the plan of God," a resistance which they had manifested both towards John the Baptist (7:30) and Jesus himself (11:53–54). Illustrating with the parables of the fig tree (13:6–9), the mustard seed, and leaven (13:18–21), Jesus underlines the positive aspect of the *kairos*, inviting the Jewish leaders and the crowd to recognize the present time as moments of opportunity for metanoia and hope for salvation.[7]

Patriarchal Judaism[8] narrows the door to salvation especially to those who are blinded by their own religious accomplishments (18:9–12) and refuse to see the urgency of liberating a stricken neighbor (14:1–6). Their blindness demands a radical change of mindset. The episode of the bent woman which is placed within the framework of the call to repentance in 12:49–13:35, underscores the need for a change of heart for law makers enslaved to the prevailing patriarchal religious and social systems.

Sabbath and Synagogue: Symbols of Jewish Male Hegemony

Jesus's opponents view the healing as a breach of the Sabbath law, while Jesus explains how his actions bring out the significance of God's decisive act. The woman's sickness is described as "having a spirit of infirmity" (13:11) and "whom Satan bound for 18 years" (v 16). Jesus's works of healing are a means of overpowering Satan and its kingdom and re-establishing God's reign (4:18). This we see taking place in the healing of the bent woman.

We shall not enter into the details of the Sabbath healing narrative but rather the consequences of it because these are pertinent for women in the Indian context. Healing the bent woman in the Synagogue, results in a debate about the Sabbath laws. It is important to note that the Sabbath and synagogue function as symbols of Jewish male hegemony. The synagogue *ochlos* include men and women, though the latter were segregated with special chambers provided for them. Supremacy of the Law and sanctity of the Sabbath day were upheld at the expense of human needs and life. A similar practice is prevalent in India. In the Hindu society, the *Manusmriti* and other Holy Scriptures and the temple function as symbols of patriarchal control. Religious laws and social taboos that are sanctioned by religion are upheld at the expense of the Indian woman's identity and dignity, "A woman is not fit for independence. . . . Men must make their women dependent day and night" (*Manusmriti* 9:2–3).

Jesus regarded social discrimination as a human barrier to equality in human dignity. Going against the traditions of the Jewish-Greco-Roman society, he adopts a more humane and liberal attitude towards women (Lk 7:36f.). Jesus restores the woman's lost dignity "and she was made straight" (13:13) for the prime purpose of including her in God's reign and its mission.[9]

The episode is significant because by freeing the woman from her bondage, Jesus manifests the life-giving power of God that moves the woman from margin to center, from invisibility to visibility, from being nameless to being called a daughter of Abraham/Sarah. The woman who was once bent over now looks up and is empowered (cf. Heb 12:12, Acts 15:16) to proclaim the liberating power of God that she has experienced.[10] It also creates a conflict between the prevailing patriarchal cultic and social customs and Jesus's breakthrough of them; between the blindness of the Jewish opponents and Jesus's openness and mercy.

The episode is also special because it presents for the first time, a ruler of the synagogue as an opponent of Jesus. The ruler opposes the cure as a breach of the Sabbath laws (v 14 cf. Dt 5:13). The indignant rebuke was directed towards Jesus, whose initiative to heal the bent woman was a violation of the Jewish religious laws and social custom. The Jewish opponents are so wrapped up in externals that they fail to recognize the Reign of God present in their midst.

The Controversy: Refusal to Save Life is to Destroy It

In his controversial response, Jesus appears to be the authority over the law. He who had declared that the disciples were worth more than sparrows (12:6–7) now pronounces that a woman is worth more than an ox or an ass (v 15). Jesus's apparent violation of accepted traditions can be explained thus: Any refusal to do good is to do evil. In the context of his mission, all life is subject to death and therefore under demand for decision (cf. 13:3, 9:23f, 59). To refuse to "save life" is "to destroy it." Jesus's liberative action in the case of the bent woman is an interpretation and continuation of his mission of God's reign. It is redemptive and salvific, a choice for freedom rather than enslavement.

In his response, Jesus does not address the ruler of the synagogue directly. Instead, he speaks to the "hypocrites," including both the "rulers" and those in the crowd (cf. 12:1–13:21). In 12:1–3, Jesus warns his disciples against the yeast of hypocrisy and in 11: 39–44 and 12:1–13:9, he exposes the hypocrisy of the Pharisees and the disciples who do not recognize the signs of the Reign of God because of their bondage to false legalism. In 13:15 Luke narrates a concrete manifestation of the walls of division created by the hypocrisy of official religion. This is evident in the refusal to accommodate the Sabbath rules to the urgency of freeing the bent woman.

Jesus criticizes the legalism and hypocrisy of the Jewish Pharisees, which today would be extended to leaders of different religions who make laws to safeguard their own interests and are blind to human need and suffering. The movement of logic involved is *a minori ad majus*. If the law is applicable to animals, it is even more in the case of human beings. Jesus argues from the lesser to the greater in a series of parallels that is characteristic of the Lucan literary style.

- If an animal, how much more the daughter of Abraham? daughter of Arbaaz Khan in Gujarat, wife of Sharma in Delhi, mother of Arockiadoss in Tamilnadu?
- If one whom you have bound for a few hours, how much more one whom human made satanic laws have bound for 18 years? And how much more a raped girl, a sonless mother and a young widow who are bound for life by sociocultural taboos and religious laws?
- If you can loose the bonds of an animal on the Sabbath as well as on the other six days of the week, how much more is it necessary for God to loose this woman's bond on the Sabbath?

Thus, the question does not concern breaking the Sabbath law but applying the law of human concern to suffering humanity. If it is permitted to untie an ox or ass on the Sabbath and lead it out to drink, then much more to liberate a daughter of Abraham/Sarah who was bound for eighteen years. The issue at stake is not Jesus's attitude or interpretation of the Sabbath law. The central issue is the hardness of heart of Jesus's opponents, who permit "sacred" rituals to segregate this needy woman from divine help, and the blindness that prevents them from recognizing the presence of God's reign in their midst. Similarly, with regard to the situation of Indian women who are bound by laws and taboos at every stage of their life, the main issue is the blindness of contemporary lawmakers—the Indian family, political rulers, religious leaders—who refuse to see women as human beings created in God's image and with a right to live as free persons.

The Divided Response: Shamed Adversaries and Rejoicing Crowd
Jesus makes a further attempt to bring about a change of heart among his adamant opponents. He addresses the woman as "daughter of Abraham/Sarah" (v 16) to remind them that as an Israelite she has a claim to the special covenant blessing promised to Abraham and Sarah (Gn 17:7; 22:17; Mic 7:20).

While the laws of patriarchal Judaism blind Jesus's opponents to the importance of liberating the woman and their narrow legalistic outlook prevents them from seeing the presence of God's reign in his works, *pas ho ochlos* (the crowds cf. 3:21, 7:29, 19:37) rejoice at all the glorious things done by Jesus (13:17b). This divided response (v 17) to the word and action of Jesus on the occasion of liberating the bent woman builds on what preceded and prepares for what follows. The shamed adversaries and the rejoicing crowd have their counterparts in the prophecy of Simeon that many will fall and rise when confronted by the sign of contradiction (2:34); beginning with those who accepted and those who rejected the baptism of John (7:29–30), right through Jesus's programmatic manifesto at Nazareth (4:22,28), his public ministry (5:26, 7:29–30), the cross (23:35–36, 47f) and post-resurrection times (Acts 2:12–13).

One can expect a similar divided response to the contemporary efforts being made by women activists and NGOs to free bent Indian women from a life-space that is restricted to the home, well, market place and temple. The woman's body cycle adds further temporal and spatial restrictions to her already small world. A sense of shame and powerlessness renders the woman voiceless, nameless and faceless. Any attempt to break these shackles is bound to evoke a divided response of opposition and rejoicing.

Such divided response of opposition and openness to change brings to fulfillment what Jesus told his disciples in 12:51, "I have come to bring division and not peace." One witnesses such divisions and conflicts in modern Indian families, particularly in cosmopolitan cities where girl children aspire to be educated and pursue professional careers, where young girls who are economically stable refuse to become victims of the traditional marriage market, where married women seek job opportunities outside their homes, and where wives expect their husbands to share in household chores. These may be small beginnings, a mere drop in the ocean of widespread patriarchy in the rest of India, but they are hopeful signs of constructive changes taking place. Any effort to free women from the shackles of tradition is bound to create division and disturbance in a male-dominated society. But such divisions and turbulence are signs that the reign of God is at hand and that the subjugated and marginalized are also rightful beneficiaries of fullness of life.

CONCLUSION

The passage puts in evidence the nature of the salvific mission of Jesus. His initiative to restore wholeness to the bent woman expresses God's special concern for the *anawim*—all those who are "bent" (*anah*), diminished and deprived of the means to live a full human life. His bold confrontation of those holding power and addressing them as "you hypocrites" continues to haunt the political, social and religious "rulers" of today. A few "repent" but the majority are oblivious to the grave evil of gender injustice and violence subtly invading the Indian society in new and different ways.

The episode has a special meaning to women in India. Like the bent woman ostracized for 18 years, Indian women are bent for life by the various patriarchal systems operative in India. The only answer to this painful reality lies in a radical conversion of our mindset and attitudes and in turning away from blindness to ordering our lives in working for the establishment of God's reign.

Significant institutional changes have altered women's position and destiny. The efforts of women themselves in mobilizing change are under way. We need to keep alive the memory of those outstanding women who brought women's causes to the forefront. We remember our foremothers and forefathers like D. K. Karve, Periyar, Jyotibha Phule and others who have dreamed visions to re-image women in India and reshape their destinies. Following the footprints of our pioneers, we continue to build on what our forerunners have done and advance God's reign of justice and equality.

NOTES

[1] The Laws of Manu (in Sanskrit, the *Manavadharmasastra* or *Manusmrti*) consists of 2,685 verses on topics as apparently varied—but actually intimately interrelated in Hindu thought—as the social obligations and duties of the various castes and of individuals in different stages of life. Composed sometime earlier or around the beginning of the Common Era, the *Manusmrti* is a dharma or model of how life should be lived and is a pivotal text of the dominant form of Hinduism up till the present.

[2] M. A. Joe Antony, "Impact of Media in Globalizing India," in *The Church in India in the Emerging Third Millennium* (Bangalore: NBCLC, 2005), 6.

[3] Maria Mies, *Indian Women and Patriarchy* (New Delhi: Concept Publishing, 1980), 46.

[4] Interestingly, due to education, media and the new national ideology of independence movement, some of the lower castes have also begun to accept the prohibition of widow-marriage along with other practices of the sanskritic "great tradition." Such practices give an apparent upward social mobility to women in the caste-hierarchy.

[5] Madhu Bhushan, "Women and Violence," *Sangarsh* 1985, quoted by Aruna Gnanadason, "Women's Oppression: A Sinful Situation," in *With Passion and Compassion: Third World Women Doing Theology*, ed. Fabella Virginia and Mercy-Amba Oduyoye (New York: Orbis Books, 1988), 72.

[6] R. C. Wahlberg also notes that later Medieval Catholicism stipulated that menstruating women were not to come into the church. *Jesus According to Women* (New York, 1975).

[7] Dennis M. Hamm, "The Freeing of the Bent Woman," *The Journal for the Study of the New Testament* 31 (1987): 30.

[8] The use of the term "patriarchal Judaism" is not meant to denigrate Judaism in general but simply refers to a particular strand of Judaism that seems to be dominant in Jesus's time.

[9] In the NT laying of hands is a symbolic gesture used for healing (4:40, 5:13, 22:5, Mk 6:5, Acts 28:8, 9:12); blessing (Mk 10:16, Mt 19:15) or for commissioning in connection with ordination to some office or ministry in the early Christian community (Acts 6:6, 13:3, 19:6). This symbolic gesture of laying hands appears to be for a mission. Jesus commissions the woman who "was made straight" to proclaim the Good News of God's reign concretely made present in her healing.

[10] It must be pointed out that many among those who have responded to bear witness to Jesus's salvific work are social outcasts, the "anawim" (4:18)—Samaritan leper, blind beggar, paralytic, bent woman, centurion.

BIBLIOGRAPHY

Gnanadason, Aruna. "Women's Oppression: A Sinful Situation." In *With Passion and Compassion: Third World Women Doing Theology*, 69–76. Edited by Virginia Fabella and Mercy-Amba Oduyoye. New York: Orbis Books, 1988.

Hamm, Dennis M. "The Freeing of the Bent Woman." *The Journal for the Study of the New Testament* 31 (1987): 23–44.

Joe Antony, M. A. "Impact of Media in Globalizing India." In *The Church in India in the Emerging Third Millennium*. Bangalore: NBCLC, 2005.

Mies, Maria. *Indian Women and Patriarchy*. New Delhi: Concept Publishing, 1980.

Wahlberg, R .C. *Jesus According to Women*. New York, 1975.

The Body:
A Testimony to Discipleship

(John 19:25–27)

Mary Cecilia Claparols, RA

9

In the light of the symbolic presence of Mary and the Beloved Disciple in the "event" of Jesus's words and actions before His death, this essay explores the evangelist's deliberate insertion of the women "standing near the cross" as a symbol revelatory of the meaning and the implications of discipleship for women. "Meanwhile, standing near the cross of Jesus were his mother, and his mother's sister, Mary the wife of Clopas, and Mary Magdalene" (Jn 19:25). This work presents another focus in the history of the interpretation of the text,[1] describing how in the manifestation of "standing near the cross," the women gave a testimony to discipleship through another language: the body.

> The "voice" of the physical can lead to words, but does not, in and of itself, use words. Its language is one of gesture, action, interaction, and the silent witness of presence.[2]

This article contextualizes the event in its historical period as seen through recent historical critical interpretations of the text and the sociohistorical study of Kathleen Corley on the "Role of Women during

Death and Burial Rituals of Jesus's Time." The text will then be studied in relation to aspects of the literary structure of John's Gospel while the feminist spirituality approach[3] will be the major perspective to uncover the reality of the discipleship of women.

The symbolic character of the Fourth Gospel opens it to transformative encounters and endless potentials for meaningful interpretations. "The only path to understanding (the text) is participation."[4] Aside from scientific research, I engaged with the text through my body.[5] My eyes allowed the text to be "seen" and understood by my body and my mind. My senses responded to the text as the words repeatedly echoed in my being. With no more words, I danced in various movements allowing my body to "touch and listen" to the recovered memories. I listened until I understood. Where everything collapsed I heard: *even there, I never left you!*

Very soon, images of Asian women shattered their silence, ferrying me through my buried fears. Deep within, a discovered space, indestructible—a creativity unleashed a courage to ACT. Text embodied is indeed transforming!

THE BODY AS LANGUAGE

The body is language. As such, the body is not merely the necessary physical substructure through which the spoken and written word must come, as if the body were only vocal cords or fingers on typewriter keys. The body can be word itself as Christians recognize in Jesus Christ, the word made flesh.[6]

The Body, a Language of the Divine

The Johannine Jesus is "*Logos* (pre-existent, eternally in communion with God, an agent of creation, the source of life and a light shining in the darkness)." At the same time this Logos becomes *sarx* (human, limited, tangible, frail, visible) as opposed to the spirit and becomes "tabernacled" (*eskēnōsen*) among us humans.[7]

The verb *eskēnōsen* is used with double meanings: flesh (sarx) and glory (*doxa*). The verb eskēnōsen and the noun *skēnos* (tabernacle) are closely connected, and skēnōs is used to refer to both the human body

(Wis 9:15; 2 Cor 5:1,4) and the Ark of the Covenant where God's living presence was manifested during the Exodus journey (Ex 40:34).[8]

Thus God's Logos in the human body (sarx) manifests God's living presence (doxa) among us.[9]

Our Christian faith is a faith in the "repeatable and continuing incarnation of God." To know God is to know and experience God through our bodies. The Divine presence is known to us through materiality, and human presence—therefore always as an embodied presence.[10]

Thus body language is inescapably the material of Christian theology, bodies are always sexual bodies, and our sexuality is basic to our capacity to know and experience God. . . . As body-selves we participate in the reality of God.[11]

My own journey and process authenticate how I have experienced God through my body. These brought about lasting shifts in my consciousness. What I know of God, my own being, and the cosmic community have never been the same again after these experiences "Our bodies tell us that we are one with the whole earth. Our bodies are revelations of God's new heaven and new earth."[12]

Woman's Body: A Challenge to Re-member

Re-membering is to "collect the members, the pieces, the parts—to put them back together again. . . . The word "remember" is related to "record," from the Latin root *recordari* . . . which literally means "to pass again through the heart."[13] The story of Isis is a story of remembering. She investigates and finds the determination to seek all places where pieces of Osiris's body are hidden. Once complete, she reconstructs the pieces into new life!

In Genesis, man's punishment relates to the external world: the ground, toil (v. 17–18) whereas for the woman, it concerns her body: childbearing and desire (which after the fall is accompanied by pain and experience of domination).[14]

Each morning on my way to Church, I see and experience this domination and distortion as I pass by a makeshift newsstand. Tabloids pervert beauty, particularly that of women's bodies, to lure, to entice, to sell merchandise, especially to male passersby. Women's bodies have become a "currency" in today's market. In wars, the body has become the political battleground and scapegoat for wounded human consciousness (abuse of prisoners, killing of innocents, rape, etc.). More so, women's bodies. Joan Chittister writes: "Women's bodies like nuclear bombs are men's newest weapons of mass destruction."[15] This is the context of reinterpretation and reconstruction.

> It is a challenge for the eye, enlightened by love and faith, to try to contemplate woman's body in a new way. As a symbol, it is able to refer to a variety of things at different times and places. . . . Deeply and genuinely felt emotion, and even any thought is expressed in our whole organism.[16]

In her study, Teresa Santiso points out that in the synchronic aspect of the woman's body, woman is "within," actively open and receptive. Woman knows the time of life through the presence of blood. The same space of reception becomes a space of growth and life. Her body is the first space of life together, the first sharing in intimacy and communion that the human being knows in life. Woman is familiar with labor which opens her body towards letting go what has grown out of her flesh. All this with the known risk of losing either her life or that of the child. Even after the child comes into the world, the woman's body is still able to nurture that life. No wonder the Bible uses this capacity of woman to describe God's love (Hos 11:4; Ps 131:2) and the calling of a messianic people to joy, delight and consolation (Is 66:12).[17]

Like Isis, women must search for places where they can find the pieces of who they truly are, letting go of whatever has been learned in the past which limits the soaring of their spirit. Women need to open themselves to the centuries of women's experiences to re-interpret where and how the Divine and the Spirit (*Ruach*) renews and recreates Life!

LOCATING THE MYSTERY[18]

The true role of biblical and theological science is to locate the divine mystery in the text, in the body of our lives.[19] To locate the mystery, the Divine revealing, we need to really know (with the body), to understand the contexts, the world, humanity "groaning" to be born! It is in this reality that the *Logos* has chosen to "dwell" and "remain." This process requires developing the intuitive and contemplative organ and capacity, the *Budhi* (to the Indian Sages).[20] This *Budhi* opens us to the "depth" level of reality beyond fragmentation and separateness. This is Oneness: Mystery continually experienced!

Women's Lament: A Potential Feared

The lament of women became a feared potential for the manifestation of grief as seen in Kathleen Corley's study on the "Death and Burial Ceremonies of the Ancient Roman, Greek and Jewish Customs."[21] While women had specific roles toward the deceased like washing, anointing the dead, "catching the last breath to give the final kiss, to close the mouth and place a coin in the mouth" very soon, restrictions curbed the prominence of women's presence in burials.

In Jewish communities, mourning after an execution was banned because women's lament after the death of a criminal expressed latent opposition to the religious court's decision and was potentially incendiary of national protest. As it was usual to have only male disciples and male friends attending the death of heroes, a new male genre, the funeral oration which could be delivered only by men, came into use, effectively excluding women from funerals altogether. Women's public expressions of grief and loss therefore came to be restricted by law and considered inappropriate and unnecessary. Despite these restrictions and possible punishment by a "board of censors for women," women could not be deterred from going and visiting the dead.[22]

The simplification of Roman burial practices, however, was part of the consolidation of the power of the state and creating a culture of "uniformity and prosperity in the Imperial Age.[23]

The women's behavior at the crucifixion does not fit the stereotypical role of women in that context but is more apt for a dying hero's close associates, disciples, or friends, usually male. Women's lament rituals were often considered theologically suspect because of their necromantic associations, however. The significance of women's presence during the crucifixion therefore had to be modified. According to Corley, the creedal tradition that Jesus 'was buried' and raised on the third day, and the commonly practiced Hellenistic custom of tomb visitation, often three days after death, may have suggested the empty tomb tradition as a way of marginalizing women followers of Jesus and weakening their claim to have seen the risen Christ.[24]

A Shared Universe Threatened

The Johannine community composed of followers of John the Baptist, Jews openly professing as followers of Jesus, Jews secretly following Jesus, and Samaritans who followed Jesus. All these faced pressure from the divergences within and, because of their Christological confession, from the Jewish authorities (of that time). Their expulsion from the synagogue "threatened their entire universe of shared perceptions, assumptions, beliefs, ideals and hopes that had given meaning to their world within Judaism."[25] The Johannine community had to make very serious choices knowing the consequences in relation to their membership to the existing religious institution. Even as the community faced this crisis, the Johannine crucifixion is less concerned with the fate of Jesus than with the significance of that fate for his followers. The Crucifixion is the fulfillment of Jesus's promise in 13:1 that in "the hour" he would show to the very end his love for his own and his lasting concern for the community of those he leaves behind (17:9–19). Bowing his head and handing his spirit indicates that the Spirit will now take up the work of Jesus (16:7).[26]

> In the face of this collapse, the action and words of Jesus were revelatory of the love of God for his followers. As brothers and sisters, they too were invited to "love till the end," ready for the unconditional gift of their life. In the cross, they witnessed the power: Life unveiling the Sacred.

A Challenged Testimony

The critical situation of the Johannine community and the findings in the sociohistorial study of Kathleen Corley show how difficult it was for the women disciples to follow Jesus. When it came to women, there was a constant double-standard, although there was also an acknowleged awareness of the powerful potential in the presence of women. Women were thus the first to be controlled and restricted even for the sake of political supremacy, the men fearing the power over birth, life, and death attributed to them.

Why is there a fear of those considered "weak?" What is being suppressed in marginalizing and restricting women so that legislation in some cases had to be issued to limit their expressions and their form of presence in significant events?

Two particular texts in the Gospel of John show how Jesus's affirmation of the unconventional roles played by women creates uneasiness and even triggers objections from the men, whom Jesus publicly reprimands each time. On the other hand, the synoptic Gospels, do not record the testimony of the women (Mt 28:8–10) and when the women were commissioned, they were not believed (Lk 24:9–12).

The intensity of the "competition" between the male and female testimonies and the male attempts to discredit the women's testimony is seen clearly in some apocryphal materials. The male disciples refused to believe that Jesus would choose to appear to a woman.

> . . . since it was to this point that the Savior had spoken to her. But Andrew answered and said to the brethren, Say what you wish to say about what she has said. I at least do not believe that the Savior said this. For certainly these teachings are strange ideas. Peter answered and spoke concerning these same things. He questioned about the Savior: Did He really speak privately with a woman and not openly to us? Are we to turn about and all listen to her? Did He prefer her to us? . . . Levi answered and said to Peter, Peter you have always been hot tempered. Now I see you contending against the woman like the adversaries.

But if the Savior made her worthy, who are you indeed to reject her? Surely the Savior knows her very well. And when they heard this they began to go forth to proclaim and preach.[27] ("The Gospel of Mary")

In the Jewish tradition, Jewish law according to Josephus disqualifies women as witnesses because their questionable morality casts doubt on their testimony. During the second temple period, however, a woman's testimony could be accepted as equal to those of a man.[28]

In John's Gospel, the women are given roles traditionally associated with Peter, and with an apostle through whose word people come to believe in Jesus (4:42). Mary Magdalen who receives the first Christophany, is commissioned to announce to the disciples, the exaltation of Jesus and its salvific effects (20:11–18).[29] Thus the women's presence near the cross testifies to their faith in Jesus, but also that their being considered as "his own" (13:1), and their testimony as important as that of the male disciples.

Despite these complexities, other apocryphal writings: "The Gospel of Mary" and "The Gospel of Peter," as well as John's Gospel and the Synoptics (Jn 20:11–18; Lk 24:10, Mt 28:1–10, Mk 16:1–8) show that they could not silence the memory of women witnessing the significant events of Jesus's life nor reject the testimony of women.[30]

UNVEILING THE MYSTERY

This search has put me in touch with a reality that I bear in my body and in my psyche. It is an energy that has often used the language of silence, withdrawal in shame and tears. Its other face is anger which society does not always deem appropriate to express. Anger is often masked in politeness; a mask of self-denigration. However, the same text has shown me another language which I discovered I also find within me. Creative energy literally gushed forth freely when I found that place once more—a place of compassionate strength.

Ministry has gifted me with opportunities to accompany women from a few countries of Asia. Some of these women have been profoundly hurt and violated in various ways. But it is through their wounds courageously faced that they experience "the Hand that holds them (their bodies) lovingly" in contrast to the "hand" that molested them. In the depths of their spirit, while remembering the violence, they find the Hand that accepts and loves them unconditionally. It is there that they encounter Trust being offered to them once more. In that body, amidst the shame and tears—fear lingering still—a gentle whisper is heard: *"even there, I never left you."* In that place, they stand remembering from another space: no longer as victims. With time, trust is now a growing possibility.

> The cross can be understood as a symbol for this process of transformation, but it is more than a symbol; it is also that process itself . . . continual event going on all the time in their lives of human beings in the here and now whenever their consciousness is transformed as they bear their own process of suffering and thus find the deeper Center within themselves.[31]

A Confronting Presence

None of the synoptics develop the trial before Pilate as John does. In seven scenes, there is movement back and forth between Pilate's confronting the crowd outside and his interrogating Jesus inside. Pilate is on trial. On whose side are you?

The passion narrative builds itself through irony, with the tension mounting in the encounters with Pilate and the evil one, both of whom try to assert their authority and power, only to be confronted with the loss of their hold on Jesus. "No one takes it (my life) from me, but I lay it down of my own accord (10:18)." This is a revelation: the freedom of Jesus challenging the desperate attempt to impose power over him. Pilate realizes that he has no power over Jesus and that he is in the presence of an innocent man. "Look, I am bringing him out to you to let you know that I find no case against him (19:4)."

In John, Jesus's death is never presented as a *kenōsis* but Jesus is glorified in and by his Death. The cross is his exaltation. It is the supreme manifestation , the final and definitive revelation of who he is and what God desires for humankind.[32]

By their Testimony

Testimony regarding the event of the cross was very crucial to the Johannine community in order for it to survive and become real in the present. Without testimony, the event would disappear and be lost in history. There was need for persons who could communicate the event accurately. To witness meant being part of that reality, being transformed by it so that it becomes a present event in the life of the community. Actual involvement guaranteed the authenticity of the testimony, more so if the witnesses' lives coherently manifested their proclamation. Thus, the women's testimony could not easily be dismissed.

Meanwhile v. 25 suggests that the women were present throughout the entire event and the Greek preposition *para* is translated as "near," which may mean physical and spatial nearness but may also refer to a closeness in relationship.[33] This tells us that there was an intimate and personal interaction between Jesus and those whom he loved. I would also like to take the suggestion that the formula used in this text "Behold... here is..." in John 19:26, 27 indicates a revelatory moment. Jesus reveals Truth to Mary, to the Beloved disciple, and to the women present.

Recognizing, they were Transformed

According to R. Alan Culpepper, the Fourth gospel makes use of a literary genre: recognition (*anagnorisis*). Aristotle in his definition of *anagnorisis* points to three parts: the encounter leads to a discovery of the true identity of the recognized; a change occurs in the relationship between the two, either to affection or enmity; the change affects the direction or fate of the people involved.[34]

"Standing near," the women bear witness to what they had seen, heard and learned from Jesus while following Him. They recognized Him whom they followed.

Being near the cross was a big risk. They publicly proclaimed: "I am one of them," a follower and disciple of Jesus. The choice was taken by them especially in the context of 6:51–58 to be among those who didn't "turn back" (6:66). This was done at the threat of expulsion from what has been "home (the Jewish institution, the synagogue)" for them. This could have led them to suffer the same fate as Jesus because crucifixion of women did exist at that time.[35]

What else was revealed to them? The categories of inequality were shattered. The women experienced in a deeper and more intimate way, the "love to the end" which Jesus had spoken about in 10:1 and especially during the washing of the feet (13:1). Now, Jesus was fully manifesting the extent of this love. The shocking challenge was for them to realize confidently that they had a place as women and had received the power to live that same kind of love and friendship in a situation that rejected that possibility. "If you make my word your home, you will indeed be my disciples, you will learn the truth and the truth shall make you free" (8:31–32).

In a context in which "your place" is continually threatened, and being oneself is not acceptable, the women must have experienced a growing sense of "home" which led them to keep following Jesus and to be present when all that was real was being challenged.

The women were not just witnesses to the birthing of a new relationship. By being there, they themselves were the manifestation of that birth. The experience of revelation had affirmed and transformed these women into persons who could stand near the cross, drawing from the newfound courage and strength within them, from their experience of being "beloved disciples." As disciples they remain where the birth of the new relationship has taken place: awakened to their found Center.

To give testimony is to give "voice" to this silent presence near the cross. The body manifests this testimony. "Standing" is not just a symbol but a bodily manifestation of a recovered identity, another language. To live from this "revelation experience" is to give oneself to Jesus and to create the conditions so that this friendship of equals can become a reality. The experience of being loved draws out the capacity to love. To "abide" in response to a context of persecution, manifests an inner freedom, an entrance into the deep mystery of the Father: Jesus who will never leave them. He now lives on in this new community. Having stood near the cross, the women can be witnesses to who Jesus truly is (8:28), and to the reality that in Jesus, light and life are indestructible. Evil and violence have lost their power! The human categories of culture, the paralysis of fear and illusions created by the mind can be deconstructed. A new consciousness is born and the entire cosmos participates in it.

Women Standing Near the Cross in Asia

To an Asian woman, the body is an important expression of witness and testimony. In some countries, the body is destroyed even in the womb through amniocentesis. As they are born, women's bodies are controlled and their labor exploited. "Their bodies are beaten, torn, choked, burnt and dismembered. Asian women's self-understanding grows out of this brutal reality. If you start to ask the meaning of pain and suffering, you begin to know God."[36] To recover memory, allowing the broken body to articulate its longings, its discovered meanings and its own voice, is to "stand near the cross." To "stand," is to be in the locus where violence and pain take place, where deep suffering finds its voice. Rising after being forced to crawl, women "stand" to resist marginalization and commit themselves towards "welcoming all as equals regardless of race, culture, social status and religious beliefs. Standing is the posture to encounter beauty—the Spirit that renews, recreates endlessly. It is to be mother, giving birth to new relationships of friends in a context of unfair inequality, the historical burden of caste, the distorted self-image that has come from colonization and patriarchy. There in the very experience of threat and insecurity, to experience the revelation of Jesus is to come home to this love. In this mystery, transformation begins to take place: the veil of fear and shame tears open towards a new life of compassion, communion and creativity. "I when I am lifted up from the earth, will draw all people to myself" (12:32).

Remain in my Love

Discipleship in John is not an ecclesiastical position. It is learning a life of love, "being interiorly taught by God" and the "final examination" is the willingness to lay down one's life for another.[37] This discipleship is learning how to recognize the Risen presence in the very circumstances of one's life, unconditional openness to divine intervention whenever and wherever God's revelation manifests, and readiness to lose one's life to God's Glory, "no matter how frightening or costly it appears to be without tampering with reality in order to preserve the situation with which one is familiar."[38] Finally it is to bear witness to that life in the unfolding of time within the community, no matter what the consequences. "*Even there, I never left you—never will!*"

Many women in Asia live this discipleship. They witness to this victory and transcendence from the "place of birth" in their being. They have walked through the impasse with the readiness for the supreme surrender of their lives. Their lives speak of this new consciousness, the freedom to give their lives for their people.

> I had learnt early in my life never to give up. I had learned to fight what was morally repulsive—to continue to—irrespective of the consequences. I never measured the depth of the whirlpool before plunging into it, but done so because my conscience demanded it. For me being able to live with my ethical self was more important than the consequence. (Kiran Bedi-India)

When asked whether she was afraid after years of being under house arrest, Aung San Suu Kyi replied: "We are only afraid when we consider the other, an enemy." More than her words, her life bears testimony to a choice she has made assuming all the consequences of that choice.

> Somehow I have survived, a witness to the voices of my dying compatriots, my family and friends. Those I once knew are gone, and I have given them my solemn promise that somehow their lives will not be wiped out, forgotten and confused within a web of history that has been rewritten by those who find it useful to destroy the memory of those I have known and loved. Fulfilling this promise is the only purpose remaining in my life. Yet an exile can never forget the severed roots of beginnings. . . . My greatest desire is to return to the land of my birth. At this time, I am considered an outlaw by the Chinese administration because I have not chosen to lower my head and try to forget the years of slavery that so many of my people have endured. (Ama Adhe, an illiterate village woman, one of the leaders of the Tibetan liberation movement; imprisoned for twenty-seven years, now living in Dharamsala, India).

Every atom of silence has the possibility of a ripened fruit.[39]

NOTES

[1] The early Fathers focused on sexuality, using the text to prove the virginity of Mary. There was an obvious image of superiority attributed to John (to whom was entrusted all the teachings) in contrast to the pious women who had to care for the holy apostles. Mary is portrayed by Cyril of Alexandra as one who doubted. To help resolve her doubts, she is entrusted to the Beloved Disciple, the best teacher and theologian to teach and care for her. Her role in redemption is, however, acknowledged. Rudolf Bultmann in the recent times states that the evangelist altered the episode with the women present to make possible v. 26–27, but the evangelist was not interested in these women. His interest centers on the mother of Jesus who represents Jewish Christianity and the Beloved Disciple representing Gentile Christianity. Rudolf Bultmann, *The Gospel According to John: A Commentary* (Philadelphia: Westminster, 1971), 673. Francis Moloney sees this scene as reversing the prologue. Whereas He was not received (in the prologue), here a new family of Jesus has been created. Francis Moloney, *Glory and Dishonor* (Minneapolis: Fortress Press, 1998). Alexander P. Kerrigan, however, suggests that in the light of Johannine theology and the Old Testament, the women at the cross are witnesses, seeing and hearing what happened; but actually it is Jesus's mother who has a role in the episode, and the witness of the Beloved disciple suffices. Alexander Kerrigan, "Jn 19:25–27 in the Light of Johannine Theology and the Old Testament," *Antonianum* 35 (1960): 375. Female scholars suggest the apostolic function of those who have been addressed "woman" in John's Gospel. "The silence and the positive portrayal indicates that gender was not a basis for exclusion from the Johannine community or from the vision of salvation described in the Gospel." Adele Reinhartz, "The Gospel of John" in *Searching the Scriptures*, vol. 2, ed. Elisabeth Schüssler Fiorenza (New York: Crossroad, 1994), 569, 591.

[2] Sandra Stacey, "Words from the Body's Spirit," a paper submitted for the class, Elements of Christian Spirituality, Graduate Theological Union, Berkeley (Fall 1999): 2.

[3] Sandra Schneiders summarizes this strategy into: "challenging the translation, focusing on texts with liberating potential, raising women to visibility, revealing the texts "secrets," the use of rhetorical criticism and rescuing the text from misinterpretation" (*Written That You May Believe: Encountering Jesus in the Fourth Gospel* [NY: Crossroad, 1999], 131–34).

[4] Ibid., 73–74.

[5] I explored the possibilities of the "body as a hermeneutical tool."

[6] James B. Nelson, *Embodiment: An Approach to Sexuality and Christian Theology* (Minnesota: Augsburg Publishing House, 1978), 35.

[7] Rekkha Chennattu, "The Intra-religious Dialogue of the Johannine Community as a Model for the Indian Church in Dialogue," a paper delivered in the Institut d'été in Lyon, France, 21–26 Aug. 2003, 6.

[8] Ibid., 7.

[9] Ibid.; C. R. Koester, *The Dwelling of God: The Tabernacle in the Old Testament, Intertestamental Jewish Literature, and the New Testament* (CBQMS 22; Washington, DC: Catholic Biblical Association of America, 1989), 102–5.

[10] Nelson, *Embodiment*, 36.

[11] Ibid.

[12] James B. Nelson, *Between Two Gardens: Reflections on Sexuality and Religious Experience* (New York: The Pilgrim Press, 1983), 35.

[13] China Galland, *The Bond Between Women: A Journey Towards Fierce Compassion* (New York: Putnam Inc., 1998), 217.

[14] Maria Teresa Procile Santiso, "Woman the Language of Life," *Ecumenical Review* 33 (1981): 367.

[15] Joan Chittister, "Beware What You're Not Aware of, It Measures Your Humanity," *National Catholic Reporter* 2, no.19 (26 Aug. 2004).

[16] Procile Santiso, "Woman the Language of Life," 369.

[17] Ibid., 370–74.

[18] Ibid., ix. This is an expression used by Demetrius R. Dumm, OSB, to indicate an approach to the Johannine text which uses symbolic language appropriate for biblical revelation that is transforming. This implies an encounter in the mystical level.

[19] Demetrius R. Dumm, OSB, *A Mystical Portrait of Jesus: New Perspectives on John's Gospel* (Collegeville, Minnesota: The Liturgical Press, 2001), xvi–xvii.

[20] The *Budhi* is one of the faculties of perception recognized by the Upanishadic sages.

[21] Kathleen E. Corley, "Women and the Crucifixion and Burial of Jesus," *Forum* 1 (Spring 1998): 181–217.

[22] Ibid., 201.

[23] Ibid., 189.

[24] Ibid., 204.

[25] David Rensberger, *Johannine Faith and Liberating Community* (Philadelphia: The Westminster Press, 1988), 2–27.

[26] Raymond Brown, *The Gospel According to John,* vol. 29: *Anchor Bible* (New York: Doubleday, 1970), 907–12.

[27] "The Gospel of Mary," available from www.earlychristianwritings.org; Internet, accessed 20 Sept. 2004.

[28] Tal Ilan, *Jewish Women in Greco-Roman Palestine* (Peabody, MA: Hendrickson Publishers, Inc. 1996), 163–64.

[29] Schneiders, *Written*, 110.

[30] Carolyn Osiek, "Women at the Tomb: What are they Doing There?" *Ex Auditu* 9 (1993): 106.

[31] John A. Sanford, *Mystical Christianity: A Psychological Commentary on the Gospel of John* (New York: Crossroad, 1997), 329.

[32] Schneiders, *Written,* 57.

[33] Mary Thompson, *Mary of Magdala: Apostle and Leader* (New York: Paulist Press, 1995), 27.

[34] R. Alan Culpepper, *The Gospel and Letters of John* (Nashville: Abingdon Press, 1998), 72.

[35] J. Massyngbaerde Ford, *Redeemer, Friend and Mother* (Minneapolis: Fortress Press, 1997), 60–71.

[36] Chung Hyun Kyung, *The Struggle to be the Sun Again* (New York: Orbis Books, 1991), 38.

[37] Schneiders, *Written,* 87–88.

[38] Ibid., 88.

[39] Paul Valéry.

BIBLIOGRAPHY

Brown, Raymond. *The Gospel According to John.* Vol. 29: *Anchor Bible.* New York: Doubleday, 1970.

Bultmann, Rudolf. *The Gospel According to John: A Commentary.* Philadelphia: Westminster, 1971.

Chennattu, Rekkha. "The Intra-religious Dialogue of the Johannine Community as a Model for the Indian Church in Dialogue." A paper delivered in the Institut d'été in Lyon, France, 21–26 Aug. 2003.

Chittister, Joan. "Beware What You're Not Aware of, It Measures Your Humanity," *National Catholic Reporter* 2, no.19 (26 Aug. 2004).

Chung Hyun Kyung. *The Struggle to be the Sun Again.* New York: Orbis Books, 1991.

Corley, Kathleen E. "Women and the Crucifixion and Burial of Jesus." *Forum* 1 (Spring 1998): 181–217.

Culpepper, R. Alan. *The Gospel and Letters of John.* Nashville: Abingdon Press, 1998.

Dumm, Demetrius R., OSB, *A Mystical Portrait of Jesus: New Perspectives on John's Gospel.* Collegeville, Minnesota: The Liturgical Press, 2001.

Galland, China. *The Bond Between Women: A Journey Towards Fierce Compassion.* New York: Putnam Inc., 1998.

"The Gospel of Mary." Available from www.earlychristianwritings.org; Internet, accessed 20 Sept. 2004.

Ilan, Tal. *Jewish Women in Greco-Roman Palestine*. Peabody, MA: Hendrickson Publishers, Inc. 1996.

Kerrigan, Alexander. "Jn 19:25–27 in the Light of Johannine Theology and the Old Testament." *Antonianum* 35 (1960): 369–416.

Koester, C. R. *The Dwelling of God: The Tabernacle in the Old Testament, Intertestamental Jewish Literature, and the New Testament*. CBQMS 22. Washington, DC: Catholic Biblical Association of America, 1989).

Massyngbaerde Ford, J. *Redeemer, Friend and Mother*. Minneapolis: Fortress Press, 1997.

Moloney, Francis. *Glory and Dishonor*. Minneapolis: Fortress Press, 1998.

Nelson, James B. *Between Two Gardens: Reflections on Sexuality and Religious Experience*. New York: The Pilgrim Press, 1983.

Nelson, James B. *Embodiment: An Approach to Sexuality and Christian Theology*. Minnesota: Augsburg Publishing House, 1978.

Osiek, Carolyn. "Women at the Tomb: What are they Doing There?" *Ex Auditu* 9 (1993): 99–107.

Procile Santiso, Maria Teresa. "Woman the Language of Life." *Ecumenical Review* 33 (1981): 366–77.

Reinhartz, Adele. "The Gospel of John." In *Searching the Scriptures*, ed. Elisabeth Schüssler Fiorenza, 2:561–600. New York: Crossroad, 1994.

Rensberger, David. *Johannine Faith and Liberating Community*. Philadelphia: The Westminster Press, 1988.

Sanford, John A. *Mystical Christianity: A Psychological Commentary on the Gospel of John*. New York: Crossroad, 1997.

Schneiders, Sandra. *Written That You May Believe: Encountering Jesus in the Fourth Gospel*. N.Y.: Crossroad, 1999.

Stacey, Sandra. "Words from the Body's Spirit." A paper submitted for the class, Elements of Christian Spirituality, Graduate Theological Union, Berkeley (Fall 1999): 2

Thompson, Mary. *Mary of Magdala: Apostle and Leader*. New York: Paulist Press, 1995.

IV

Body and Sacraments

Re-imaging the Body of Christ

Women's Body as Gospel Proclamation

Antoinette Gutzler, MM

10

One day, a dying Hindu man was brought into a small hospital run by Catholic sisters. A young sister was put in charge of him and every day saw to it that he was bathed, and given the nourishment and medicines he needed. Contrary to all expectations, the man began to get well and soon was well enough to begin preparations to leave the hospital. One day when the young sister was with him he said: "Can I ask you a question? When I was brought in here you didn't know me and yet you treated me so kindly. Each day you saw to it that I was clean, had food to eat and the medicines I needed to get better. Why did you do all that for me when you never knew me before?" The sister explained, "Well, you see, I am a Christian and believe in Jesus. When I see you I see the face of Christ and I want to do everything I possibly can for you." The man looked at her and said, "Oh, so you didn't do it for me?" He died the next day.[1]

Reflection on this story that comes from Asia provokes questions about what this man was really saying. After receiving such tender care, what was it that moved him so quickly from life to death? One can only speculate. I wonder if the answer lies in the *body*? Is it possible that this sister, though she ministered to his bodily needs, only saw him "spiritually?" Is it possible that he wanted to be acknowledged for himself: "I am *me*. I *am* my *body*." This story touches the desire deep within the human heart to be seen and loved for one's person, as expressed in and through our body, rather than loved *in spite of* our body. This article is an attempt to flesh out and honor this desire.

From the perspective of the Gospel and insights of feminist theology, this article discusses the warrants for the Christian attitude toward bodiliness, with particular attention to woman as image of God, body of Christ and vicar of Christ. The warrant for acknowledging the importance of women's body *as body* is derived from the meaning of the Incarnation and the concrete praxis of Jesus in his healing ministry. The incarnation of God in a body and attention to our bodies *is* Gospel proclamation. This work maintains that "body" is constitutive of the "Christic-ness" in which all human beings share including women and the non-Christian poor of Asia.[2] My thesis and my concern is that as long as the "Christic-ness" of women continues to be violated and her body as Gospel proclamation denied, the Gospel does not bring "Good News" to Asia and will not find a place in the hearts of Asia's people.

BODILINESS AND THE IMAGE OF GOD

At the heart of the Judeo-Christian understanding of the human person is the affirmation that human beings are made in the image and likeness of God: "Then God said: 'God created man in his own image, in the image of God he created him; male and female he created them"(Gen.1:26-27). From her study of the Fathers of the Church, Rosemary Radford Ruether maintains that they would have been happier without the "male and female" part of the text. She writes:

> About the character of the image of God in man they had no doubts. This referred to man's soul or reason. . . The problem came with reconciling this spiritual interpretation of the image of God with the subsequent reference to bisexuality. . . Since it was anathema to think of God as bodily, with male and female characteristics, the two parts of the text must be separated so that the "image" could be defined in a monistic, spiritual way, and bisexuality could refer to something other than the nature of God as reflected in man.[3]

However, throughout Judeo-Christian history, images of God have been used to guide the imagination, prayer and praxis of the community. Most of these images have been male and their literal, exclusive and patriarchical usage has subtly drawn Christians into believing that this male imaging of God is the most excellent way to talk about the One who is beyond anything we could say or imagine. The problem is compounded when this "maleness" of God—rather than "humanness"—is posited as constitutive of the Incarnation and the maleness of Jesus becomes a warrant for speaking of the maleness of God to the detriment of women who are led to the conclusion that they do not image God in any particular way.[4] Feminist scripture studies after the Second Vatican Council uncovered and reclaimed female images of God in the scriptures but after millennia of androcentric catechesis it is difficult to believe and accept that women *truly* are "image of God."

Incarnation

It would be unthinkable (as well as anachronistic) for Jesus, as a religious Jew, to regard the body as "image of God" as we do today, or heal bodies because they are this image. The task, therefore, is to look to the praxis of Jesus and his acknowledgement of "bodiliness" as an intrinsic element of salvation in order to discover the "image of God" he is unveiling and begin to grasp in a deep and unbreakable way how the Incarnation is a pivotal turning point in the understanding of what it is to be created in the "image of God." Catholic theology not only acknowledges that Jesus shows us how God would act, it affirms in dogma that he *is* God acting among us.[5] "He is the image of the invisible God" (Col 1:15). The reality and the mystery of Incarnation comes among us: God has, in fact, become what God was not, i.e., human. In writing of the Incarnation, Karl Rahner explains that "the man Jesus must be the self-revelation of God through who he is and not only through his words, and this he really cannot be if precisely this humanity were not the expression of God."[6] From this perspective humanity can be understood "'as that which comes to be when God's self-expression, his Word, is uttered into the emptiness of the Godless void in love,' or by saying that 'when God wants to be what is not God, man [the human person] comes to be.'"[7]

In Jesus, then, we see God *in the flesh*. Through his healing ministry, Jesus affirms the importance of our bodies and the care that God wants to give them. The salvation that comes to us from God in Jesus brings healing and wholeness to bodies that are crippled, ravaged by disease, inhabited by evil spirits, considered "unclean" by religion and society, and "marginalized" because of engagement in unacceptable "professions." Jesus—the enfleshment of the God in whose image we have been created—calls nothing external unclean or profane. What defiles lies within the human heart. The following stories of healing—the healing of a leper (Mark 1:40–45), the woman bent over (Luke 13:10–17) and the woman with a hemorrhage (Mark 5:25–34)—make this point.

Healing of Bodies

The following analysis by anthropologist Mary Douglas gives the background for these stories of healing. In *Purity and Danger,* Douglas writes:

> The body is a model which can stand for any bounded system. Its boundaries can represent any boundaries which are threatened or precarious. The body is a complex structure. The functions of its different parts and their relations afford a source of symbols for other complex structures. We cannot possibly interpret rituals concerning excreta, breast milk, saliva, and the rest unless we are prepared to see in the body a symbol of society, and to see the powers and dangers credited to social structure reproduced in small on the human body.[8]

Healing of a Leper (Mark 1:40–45)

Leprosy, the collective name for a number of dreaded skin diseases, was a greatly feared disease in the ancient world. Leviticus states clearly that: "The person who has the leprous disease shall wear torn clothes and let the hair of his head be disheveled; and he shall cover his upper lip and cry out, 'Unclean, unclean.' He shall remain unclean as long as he has the disease; he is unclean. He shall live alone; his dwelling shall be outside the camp" (Lev 13: 45–46). *Because of their bodies,* lepers must dwell outside the community. "According to Josephus, Jewish 'lepers' were expelled from the city."[9]

Judaism was particular about its boundary symbols and boundary markers that clearly delineated who was "inside" and who was "outside" the bounds of the community. As an observant Jew, Jesus is aware of this fact but it appears that it is not a concern for him. What is of importance is the physical and psychological suffering caused by bodily disease. In this healing, Jesus *touches* the body of the leper—thus rendering himself unclean—so that the other can become "clean." Jesus, "image of the invisible God," visibly attends to a suffering, diseased body and, by his healing touch, affirms that "it is good." The body which has been a source of defilement, exclusion and suffering is now a witness to Gospel Proclamation. **Good News for all diseased ones!**

The Woman Bent Over (Luke 13:10–17)
This woman, "crippled by a spirit, bent over and completely incapable of standing erect" is a symbol of what has been done to women's sense of self through patriarchy and its attendant exclusive male imaging of God. "Bent over" describes her inability to see herself as she really is, she is dependent on others for a sense of who she is. "Incapable of standing erect" gives a *picture-image* of the paralysis that partners her powerlessness to change her life situation. She mirrors the situation of many women in Asia: women whose bodies are raped and burned; women who are "trafficked,"[10] and beaten down; women who are powerless to protect themselves from HIV-AIDS; women who are told they do not bear a likeness to Christ. This woman's healing comes through call and "touch:" Jesus "laid his hands upon her." The ensuing criticism of the synagogue official, who perhaps would rather she be kept *in her place* and certainly not healed on the Sabbath, is challenged by Jesus who acknowledges her as "Daughter of Abraham" and thus her inclusion in the family of God. Being crippled does not mean loss of God's original blessing in creation; one still has the power to become whole. Her act of "standing up straight" is **Body as Gospel Proclamation!**

The Woman with a Hemorrhage (Mark 5: 25–34)
This pericope details the desperation of a woman whose hemorrhaging

body is the cause and vehicle of her uncleanness. "No other miracle story in the Gospels centers on the delicate question of a gynecological problem (perhaps chronic uterine hemorrhage), which would not only be a sensitive private matter for the woman but also a constant source of ritual impurity according to the laws of Leviticus."[11] This unnamed woman, impoverished by her illness and unable to participate fully in the life of the family and larger community, finds her own road to healing. The story is well known. Hearing of Jesus's healing reputation she sneaks up behind him in the crowd and touches his garment. Instantly, "she *felt in her body* that she was healed." Her realization of this tremendous happening (and our access to her inner thoughts) brings poignancy to this story. Not only is she healed but she reclaims her voice and has the courage to tell Jesus her "whole story." Perhaps through this release of power and meeting the woman "heart to heart," Jesus now understands on a deeper level the suffering that is borne by women's bodies. Joanna Dewey writes that "several words appear only in the depiction of the hemorrhaging woman and of Jesus himself: 'suffer many things,' 'blood,' 'body,' and 'plague.' The language suggests that 'Mark dared to identify her suffering with Jesus.'"[12] This bleeding, unclean body—now healed—becomes a sign of the Good News and a witness to the call to meet the Lord "heart to heart." **This is Body as Gospel Proclamation!**

"All Theology is Anthropology"
Karl Rahner's famous dictum—"all theology is anthropology"—crystallizes the affirmation that any talk about "God-with-us" needs to begin "from below," that is, from our bodies. The previous examples from the Gospels showed Jesus's attitude toward the bodies of others but what about his own body? The Cross of Jesus draws us into an answer for on the cross Jesus's body "becomes" a collective "we." Throughout his life, Jesus was in solidarity with those who suffer and gazing upon the cross, suffering humanity sees itself in the image of God—not the pristine, innocent, unblemished "image" of Eden – but the image that has borne and continues to bear suffering and crippling indignities that

causes one to be bent over, quite unable to stand up straight. On the cross Jesus is upright and the "Ecce Homo"—"Behold humanity"— "Behold God who has become totally one with us"—rings out for all to hear. In this upright, crippled one, who experienced and endured human suffering, women see *their* suffering acknowledged and honored. In Jesus's resurrection—witnessed first by a woman and proclaimed to the community by Mary Magdalen—they see the possibilities of standing up straight. Woman—as she is—her body intact and delighted in—experiences resurrection. **This is Body as Gospel Proclamation!**

BODILINESS AND THE BODY OF CHRIST

The points of interface between women's body and the body of Christ begin with St. Paul's confirmation of the Christian community as "the body of Christ" (1 Cor 12:13) and the oneness and egalitarianism that is constitutive of this body (Gal 3:28).[13] Classical theology understands "body of Christ" as "a term which designates the human body of Christ, his risen body, his Eucharistic body and the church."[14] Feminist theologian Kathleen Cannon writes eloquently of the "body of Christ" as the corporeal reality of the risen Christ. The continuity between the crucified body and the risen body means that Jesus has moved into a divine dimension of existence and yet at the same time, in a very real sense, he remains entirely in this world, though in a new way given him by God. Paul speaks of the risen body as *soma pneumatikon* (Gk.), "spiritual body" (1 Cor 15:44), by which he does not mean some sort of spiritualized mater or ephemeral substance, but a body existing in the domain of the Spirit. Christ's body, now suffused with the light of God's glory, is the foundation for a new creation. Thus it can be said that the Eucharist is truly the body of Christ; and so, too, is the Church, the place where Christ dwells in the midst of his people, the Body of Christ.[15]

Elisabeth Schüssler Fiorenza's scholarly work, *In Memory of Her,* brings invaluable insights into this discussion. Her phrase "discipleship of equals" as a description of the egalitarian spirit that existed among the first followers of Jesus has captured the imagination of many Christian feminists (men as well as women!). She notes that after the death and resurrection of Jesus, this early community was engaged in the struggle for survival within the Roman political order and employed a strategy which "gradually introduced the patriarchal-societal ethos of the time into the church. As a result, in the long run it replaced the genuine Christian vision of equality, by which women and slaves had been attracted to become Christians."[16] Many examples of the introduction of this patriarchal-societal ethos into the early community can be found in the letters of the New Testament exemplified in the household codes in Ephesians. These codes detail the relationship of husband and wife within the bonds of a decidedly unegalitarian patriarchal marriage. "The relationship between Christ and the church, expressed in the metaphors of head and body as well as of bridegroom and bride, becomes the paradigm for Christian marriage and vice versa. . . . [Eph] 5:22 insists that the submission of the wife to her husband is on a par with her religious submission to Christ, the Lord. The instruction to the wives thus clearly reinforces the patriarchal marriage *and justifies it christologically*" (italics mine).[17]

However, despite the codification of the discipleship of equals into the bonds of patriarchal marriage and household codes, the image of "Christ" having a "body" continued to live on in the bodies of those who follow him and has shaped Christian tradition (the spiritual and corporal works of mercy) and imagination (St. Vincent de Paul: "Christ now has no hands but yours") over the past two millennia. Christian interpretation of Matthew 25:31–46 understands "whatsoever you do to the least . . . you do to *me*" as a Christian imperative to reach out to the poor and suffering of our world.

Women as "Body of Christ" in Christian Tradition

Christian tradition is a history of paradox and contradictions. It harbors a history of misogyny as well as high praise of women as virgins.[18] Over the past thirty years feminist theology has opened a path into these areas of Christian history and tradition and brought to light attitudes of male theologians such as Tertullian, Augustine, Thomas Aquinas (among others) on women. Their writings have shaped and continue to shape church attitudes towards female bodiliness. It is a matter of record that the Fathers of the Church considered "man to be the paradigmatic human being and maleness to be symbolic of the divine." Woman was considered naturally inferior and her bodiliness symbolic of what was not God-like. However, since these Church Fathers also affirmed that all the baptized are equal they found themselves in a theological conundrum.

How can a Christian woman who was made inferior by nature, law, and the social-patriarchal order achieve in her life the Christian equality which belongs to her as a disciple of Christ? The Fathers answered this question by declaring that a Christian woman is no longer *woman*. While a female nonbeliever is defined by her physical sex, the believing woman, "progresses" to the "perfect man," to the measure of the maturity of Christ [cf. Eph 4:13].[19]

One chapter of church history that remains conveniently forgotten records the lengths to which the church went to purify the Body of Christ through the witchcraze that blazed through western Europe from the 15th to the 17th centuries. It is impossible to know exactly how many women were burned but numbers range from 30,000 to several million. Mary Daly claims that this witchcraze was aimed at ridding Christ's body of strong, independent women such as unmarried women (spinsters), widows and women who were independent economically, spiritually, intellectually, physically and morally.[20] Their independence and sexuality caused these women to be were feared as undesirable elements in the body of Christ.

It is undeniable that the Catholic Church was a major catalyst in this genocide beginning with the 1484 Papal Bull of Innocent VIII and the *Malleus Maleficarum* of the Dominican Inquisitors, Kramer and Sprenger. Shocking stories have come to light of the unbelievable tortures endured by the women, the use of children as witnesses against their own mothers, and daughters seeing their mothers burned alive. Daly writes, "The purification of society was legitimated as a cleansing not only of the 'body politic' but, more specifically, of the Mystical Body of Christ. Since Christ was believed to possess not only his own body but also a Mystical Body—extended to include all members of his church—this Mystical Body had to be kept pure enough to perform the functions required by its divine Head."[21] The burning of women's bodies as a way to purify the body of Christ was the ultimate denial of women as *body of Christ*. Many of the women who were condemned and burned as witches were poor.

BODILINESS AS VICARS OF CHRIST[22]

Historians of the middle ages verify that "in the twelfth century the poor were referred to as *Vicarius Christi*—the vicar of Christ."[23] This claim can be startling since, for centuries, Catholics throughout the world have acknowledged the Bishop of Rome, as the vicar of Christ on earth. This difference of perspective may be seen only through a return to Jesus and retrieval of a little known fact in church history. In the Gospel of Matthew, Jesus clearly designates the poor as his vicars on earth. They are the ones who will judge the nations at the end of time (Mt. 25). The conversion story of St. Paul also emphasizes Jesus's identification with the persecuted ones: "I am Jesus, whom you are persecuting" (Acts 9:5) A "review of church history" uncovers the fact that "Vicar of Christ" as a designation for the Bishop of Rome is *not* a tradition handed down from the early church (that designation is "vicar of Peter") but rather a creation of Pope Innocent III (1198–1216) "who asserted that he was not the vicar of Peter, but the vicar of Jesus Christ himself."[24] This was a movement from designating the "many" as Christ's vicars to naming "one" as *the* "vicar."

The work of reclaiming women as both "body and vicar of Christ" begins to shake the male foundations of the faith community as it moves away *from* the designation of "one" as *the* vicar *to the many* poor as the true "vicars of Christ" on earth. Aloysius Pieris designates these "vicars of Christ" as a new type of magisterium for the Church. As vicars of Christ, women suffer for the life of the world: their body and blood birth new life, their milk gives nourishment and sustenance that builds up the body of Christ, their bodies and souls give physical and spiritual comfort in times of sorrow and distress. Women's bodies protest injustice against their families, children and nation; they weep with the sorrowing (as Jesus wept over Jerusalem), they rejoice with those feasting (as Jesus ate and drank with many different friends), they pray (Abba), they resist injustice, they feed their families, they are subject to "double standards" in sexuality and accused unjustly of sexual crimes.

Women are "Christa" in our midst.[25] They know Jesus in connaturality—in the sharing of natures. When they have their agonies in the garden, their betrayals, guilts, joys, longings, loneliness, and crucifixions, women experience that they touch Jesus and have a "taste of" and "feel for" his life. They know him and they know themselves for who they are and who they are called to be. Women, in their Christic-ness, open a space for the peoples of Asia to see the human face of Jesus and allow that face to change their lives.

CONCLUSION: WHITHER CHRISTIC-NESS?

"Can I ask you a question? When I was brought in here you didn't know me and yet you treated me so kindly. Each day you saw to it that I was clean, had food to eat and the medicines I needed to get better. Why did you do all that for me when you never knew me before?"

We return to the beginning. The healings from the Gospels cited in this article are those of the body—ravaged by leprosy, bent over, hemorrhaging. They are the bodies of those who were ostracized, marginalized, and stigmatized because of their suffering. If the Gospels impart the spirit of Jesus and in that spirit move us to action, then Christians must ask about today's ostracized, marginalized and stigmatized ones. *Who* are they and *where* are they? In the multi-religious context of Asia, they are found primarily "outside" the boundaries of Christianity. This reality presents a challenge and opportunity for real conversion to the Gospel of Jesus and his proclamation of the Reign of God. If Christ so identified with the poor that they can be called his "vicars," and if the majority of these poor in Asia belong to non-Christian religious traditions, then Christic-ness exists outside the church's self-constructed boundaries. The non-Christian religious poor of Asia are Christ among us waiting and wanting to be touched in their hearts and bodies with the healing power that comes from God.

The Incarnation is the light that guides our humanity to become who we really are. Karl Rahner implores us to remember that:

> If God is human and remains so for all eternity; if therefore all theology is eternally anthropology. . . it is forbidden to woman to think little of herself because she would be thinking little of God.[26]

This is Body as Gospel Proclamation!

NOTES

[1]   This story was told to me by the superior of the hospital.

[2]   This term "Christic-ness" is taken from the work of Aloysius Pieris.

[3]   Rosemary Radford Ruether, "Misogynism and Virginal Feminism in the Fathers of the Church," in *Religion and Sexism: Images of Women in the Jewish and Christian Traditions*, ed. Rosemary Radford Ruether (New York: Simon and Schuster, 1974), 153.

[4]   See Elizabeth A. Johnson, *She Who Is: The Mystery of God in Feminist Theological Discourse* (New York: Crossroad, 1992), 19–36.

[5]   Edward Schillebeeckx has written that if one wants to know how God would act, look at Jesus.

[6]   Karl Rahner, *Foundations of Christian Faith: An Introduction to the Idea of Christianity*, trans. William V. Dych (New York: Crossroad, 1978), 224.

[7]   William V. Dych, *Karl Rahner* (London: Geoffrey Chapman, 1992), 78. His reference is to Rahner, *Foundations of Christian Faith*, 224–25.

[8]   Mary Douglas, *Purity and Danger: An Analysis of Concepts of Pollution and Taboo* (London: Routledge and Kegan Paul, 1966), 115, cited by John Dominic Crossan, *Jesus: A Revolutionary Biography* (San Francisco: Harper SanFrancisco, 1994), 77.

[9]   E. P. Sanders, *Judaism: Practice and Belief 63 BCE -66CE* (Philadelphia: Trinity, 1992), 75.

[10]   This refers to the trafficking in women for the purpose of sexual exploitation which is a contemporary form of sexual slavery.

[11]   John P. Meier, *A Marginal Jew: Rethinking the Historical Jesus*, vol. 2: *Mentor, Message, and Miracles* (New York: Doubleday, 1994), 709.

[12]   Joanna Dewey, "The Gospel of Mark," in *Searching the Scriptures: A Feminist Commentary*, vol. 2, ed. Elisabeth Schüssler Fiorenza (New York: Crossroad, 1994), 481.

[13]   *Corpus Christi*, the feast that commemorates the Eucharist as Body of Christ, is not the focus of this reflection on bodiliness and the body of Christ.

[14]   See Richard P. McBrien, *Catholicism* (San Francisco: Harper SanFrancisco, 1994),1235.

[15]   Kathleen Cannon, "Body of Christ," in *Encyclopedia of Catholicism*, General ed., Richard P. McBrien (San Francisco, Harper SanFrancisco, 1995),188.

[16]   Elisabeth Schüssler Fiorenza, *In Memory of Her: A Feminist Theological Reconstruction of Christian Origin* (New York: Crossroad, 1992), 266.

[17]   Ibid., 269.

[18]   See Radford Ruether, "Misogynism and Virginal Feminism in the Fathers of the Church."

[19]   Schüssler Fiorenza, *In Memory of Her*, 277.

[20] See Mary Daly, "European Witchburnings: Purifying the Body of Christ," in *Gyn-Ecology: The Metaethics of Radical Feminism* (Boston: Beacon, 1978), 178–222.

[21] Ibid., 186.

[22] I am indebted to the work of Aloysius Pieris for this understanding of the poor as "vicars of Christ."

[23] Felix Wilfred, "Church's Commitment to the Poor in the Age of Globalization," *Vidyajyoti Journal of Theological Reflection* 62 (1998): 83. Also see Michael Mollat, *The Poor in the Middle Ages: An Essay in Social History*, trans. Arthur Goldhammer (New Haven: Yale, 1986).

[24] Eric G. Jay, *The Church: Its Changing Image through Twenty Centuries* (Atlanta: John Knox, 1980), 109, quoted in T. Howland Sanks, *Salt, Leaven and Light: The Community Called Church* (New York: Crossroad, 1992), 71.

[25] *Christa* is a well-known sculpture of Christ as a crucified woman. Some have objected to it as pornographic; others see it as capturing the human violation that was Roman crucifixion for both women and men. I am using "Christa" here in a wider in order to redeem a female imaging of "Christ" who, while neither male nor female, is usually seen to be male.

[26] Rahner, *Foundations of Christian Faith*, 225. The original translation is "If God himself is man and remains so for all eternity; if therefore all theology is eternally anthropology . . . it is forbidden to man to think little of himself because he would then be thinking little of God." Personal conversations with one of Rahner's translators, William V. Dych, indicated that, if Rahner were writing at this time in history, he would use inclusive language in his writings.

BIBLIOGRAPHY

Cannon, Kathleen. "Body of Christ." In *Encyclopedia of Catholicism*, 187–88. Edited by Richard P. McBrien. San Francisco, Harper SanFrancisco, 1995.

Crossan, John Dominic. *Jesus: A Revolutionary Biography*. San Francisco: Harper SanFrancisco, 1994.

Daly, Mary. "European Witchburnings: Purifying the Body of Christ." In *Gyn-Ecology: The Metaethics of Radical Feminism*, 178–222. Boston: Beacon, 1978.

Dewey, Joanna. "The Gospel of Mark." In *Searching the Scriptures: A Feminist Commentary*, 2:470–509. Edited by Elisabeth Schüssler Fiorenza. New York: Crossroad, 1994.

Dych, William V. *Karl Rahner*. London: Geoffrey Chapman, 1992.

Johnson, Elizabeth A. *She Who Is: The Mystery of God in Feminist Theological Discourse*. New York: Crossroad, 1992.

McBrien, Richard P. *Catholicism*. San Francisco: Harper SanFrancisco, 1994.

Meier, John P. *A Marginal Jew: Rethinking the Historical Jesus*. Vol. 2: *Mentor, Message, and Miracles*. New York: Doubleday, 1994.

Mollat, Michael. *The Poor in the Middle Ages: An Essay in Social History*. Translated by Arthur Goldhammer. New Haven: Yale, 1986.

Radford Ruether, Rosemary. "Misogynism and Virginal Feminism in the Fathers of the Church." In *Religion and Sexism: Images of Woman in the Jewish and Christian Traditions*, 150–83. Edited by Rosemary Radford Ruether. New York: Simon and Schuster, 1974.

Rahner, Karl. *Foundations of Christian Faith: An Introduction to the Idea of Christianity*. Translated by William V. Dych. New York: Crossroad, 1978.

Sanders, E.P. *Judaism: Practice and Belief 63* BCE-66CE. Philadelphia: Trinity, 1992.

Sanks, T. Howland. *Salt, Leaven and Light: The Community Called Church*. New York: Crossroad, 1992.

Schüssler Fiorenza, Elisabeth. *In Memory of Her: A Feminist Theological Reconstruction of Christian Origin*. New York: Crossroad, 1992.

Wilfred, Felix. "Church's Commitment to the Poor in the Age of Globalization." *Vidyajyoti Journal of Theological Reflection* 62, no. 2 (1998): 79–95.

The Passion of the Womb: Women Re-living the Eucharist

Astrid Lobo Gajiwala

11

Women have given their bodies to be broken and their blood to be spilt in every part of the world, responding to Jesus's call to "Do this in memory of me."

—Mary Lynn Sheetz

THIS IS MY BODY, BROKEN FOR YOU

"This is my body given up for you," she croons. "Take and eat."

Guiding her shrivelled breast to parched lips, she strokes the wisps of sun-bleached hair off her baby's face as it settles itself into the crook of her arm. It is all she has left to offer in her sacrifice of motherhood. The blood and bones have gone before, nurturing the germ of life in the warm waters deep within her. Chronic anaemia and osteoporosis are the signs of this Eucharistic ritual that binds all women together across the divides of creed, caste, race and class . . . dying to ourselves so that another may have life in a process that never ends. Being poured out, almost drained to the last drop, for another.

I was spared the unrelenting nausea but not the breathlessness and the excruciating cramps, nor the acidity and immobilizing backaches. My life was full of rules: don't bend, don't lift heavy objects, don't wear heels, don't travel by bus or rickshaw, don't stand for too long, don't sit for too long, don't go out during the eclipse . . . constant reminders that there was another heart pulsating inside me, another being who would claim my body for life. No more could I eat to live. In this maternal self-sacrifice the law of survival was turned on its head: precious calories deliberately taken in only to be given away to another.

I never questioned the price, for I had the means. But what of my undernourished sisters? Their bodies protest the repeated pregnancies that demand what they can no longer provide, and yet their spirits refuse to abandon their flesh. Little ones slung across their emaciated torsos, they continue their backbreaking work in the fields or at construction sites. Loads they cannot put down even as they walk miles in search of firewood or water. At home they set a Eucharistic meal drawing on their meager reserves, body and blood providing sustenance for hungry mouths. Too often they become a statistic in the high mortality rates for Indian mothers and infants. Death and life for them is so intimately intertwined—as it was for the sacrificial Lamb of God.

The birthing, however, also brings with it the wonder of the breath of God moving within the womb, bringing forth human life. It is a re-creation of the mystery of the Divine presence in Eucharistic flesh—one, yet different. "I remember the way I felt," says Lori Challinor, "after my children were born, holding my sleeping infant after the birth, when everyone else had finally left us alone. Two different people, when an hour before there had been only one, so newly separated that neither of us were sure if the new boundaries were real or imagined."[1] So, too, must the God-Mother hold us close, suckle us tenderly, and whisper a never to be forgotten memory, "This is my body, this is my blood" as She sends us on our way.

In women this Eucharistic bonding is crystallised in the ever-present maternal instinct that winds its way through the tears of childhood to the heartaches of adolescence and the insecurities of early adulthood. Caring and sensitive, in a flash it unleashes its power and fury when its charges are threatened, in a replay of divine retribution captured dramatically by *Kali*, the Hindu goddess of destruction. Through the prophet God asks, "Can a woman forget the child of her womb?" (Is 49:15). When the human fails, then comes the Eternal Mother to defend her bodily image as its innocent blood is spilt on the altars of power, greed and lust. She is there in the mothers of children lost in political purges, who challenge the indifference and injustice of governments; in the war widows all over the world struggling to begin life afresh; in the women in refugee camps eking out an existence for themselves and their families; in the prostitutes and victims of abuse who still find it in their hearts to love. Swooping down, Her cry rents the universe as she gathers up Her broken children to Her ample bosom and gently cradles them, wiping away their tears, breathing back life into their empty eyes.

I catch a glimpse of Her in the women who preside at Life's Eucharistic banquet, breaking the bread of their lives to feed the hungry of the world. In unconditional love these humble breadmakers sow the grain, reaping the harvest in hope and faith. In the making of the one bread of Life they allow themselves to be crushed, like the grain of wheat, its identity lost in its transformation. Into the dough they knead the yeast of gentle caresses, constant availability, listening ears, helping hands and a sense of the Absolute in and beyond all. As their hands pummel the dough into it goes the salt of their tears—of hunger, deprivations of education and growth, stunted careers, missed opportunities, frustrations and sexual humiliations. With the fire of their loving, God-fearing lives as mothers, teachers and community sustainers, they bake simple bread, making food that is accessible even to the poor, nourishing both bodily and spiritual hunger.

Theirs is a daily re-living of the Last Supper (Jn 13:33) when Jesus takes the bread, blesses it, breaks it and gives it to his *teknion* ("little ones") to eat.[2] Significantly, by this gesture Jesus not only confirms his self-giving in the sacrifice of his motherhood, but he also places himself among women, the traditional preparers and servers of family food.[3] He is the mother calling to her young children to come and eat after a hard day's work (Jn 21:9–13). His motherly heart is concerned about the late hour and the need to feed those dependent on him, and as the woman of the house he stretches the family meal to accommodate the *atithi* ("unexpected guest") (Mk 6:34–42).

The table he sets is round—without sides, margins, preferential seating, first or last, beginning or end.[4] The wedding garment he demands is neither a red cap nor a clerical collar, nor even a baptismal robe, but a conversion of heart that is inspired by the Holy Spirit (1Cor 12:3). It is reminiscent of the messianic end-time banquet,[5] when all will sit together at the table without distinctions of any kind, and God, our Mother, will fill every mouth with food.

The meal itself is so typical of the East. It brings together the human and the Divine in a communitarian dimension, that "gathers all space and time into the intense moment of remembrance, thanksgiving and hope."[6] Different generations sit down to eat together, to be strengthened and united in ways that will nourish generations to come. At the center is the woman, cooking the meal, setting the table, ensuring that there is enough for all, even as she spiritualizes the ritual. "My grandmother would always offer food to her ancestors before she sat down to eat. She would place it out for the birds to eat or give it to the cow," explains my Hindu husband. On visits to my Hindu uncle's home, before every meal I have watched my aunt prepare a *thali* (steel plate) of food for the household deities, later to be distributed as *prasad* (blessed offering). Often the woman of the house will give part of the food to the *bhikshu* (monk), in symbolic hospitality to the poor, the orphan and the outsider. It is a sign that goes beyond charity to an "observance of *dharma* with all its implications for justice and sharing."[7] "Precisely because the grain of rice is deeply spiritual," says theologian K. M. George, "we should be doubly concerned about the lack of it for millions of our humble sisters and brothers."[8] And we should never forget that in the search for food it is women, the poorest of the poor, on whom most responsibility rests.

So concerned are they about their charges, that often they forget their own bodies. Who is there to care for women? "I will give you rest and wash your tired feet," says Jesus. "Come and eat, I have prepared a banquet for you," he invites them. Perhaps that is why women have a deep affinity for the Eucharistic ritual. It brings them comfort, hope and renewal.

In a celebration that uses Christ's body and blood to symbolise deep spiritual truths, women also perceive an affirmation of the sacredness of their own bodiliness. No more "unclean" labels that desecrate women's signalling of their readiness to support new life. Gone too the "seductress," making way for the New Woman, comfortable and confident in the beauty of her body, exploring and accepting its rhythms with the passage of time. Children sometimes are catalysts in this body consciousness. "So many nights I didn't touch your hair," my seven-year-old son reproached me on my return after a couple of days away from home. His older sisters lay silently beside me, one with a finger exploring my navel, the other with her hand on my breast. It made me aware of my body in a way I had never been before, awakening me to its *Shakti* ("female energy") into which they seemed to need to plug in to sustain their human spirits.

This joyful acceptance of the body is a reversal of the centuries-old tradition of the Church that looked down on women, associating them with the "less spiritual" body. It also ties in with feminist theology's rejection of the dualistic system we have inherited that opposes men and women, spirit and nature, history and nature, soul and body.[9] If feminists today are going back in search of the goddess religions it is precisely in an attempt to recover the intrinsic sacrality of women, evident in their fertility. By doing so they hope to reconnect nature and history, body and spirit.

THIS IS MY BLOOD, POURED OUT FOR YOU

"This is the cup of my blood which shall be shed for you." When I hear these Eucharistic words, images of crucified women flash before my eyes. Sr. Rani Maria lying on the side of a jungle road soaked in her own blood; eliminated because she dared to feed and shelter the tribal poor of Udainagar against exploitation and harassment. Bhanwaridevi, a simple village "*sathin*" ("woman helper") of Rajasthan, who was gang raped for courageously opposing the practice of child marriage in the house of the *sarpanch* (village chief). Medha Patkar, whose life is dedicated to saving "expendable" tribals from submersion in the waters of development. Gladys Staines, binding the wounds of leprosy patients in Manoharpur even as she copes with the gaping wounds caused by a husband and children being torn from her side.

"When I hold up the cup I think of women's blood," says Lyn Brakeman, an Episcopal priest and pastoral psychotherapist.[10] Month after month it flows, this river of energy. No wounds or death in this uniquely woman-experience, only a readiness to receive in order to give till death to oneself brings new life. Sometimes a curse, sometimes a blessing, it marks woman's place in the natural cycles of Mother Earth, and through her, man's. Not surprisingly, tribal women bury their placentas after giving birth, returning this flesh and blood to the sacred womb from whence all life emerges.

Many celebrate this rite of passage into womanhood . . . a crimson cord that binds mother and daughter for life bringing them together in an intimate sharing of the seasons of their bodies. "Sit down and listen my daughter to the wonders your body has in store for you . . ." Wide-eyed, she listened, questions bubbling out before I could finish. An age-old ritual forged in blood that slowly opens itself to embrace all women as they narrate their stories of menstruation, childbirth and menopause, every telling a commemoration of their intuition for life, born of their closeness to the Earth, "the primary sacrament of God's presence."[11] (Can this be why that all the four Evangelists present women as the first to witness New Life?[12])

At the consecration Brakeman holds up the bread and celebrates wholesome life-giving connections. Then she breaks the bread and grieves broken connections. "These are the passions behind the Passion."[13] In them I remember passionate human love marked with the shedding of woman's blood. Man and woman offering to each other their bodies, uncovering their imperfections, savouring the sweetness of flesh and blood in unions around and beyond the womb. Tragically there is too the bloody coupling—a tearing of flesh, a letting of blood in a violation that strips a woman naked, like a lamb ready for the slaying. These are the blood ties that remind us that "amid the prettified adornments of the altar meal there lurks the dark reality of innocent slaughter"[14] of the Lamb of God.

Other covenants come to mind. My women friends sharing gospel stories, nurturing, laughing, weeping, protesting . . . in body and blood relationships, some strong and growing, others faded with time, a few damaged by human failings. Women moving across the boundaries of rich and poor, East and West, one religion and another, transforming their lives in communion, much like the Master did as he gave of himself to Pharisees and scribes, tax-collectors and prostitutes, men, women and children, Jews, Samaritans and Syrophoenicians, refusing to recognize human divisions. My thoughts go too to the women I know, denying themselves marriage and the life that comes with it, to tend to sick and ageing parents, or serve the unwashed and unwanted in institutions. I remember consecrated women and men who work with the marginalised and help them regain their dignity. They stand as Eucharistic signs, celebrating human connectedness, proclaiming one body and blood.

DO THIS IN MEMORY OF ME

Tragically, in the institutional Church, women are reduced to little more than spectators in the Eucharistic ritual. They may be the unifiers in families, close and extended, but they are forbidden to preside at the sacrament of unity. They may serve as Eucharistic ministers but without any rights of their own, only as substitutes for priests (Canon 910, 911). They cannot be installed as lectors (Canon 230:1), nor be ordained as deacons. And the final ignominy, these servants of the community cannot even have their feet washed in commemoration of Jesus's call to service. And so they sit in the pew, waiting . . . hoping . . . sharing.[15]

In a powerful poem that provokes the imagination, Frances Croake Frank brings together the key issues of "God-with-us" and women: the incarnation, women's experience of the Real Presence and gender discrimination in the Church.[16]

Did the woman say,
When she held him for the first time in the dark of a stable,
After the pain and the bleeding and the crying,
"This is my body, this is my blood"?

Did the woman say,
When she held him for the last time in the dark rain on a hilltop,
After the pain and the bleeding and the dying,
"This is my body, this is my blood"?

Well that she said it to him then,
For dry old men,

brocaded robes belying barrenness,
Ordain that she not say it for him now.

Reflecting women's spirituality, there is no distinction here of the sacred and the profane. The life-giving blood of childbirth is intermingled with the life-giving blood of sacrificial death. The words of consecration recall the consummation of the Word made flesh even as they hint at the continuing self-emptying that is women's life. And running through it all is the pain—of the womb, of letting go, of exclusion.

For women this pain is intrinsic to their experience of the Eucharist making it impossible to explore this reality without mentioning the ban on the ordination of women. This exclusion is a shadowy presence at the Eucharist, setting limits to women's participation in this community meal. For many women it stands as a counter-witness to Jesus's non-discriminatory table sharing that is without conditions of participation, for it introduces an element of separation—gender. Bad enough that the Church has replaced Jesus's welcome mat with a ticket; for women there is now also fine print. Ironically too, in a sacrament that celebrates humanity in all its fullness through the embodiment of the Divine in human flesh, women experience a denial of their humanity, thus making a mockery of the radical union of God and the human.

"Why bother to come?" I sometimes ask myself when the priest holds up the host and I hear the voice of my Church: "Male hands alone can make holy this sacrifice." But go I do, like women the world over, sifting through the patriarchal morass to uncover the Christic core in whom there is neither Jew nor Gentile, slave nor free, male nor female (Gal 3:28), taking secret comfort in the knowing that:

The Divine became human,
Penetrated a woman's womb.
(Patriarchy had no place!)
Like soft petals enfolding
A crystal dewdrop,
The seed nestled in a female form . . .
"You shall touch the Divine!"[17]

Women religious the world over experience the hurt and anger of this exclusion most acutely. They resent having to depend on a stranger for their spiritual nourishment and they are unwilling to be humiliated by priests who use the Eucharist as a weapon of power, withholding it on a whim. They are tired and frustrated by the Church's refusal to recognize their priesthood in the breaking of their bread. Increasingly, these women and their lay sisters are creating their own rituals, gathering in Christ's name, sharing bread and wine, using symbols taken out of their knowing and loving. What many of these groups miss, though, is the connection with the universal Church.[18]

Feminist theologians offer them an alternative by focusing the spotlight on the faithful. Mary Collins, for instance, suggests that women need not let the Eucharist be co-opted by the clergy as their own as the sacraments belong to the whole Church.[19] Vicki Balabanski goes further to remind us that the presence of the community at the Eucharist is not incidental to the action taking place, but of the essence. Every person is involved in this *Zikaron* ("remembrance"), and "Christ's presence is not so much in the elements themselves, the bread and wine, as in the people and in their act of participating in sharing the bread and wine."[20]

Renate Rose points out that the Eucharist in fact, was never "instituted," either by Jesus or by his disciples. Instead "it was born in the process of forming a new community ethic of love and reconciliation. It was inspired and conceived out of Jesus's life . . ." becoming a movement, flowing from the continuity of Jesus's spirit to *metanoia* in those who receive him.[21] Such an understanding places the ecclesial assembly, not the one who presides, at the center of the celebration. As Susan Ross, Associate Professor of Theology, Loyola University, Chicago, elaborates, this makes the Eucharist a lavish gift to be shared, not scarce gold to be parcelled out piecemeal only to those who qualify. Like the multiplication of the loaves and fishes, the Eucharistic feast ought to be a living symbol of the openness and generosity of the Christian community. That it so often fails to live up to this generosity is a scandal.[22]

It is a measure of women's resilience that instead of staying in the silent background that the prohibition of their ordination seeks to thrust them, they have emerged to push the discussion of women and the sacraments to deeper levels. As Ross astutely observes, "because the current official Catholic position on ordination rules out the presence of women in the priesthood, Catholic feminist theologians have the opportunity to take a more creative approach to the sacraments than simple inclusion in the present system."[23] Discarding Thomas Aquinas's definition of sacrament *instrumentally*, in terms of function, feminists have focused on Karl Rahner's *symbolic* expression to reconnect the sacraments with their personal and ecclesial dimensions.[24] It is an extension of the sacramental theology of Edward Schillebeeckx for whom sacraments are more than mere "pipelines" of grace, but rather "places where human beings live out in a symbolic way the life of the gospel."[25]

This rooting of the sacrament in ordinary life is typical of women's approach to spirituality that defies the traditional separation and grading of the "spiritual" versus the "rest."[26] For the most part their quiet moments of meditation are found not in Retreats which too often are a luxury they cannot afford, but as they stir the cooking pot, or travel in a bus to work or pat a child to sleep. Their embrace of their love partners holds a thanksgiving more powerful than any religious ritual, and scrubbing the floor or dirty dishes brings with it an inner cleansing that only God is witness to. In their contemplation of the setting sun as they walk the endless miles to fetch water is a prayer no words can capture and in the words drawn out from my computer is a consciousness of the Divine that I would not exchange for any priestly blessing. As Val Webb, author of In *Defense of Doubt* points out, "Spirituality (for women) is not a different level of being, but rather feelings, doubts, physical pain, sexuality, all intertwined, sometimes chaotically, into a life."[27] It is not a question of finding God in our selves and our lives, but becoming conscious of the ongoing activity of God and responding with love.

It is this spirituality that animates women's sacramental ministry taking it beyond the confines of ordained priesthood. Sure, women mind the exclusion—the denial of full imitations of the male bias on the wonderfully free person of Jesus Christ and the clericalization that makes of women second-class citizens in the Church. But for the rest they enjoy a priesthood that is infused with women's wisdom—their capacity for relationship that bonds not just person to person, but the human to the Earth and God within us; their spirituality that recognizes no boundaries between the sacred and life but instead leads them to live every ordinary moment in relation to God; their ability to remain connected through systems that encourage "power-with" and "power-among" and "power-for," rather than "power-over"; and their closeness to life that makes them so vulnerable to love that they cannot help but be moved to serve.

Ironically, women have come to an awareness of their priesthood because they have been denied the experience of official priestly ministry.[28] Most contemporary feminist theologians, in fact, are no longer interested in an inclusion of women in the existing ministerial set-up of the Church. They are beginning to question whether it is at all possible for them to "do this in memory of me" in the existing patriarchal design of the Church. Opt out or work for change from within—this is their dilemma.

What is becoming increasingly clear, however, is that the Church has much to gain from women's inclusion—a richer understanding of ritual activity and God's presence in human life through women's recovery of the sacredness of the everyday; a holistic approach to being human that refuses to be defined by biological sex differences; a returning of the sacraments to the whole Church, and a going back to the priesthood of the gospels where power is put to service.

THE CHALLENGE

It must be said, that women's demand for ordination cannot be reduced to a power struggle. Their exclusion addresses a deeper issue— recognition of their full humanity, not only "in Christ" but also in all of society and the Church. How is it possible, they ask to sit together to eat and drink the Passover food of freedom from bondage and yet not see women's chains of oppression? Worse, with what conscience can we receive the blessing of liberation and then join the ranks of the oppressors[29] by preventing those who faithfully set the table from setting the agenda? It is a travesty of the ritual that Paul warns, has dire consequences: "Whoever therefore eats the bread or drinks the cup of the Lord in an unworthy manner will be answerable for the body and blood of the Lord" (1 Cor. 11:27).

Women's questioning also uncovers the Church's narrow interpretation of the *faciendi* ("making") of the Eucharist. Conditioned by a patriarchal society that sees man as the head, the Church has reduced this sign to the presiding minister and his maleness. The call to make the Eucharist, however, is not realized only in the one who presides, but in all who give flesh to the Eucharist in life.[30] This understanding, coupled with women's changing roles in society, make it imperative that the Church rethink its theology of priesthood, so as to make place not only for women, but for a new kind of priesthood, one at which women excel.

And finally, women's experience of the Eucharist also presents a challenge to the Church "to transform the ways in which we live out the Christian belief that Christ lives among us in the flesh and blood of the Church."[31] Their very lives remind the Church constantly of the central Eucharistic symbols—not bread and wine, but *broken* bread and *poured-out* wine.[32] Through marginalization, exploitation and starvation women continue to provide. Can the Church with its human and material wealth spread across the globe, claim "communion with Christ" of the *anawim* and do any less? As Monika Hellwig writes in her book *The Eucharist and the Hunger of the World,* "To accept the bread of the Eucharist is to accept to be bread and sustenance for the poor of the world."[33]

Such an acceptance, however, means more than the charitable distribution of food, important though that is. It must go beyond to a solidarity that recognizes the one Body in the impoverished poor. It must dig deep and unearth the roots of the "feminization of poverty" a phenomenon that is experienced the world over. It must challenge the unchecked growth of globalization that feeds on the poor, robbing them of their lands, exploiting their labor, and driving their women and children to prostitution. It must work for debt relief and a more equitable distribution of the world's resources.

Anything less cannot be an act of remembrance of the one who is the Bread of Life.

NOTES

[1]   Lori Challinor, "The Worth of Women-Created Worship," *Daughters of Sarah*, 21, no. 4 (Fall 1995): 31.

[2]   Subhash Anand, "The Inculturation of the Eucharistic Liturgy," *Vidyajyoti Journal of Theological Reflection* 57, no. 5 (May 1993): 285.

[3]   Ibid., 280.

[4]   Christine Grumm, *In Search of a Round Table,* in the book of the same name, ed. Musimbi R. A. Kanyoro (WCC, 1997), 28–39, cited by Yong Ting Jin, "Women Reclaiming Their Place at the Table," *In God's Image* 17, no. 4 (1998): 16.

[5]   Vicki Balabanski, "Anamnesis: Remembering Through the Lord's Supper," *In God's Image* 13, no. 2 (Summer 1994): 15.

[6]   K. M. George, "The Sacred Grain," paper presented at the FABC Conference of Asian Theologians II, Bangalore, India, Aug. 1999.

[7]   Ibid.

[8]   Ibid.

[9]   Rosemary Radford Ruether, *New Woman/New Earth: Sexist Ideologies and Human Liberation* (New York: Seabury, 1975).

[10]   Lyn Brakeman, "Passions Behind the Passion: Body and Blood Remembrances in the Eucharist," *Daughters of Sarah* (Fall 1995): 22.

[11]   Anand, "The Inculturation of the Eucharistic Liturgy," 286.

[12]   Ibid.

[13]   Brakeman, "Passions Behind the Passion," 20.

[14]   Ibid., 21.

[15]   Ranjini Rebera, "A Woman's Hands," poem published in *Ecumenical Decade 1988–1998, Churches in Solidarity with Women: Prayers and Poems, Songs and Stories* (Geneva: WCC, 1988).

[16]   Frances Croake Frank, cited by Susan A. Ross, "God's Embodiment and Women," in *Freeing Theology: The Essentials of Theology in Feminist Perspective*, ed. Catherine Mowry LaCugna (San Francisco: Harper SanFrancisco, 1993), 186.

[17]   Ranjini Rebera, "A Woman's Hands."

[18]   Ross, "God's Embodiment and Women," 204.

[19]   Mary Collins, "Women in Relation to the Institutional Church," lecture given at the Leadership Council of Women Religious, Albuquerque, 1991.

[20]   Balabanski, "Anamnesis," 14.

[21]   Renate Rose and Patria Agustin, "The Eucharist Section of BEM Revisited," *In God's Image* 10, no. 1 (Spring 1991): 33.

[22]   Ross, "God's Embodiment and Women," 204–5.

[23]   Ibid., 187.

[24]   Ibid., 188–89.

[25]   Ibid., 191.

26   Val Webb, "Spirituality: A Perpetuation of Dualism for Women?" *Daughters of Sarah* (Fall 1995): 64.
27   Ibid.
28   Ross, "God's Embodiment and Women," 205.
29   Balabanski, "Anamnesis," 15.
30   Tony Charanghat, ed., *The Examiner,* Mumbai.
31   Ross, "God's Embodiment and Women," 207.
32   Balabanski, "Anamnesis," 13.
33   Monika Hellwig, *The Eucharist and the Hunger of the World* (Lanham, MD: Sheed and Ward, 1992), 72.

BIBLIOGRAPHY

Anand, Subhash. "The Inculturation of the Eucharistic Liturgy." *Vidyajyoti Journal of Theological Reflection* 57, no. 5 (May 1993): 269–93.

Balabanski, Vicki. "Anamnesis: Remembering through the Lord's Supper." *In God's Image* 13, no. 2 (Summer 1994): 11–15.

Brakeman, Lyn. "Passions Behind the Passion: Body and Blood Remembrances in the Eucharist." *Daughters of Sarah* (Fall 1995): 20–23.

Challinor, Lori. "The Worth of Women-Created Worship." *Daughters of Sarah*, 21, no. 4 (Fall 1995): 30–33.

Charanghat, Tony, ed. *The Examiner*. Mumbai.

Collins, Mary. "Women in Relation to the Institutional Church." Lecture given at the Leadership Council of Women Religious, Albuquerque, 1991.

George, K. M. "The Sacred Grain." Paper presented at the FABC Conference of Asian Theologians II, Bangalore, India, Aug. 1999.

Hellwig, Monika. *The Eucharist and the Hunger of the World*. Lanham, MD: Sheed and Ward, 1992.

Radford Ruether, Rosemary. *New Woman/New Earth: Sexist Ideologies and Human Liberation*. New York: Seabury, 1975.

Rebera, Ranjini. "A Woman's Hands." Poem published in *Ecumenical Decade 1988–1998, Churches in Solidarity with Women: Prayers and Poems, Songs and Stories,* 78. Geneva: WCC, 1988.

Rose, Renate and Patria Agustin. "The Eucharist Section of BEM Revisited." *In God's Image* 10, no. 1 (Spring 1991): 33–35.

Ross, Susan A. "God's Embodiment and Women." In *Freeing Theology: The Essentials of Theology in Feminist Perspective*, 185–210. Edited by Catherine Mowry LaCugna, San Francisco: HarperSanFrancisco, 1993.

Ting Jin, Yong. "Women Reclaiming their Place at the Table." *In God's Image* 17, no. 4 (1998): 10–16.

Webb, Val. "Spirituality: A Perpetuation of Dualism for Women?" *Daughters of Sarah* (Fall 1995): 61–64.

Reflections on the Spirituality of Ageing Korean Women

The Empowerment of the Sacred in their Body-image and Inner Life

Han Soon Hee, RSCJ

12

The average life-span of people in Korea is increasing and women are living relatively longer than the men. According to the Korean Bureau of Statistics, those aged over 65 was 3.9 percent in 1990, but in 2000 this increased to 7.1 percent. The Bureau foresees that in 2010, the age of those 65 and over will increase to 9.9 percent. Since the female population is increasing more than the male, in 2030, one woman out of 5 or nearly 21.4 percent of the female population will be more than 65 years old.

Although living longer and healthier than our ancestors is a wonderful thing, aged people want to live gracefully and in a meaningful way. No one wants to live solely for the sake of a longer life. For this reason we have to prepare for old age. What is the secret of growing old gracefully?

Up to the beginning of the twentieth century, old people had a recognized place in the family circle and life in old age was reserved for religious development. After the heat and struggle of the day, men and women turned their attention to making their peace with God through prayer and meditation. The culture of the inner life was recognized as the specific task of the elderly.

Today a lot of research concerning old people—the physical, psychological, sociological and economic dimensions of their life—is being done. However, more needs to be known about how people face retirement. Carl Gustav Jung, in studying the problems of older people, writes:

> The afternoon of life is just as full of meaning as the morning; only, its meaning and purpose are different. Man has two aims: the first is the natural aim, the begetting of children and the business of protecting the brood; to this belongs the acquisition of money and social position. When this aim has been reached a new phase begins: the cultural aim.[1]

Old age is no longer just a family issue but a societal one that needs to be given more attention. The solution is principally personal, however, for each individual to prepare for and work out. Above all, inner preparation is the most important task, requiring as much consideration as economic preparation.

It is not an easy job to grow old gracefully; one has to constantly work at it. In old age people often feel that they have lost everything. After age sixty, they are not as strong and they begin to face the shock and pain of aging. This pain often begins with retirement; having no work to do they must adjust to a new life. Life does not end; it changes. After a president of one university retired he became a reporter for a small newspaper. He had dreamt of this since childhood, and he was very much satisfied with it. A well-known businessman finally retired and got a job at a hotel restaurant serving food to guests. These people were satisfied because they found a way to adjust. The majority of old people in Korea, however, lack economic security. Not having the independence that would permit radical alternatives, there is no psychological space to enjoy preparing for inner life.[2]

In general, older religious women are well equipped by their community for later life. They usually have medical care and are empowered through their spiritual life and the care of the religious community. David Snowdon who did his work with the Notre Dame sisters discovered that psychologically and spiritually, the sisters spend a long and happy old age. He found their lifestyle and attitudes to be excellent, thus making them good examples for others.[3]

In this article I explore the difficulties accompanying the aging process of women, and how personal and societal images of older women constrict their sense of worth and their potential. I then discuss ways in which they can embrace new visions of themselves strengthened by a spirituality which acknowledges human limitation and powerlessness. Next I look into the place in women's spirituality of transitions, especially changes in the body-image and the inner life.

There is often a central paradox that accompanies aging: interior awareness often becomes richer while physical abilities slowly lessen. There can be a greater relationship between body and spirit. How can we continue to affirm the sacredness of the body even as we experience its decay? Bodily decline is frequently one of the most difficult aspects of growing older. There comes a time when what we most fear is not aging, but disability; not death itself, but the dying process.

Many women struggle throughout their lives with negative body images, seeking to find a way through centuries of both idealizing and loathing the female body. It is not surprising that we find it hard to talk about our aging bodies, difficult to like our own bodies and those of friends as we begin to show the accumulation of years. How can aged women be empowered to have confidence in their declining body? These days in Korean society, women are very fond of cosmetic surgery and they give great value to it. This is not good nor is it the Christian way. Does anyone know how to live their last years meaningfully and joyfully? It is precisely here that the need for a spiritual perspective is most acutely felt. Perhaps "religion" whether it is Buddhism, Christianity, or others, can help us.

THE REALITIES OF AGED KOREAN WOMEN

Kang Eu-Jin studied the life experiences of elderly Korean women and their process of adaptation to old age.[4] She found that earlier life experiences influence how the later years turn out; also that the women themselves are critical agents in shaping their lives. In her study she interviewed thirteen elderly women and analyzed the key issues in their personal lives. She found the following:

First, based on elderly women's narratives of their own life stories, their role as "mother" gave meaning to their existence. Being "mother" was an essential part not only of the life of their children and the family but of the mothers themselves.

Second, some elderly women continue to search for meaning in old age, while others are not able to reinvent themselves in their later years. Adverse life experiences such as poverty or the 1950 Korean war seem to contribute to a very low self-image and a lack of inner strength in old age. There are, however, those who remained resilient due to the support they received from their families.

THE DEVELOPMENTAL TASK IN AGING

Erik Erikson's "Eight Ages of Man"[5] represents the psychosocial stages of maturation in human development. According to Erikson's theory, at age sixty and above is the period of late adulthood, the era of maturity. Here one can reach integrity of life and be influential as a wise senior in society; not reaching this stage can be a source of despair. James Fowler, in his study on faith development sees this era as the phase of universalizing faith. One who reaches this stage can be concerned with world issues or have a personal interest in family, society and the nations of the world. Examples of people who seem to have attained this stage of development are: Mahatma Gandhi, Martin Luther King, and Mother Teresa. As Daniel Helminiak noted,[6] some significant aspects of this stage of Faith are:

First, more than in the other stages, in Stage-6 Faith, Fowler emphasizes the subject's actual being and doing rather than the subject's way of construing a world of meaning and purpose. The self-constitutive dimension of faithing comes to the fore here so much as to suggest a sharp contrast with presentation of previous stages. Second, Fowler implies that to say someone embodies Stage-6 Faith is not to say that he or she is perfect, neither in a moral nor psychological or leadership sense . . . to Gandhi for his unfair and mutely violent treatment of his wife, . . . Fourth and finally, Fowler admits that the Jewish-Christian image of the kingdom of God . . . are the dominant influences in his conception of Stage-6 Faith.[7]

Jane Loevinger's notion of ego development sees the last stage as the integrated stage, it can transcend conflicts and consolidate a sense of identity; it is open-ended and self-actualizing. Admitting that as the highest, this is the hardest stage to describe, Loevinger points to Maslow's account of self-actualization as the best likely description of the integrated stage.

The characteristics of self-actualization, according to Abraham Maslow, are as follows: it is not a fixed state but a changing process, thus, there is openness to development; a more efficient perception of reality, that is, "lesser blindness"; availability of inner life, vivid perception of the outer world; capacity for both abstractness and concreteness; tolerance for ambiguity; capacity for guilt and sense of responsibility; capacity for spontaneity, as opposed to intensive striving; existential as opposed to hostile humor; gaiety, particularly in sexual and other love relations; transcending of contradictions and polarities; acceptance of reality; greater integration, autonomy, and sense of identity; increased objectivity, detachment, and transcendence of self; democratic character structure.[8]

Naturally we have to acknowledge that where the spiritual care of the later years is concerned, an urgent task is to prepare the aged to integrate all seasons of life: spring, summer, autumn, and winter. The spiritual dimensions of life are intimately related with all the other dimensions people have lived through. As we reflect on the life of the aged we need to pay attention to the meaning of life and how God enters into life's ups and downs. We have to see the mystery inherent in the aging process. Unless we grasp the meaning of this period it is hardly possible to perceive a deeper and fuller insight into human life.

Is aging a declension or ascension? Aging is really ambiguous. If life is a meaningful journey, then each stage has purpose from birth till death, from beginning till the end. The quality of life and the emphasis we place on our role will be appropriate in each different stage. Regrettably, in modern society aging has very negative connotations.

SPIRITUALITY AND AGING

We cannot learn to understand aging if we undervalue or overvalue its realities, or if we simply try to make it appear as much like midlife or youth. As the anthropologist Barbara Myerhoff says of the Jewish elderly portrayed in her book, externally they are cut off, poor, and immobile. However, they are also engaged, resourceful, vigorous, and independent.[9] Psychologist Robert Coles interviewed old people in New Mexico, and he witnessed the same qualities. These older people remembered the hardship in their lives and were deeply convinced that they were eminently valuable human beings, worthy of love, admiration, and respect.[10]

It is a reality that aging is both a descent and an ascent, both loss and gain. Every stage of the life cycle: childhood, adolescence, midlife, and old age, encounters a similar ascending and descending process. Every activity we undertake in the human journey we later have to let go of in order to step forward. A little dying is involved each time. The process seems like riding a wave, we need to have faith and courage to transform our lives, to become more integrated, wise and deep.

Jesus challenges us by saying: "I came so that they might have life and have it more abundantly." (John 10:10) He is the one who gives the fullness of life. Even if aged people seem to be losing, descending, suffering and dying, he is saying: "Whoever wishes to come after me must deny himself, take up his cross, and follow me. For whoever wishes to save his life will lose it, but whoever loses his life for my sake will find it" (Mt.16: 24–25). This is real contradiction, learning to lose in old age so Christ will fill us. "A spirituality of aging must help us find a way to turn losses into gains, to learn how the stripping process which often accompanies aging can be a gradual entrance into freedom and new life, how in fact, aging can be winter grace."[11]

Winter is a season of real losses. There are no flowers of spring, no green leaves of summer, and above all no autumn leaves, just nude trees, waiting for completion. However, there is life in water running through the branches of a tree. "Winter grace is also the capacity to affirm life in the face of death."[12]

In old age we need to keep in mind the vision Jesus showed us. "I say to you, unless a grain of wheat falls to the ground and dies, it remains just a grain of wheat; but if it dies, it produces much fruit. Whoever loves his life loses it, and whoever hates his life in this world will preserve it for eternal life" (John 24–25).

We may need to understand the spirituality of imperfection by learning to accept human limitations and powerlessness.[13]

> Spirituality helps us first to *see* and then to *understand*, and eventually to accept the imperfection that lies at the very core of our human be-ing. . . . This is spirituality not for the saints or the gods, but for people who suffer from what the philosopher-psychologist William James called "torn-to-pieces-hood." We have all known that experience, for to be human is to feel at times divided, fractured, pulled in a dozen directions . . . and to yearn for serenity, for some healing of our "torn-to-pieces-hood."[14]

Older people have to come home to themselves by being able to accept their life-long imperfect humanness. It involves self-forgiveness, simply the opening of one's self to experiencing forgiveness, which begins with allowing another to forgive us. As a result we find ourselves to be-at-home with both self, others, and the world so that we can really trust God and others.[15]

Teilhard de Chardin captured something of the very essence of our intimacy with God during the later years of life as he prayed:

I may recognise you under the species of each alien and hostile force that seems bent upon destroying or uprooting me. When the signs of age begin to mark my body, and still more when they touch my mind; when the ill that is to diminish me or carry me off strikes from without or is born within me; when the painful moment comes in which I suddenly awaken to the fact that I am ill or growing old; and above all that last moment when I feel I am losing hold of myself and am absolutely passive within the hands of the great unknown forces that have formed me; in all those dark moments, O God grant that I may understand that it is you . . . who are painfully parting the fibres of my being in order to penetrate into the very marrow of my substance and bear me away within yourself.[16]

THE AGING BODY AND BODY-IMAGE

The approach of old age brings with it a gradual deterioration of the body itself. A woman must face the loss of many of the characteristics of youth, which have been among her chief assets. Not only will her strength and elasticity diminish as the years go by, but her complexion and figure will lose their youthful beauty. Because of the great value placed on feminine beauty, the loss of youth is of far more a concern to women than to men. A man may be seriously hampered by the diminution of youthful vigor, but few men worry when the color of their complexion changes or when wrinkles replace the smooth contours of youth.[17]

However, it has also been said that in youth a woman's good looks depend on her natural charms, but that after she passes forty it is her own fault if she is not beautiful. After forty, a woman's beauty depends much less than formerly on physical features and far more on her character and how she passes through the journey that is her life. An older woman with her individual experiences of living, suffering and joy is beautiful or ugly according to the kind of spirit that looks out of her eyes; she attracts or repels by the kindliness or bad temper that is expressed by the lines around her mouth. In other words it is her essential "being" that counts rather than the accidents of her physical makeup. As a woman ages she has to realize and learn to see the importance of shifting from the outer world to her inner world.

Women especially struggle through life with negative body images, inherited through the centuries; concepts which either idealize or despise the female body. It is not surprising that they find it hard to talk about their aging bodies and difficult to like their own bodies and those of their friends. One way to help is to let the women share about their understanding of themselves and their attitudes toward their bodies. Such sharing will increase self-confidence and acceptance of their real bodies whatever these look like. Even if the women suffer through sickness, they have to learn to honor the weak body as sacred and to realize that their fragile body has to go through hardship to come to spiritual depths.

Recent years have been characterized by a frantic search for self-improvement; diets for good looks and good health are numerous. The messages we get from the outside world often make us feel dissatisfied with what we have. We pour far too much energy into lamenting our flaws. The body and the being inside were originally designed to work seamlessly together; one "body-self" moving naturally through the world. But when we agonize so much over how we look to others, we fragment this natural unit into two pieces. The result is a continual conflict between the "appearance of our body-self" (how we actually look, how we want the world to see us, how we believe the world sees us from our "body-self").[18]

An essential part of being "in shape"—the part most of us forget— is related to our internal fitness, our joy of living, our relationship to ourselves from the inside out. Once we understand that society's demands on us often go against natural embodiment, we can actively participate in changing our mental/emotional environment to match the basic needs of natural health. We can consciously get back into balance. The first step is to get to know the body we have, to accept it appreciatively, and then ask and dialogue about how I deal with my body.[19]

Aged women need to accept their aging and/or disabled body through the healing of the psyche, and through spiritual activities such as prayer, meditation, exercise, cultural activities and the appreciation of nature.

A METHOD OF SPIRITUAL REFLECTION
FOR EMPOWERMENT OF THE SACRED IN
BODY-IMAGE AND INNER SELF

Following is a pastoral program for women fifty-five years and over. I recommend a two- or three-day workshop. This amount of time is necessary to help people discover the sacredness in their body and to strengthen their inner life. The workshop schedule includes prayer, reflection, sharing, talks and a lecture by a medical doctor. The aim is to give some understanding of the characteristics which accompany aging, so that participants can be happier persons through their remaining years. The workshop will help to heal and restore self-dignity to those who want to become more deeply in tune with the inner guidance of their bodies, minds and spirits.

Day 1
   Opening Prayer

   Step 1
   Talk by a medical doctor about the ageing process: physical, psychological and cultural.

   Step 2
   Form small groups of four or five people.
   Each one chooses and shares from his/her own aging process, an experience that catches his/her attention and energy now and in recent years (one hour, including the feedback from the groups).

   Step 3
   Deepen this experience with prayer and reflection.
   This is done alone and in silence, perhaps in the garden (half an hour).

Step 4
Power-point presentation: fifteen women models of people who have journeyed through their lives, especially focused on older women's real images. In some cases, the body is deformed telling of the harsh life they have led. Use these pictures and try to see in them, inner beauty, dignity and sacredness. Try to see positive and negative images through the light of your own spirituality.

Step 5
In the small group share your thoughts and feelings while looking at the photos of models of women (from step 4).

What kind of life has the woman lived?
What kind of self-image can you see
    through the appearances of the photos?
Do these photos remind you of any parts of your own life journey?

(probable end of Day 1)

Step 6
Dialogue with yourself about how you see your body and your life's journey (alone, but you might speak it out)
Each participant prays, reflects and might embrace herself actually or symbolically. She tries to find beauty and sacredness in herself and learns to respect her body and acknowledge a higher power or inner wisdom[20] (one hour).

Step 7
Listen to the input on "How to Become Gracefully Older; Psychology and Spirituality" Group sharing after the lecture. In the first part "middle age" is considered and in the second part, old age.

(probable end of Day 2)

Step 8

Plan a future for yourself that appreciates God's gift to you including the gift of your body with its strengths and weakness. Plan to empower and care for your body as something beautiful, sacred and full of dignity. If necessary you have to heal and reconcile with yourself and your past life.[21]

"Forgiveness frees us. It heals our bodies and our lives."[22]

The hope is that the participants become happier, freer and empowered to enjoy life. Time can be given to cultural and recreational activities. Creation spirituality is recommended as nature heals and takes us to God.

CONCLUSION

In later life we encounter what may be the advent of darkness. The body becomes weak, even deformed, and movement is difficult so that one can be easily discouraged and disappointed. "These 'dark moments' of which God speaks, these deprivations, are not confined to those which touch the body. God's coming to invade our lives may be through the loss of role, of status, power and influence, even of home and cherished friends, sometimes through financial hardship or through isolating loneliness. All these are part of the emptying by which we are opened to the transforming action of God. We are reminded of the 'kenosis' of Jesus."[23]

How can older people bring the empowerment of the Sacred to their low self and body-image? What is the best means to empower them to have strong self-esteem to overcome the trials of the diminishing years of life? In this article I suggested a pastoral module to help people grow old gracefully, and develop a trusting relationship with their bodies even if they look weak and deformed.

NOTES

1   Carl G. Jung, *The Collected Works of C. G. Jung,* vol. 7: *Two Essays on Analytical Psychology* (New Jersey: Princeton University, 1977), par. 114, cited by M. Esther Harding, *The Way of All Women* (New York: Harper and Row, 1975), 246.
2   Harding, *The Way of All Women,* 244.
3   David Snowdon, *Aging With Grace,* trans. in Korean Yoo Eun Sil (Seoul: Sciencebooks, 2003).
4   Eu-Jin, Kang, *Korean Women's Life Experiences and Adaptation to Old Age* (Seoul: Seoul National University Press, 2002), 161–63.
5   Erik Erikson, *In Childhood and Society* (New York: W.W. Norton and Co., 1963).
6   Daniel A. Helminiak, *Spiritual Development* (Chicago: Loyola University, 1987), 45, 60–61, 72–73.
7   Ibid., 61.
8   Jane Loevinger, *Ego Development* (San Francisco: Jossey-Bass, 1977), 140, cited by Helminiak, *Spiritual Development,* 68. There are some similarities and differences between Fowler's and Loevinger's explanation on the final stage of development. The two are not correlates, but they both share the same developmental direction. Helminiak, *Spiritual Development,* 69.
9   Barbara Myerhoff, *Number Our Days* (New York: Simon and Schuster, 1980), cited by Kathleen R. Fischer, *Winter Grace* (New York: Paulist, 1985), 3.
10 Robert Coles, *The Old Ones of New Mexico* (Albuquerque: University of New Mexico, 1973), 4, cited by Fischer, *Winter Grace,* 4.
11 Fischer, *Winter Grace,* 4.
12 Ibid., 7.
13 Ernest Kurtz and Katherine Ketcham, *The Spirituality of Imperfection— Storytelling and the Journey to Wholeness* (New York: Bantam Books, 1992), 6.
14 Ibid., 2–3.
15 Ibid., 232.
16 Pierre Teilhard de Chardin, *Le Milieu Divin* (Great Britain: Collins, 1964), 89.
17 Harding, *The Way of All Women,* 256.
18 Ibid., 28.
19 Ibid., 28–29.
20 Christiane Northrup, M.D., *Women's Bodies, Women's Wisdom* (New York: Bantam Books, 2002), 606–15.
21 Ibid., 17, 630.
22 Ibid., 630.
23 Mary d'Apice, *Noon to Nightfall: A Journey through Mid-life and Aging* (Victoria, Australia: Harper Collins, 1995), 236.

BIBLIOGRAPHY

d'Apice, Mary. *Noon to Nightfall: A Journey through Mid-life and Aging.* Victoria, Australia: Harper Collins, 1989.

Erikson, Erik. *In Childhood and Society.* New York: W. W. Norton and Co., 1963.

Eu-Jin, Kang. *Korean Women's Life Experiences and Adaptation to Old Age.* Seoul: Seoul National University, 2002.

Fischer, Kathleen R. *Winter Grace.* New York: Paulist, 1985.

Harding, M. Esther. *The Way of All Women.* New York: Harper and Row, 1975.

Helminiak, Daniel A. *Spiritual Development.* Chicago: Loyola University, 1987.

Harding, M. Esther. *The Way of All Women.* New York: Harper Colophon Books, 1975.

Kurtz, Ernest and Katherine Ketcham. *The Spirituality of Imperfection—Storytelling and the Journey to Wholeness.* New York: Bantam Books, 1992.

Northrup, Christiane, M. D. *Women's Bodies, Women's Wisdom.* New York: Bantam Books, 2002.

Snowdon, David. *Aging With Grace.* Translated into Korean by Yoo Eun Sil. Seoul: Sciencebooks, 2003.

Teilhard de Chardin, Pierre. *Le Milieu Divin.* Great Britain: Collins, 1964.

V

Sexuality and
Church Leadership

Facing the Reality of Clergy Sexual Misconduct in the Church

A Step toward Justice and Healing

Leonila V. Bermisa, MM

13

She stood up. My lilac crystal vase tipped over and fell to the cold cement floor under my chair. She bent down to pick up the broken pieces. I said "Go on. Don't worry, I'll take care of it." She walked out of the door. I looked at my favorite vase on the floor. Broken . . . like her, I thought. I picked up the broken pieces. "My favorite vase . . . it's gone" I sighed.

But, unlike my crystal vase, it is not the end of her. She is broken indeed but it is not the end of her. The fact that she came to share her story was an indication that she is ready to reclaim her dignity and spirit. That to me is the beginning of new life for her. The broken woman hears the holy voice from the depth of her being "Talitha Cum!" and she rises, walks about, seeking truth and justice.

Perhaps you've heard similar stories of women victims of sexual abuse. And you too have encountered women (as well as men) who have gathered enough courage to speak up and to seek justice for themselves and for others.

Recently you and I have heard experiences of victims and survivors of clerical sexual misconduct within the Roman Catholic Church. The fact is that these recent exposés have rocked the Catholic Church both as an institution and as a faith community.

The Philippines is one of the countries where this abuse was most publicized and this appears to be an indication of the Philippine Catholic Church's power and influence. It is this same power that has seemingly been corrupted, giving way to sexual violence against women and men by diocesan clergy and religious priests, and brothers. As research shows that for the most part, the victims and/or survivors of this violence are women, the focus of this presentation is clergy sexual misconduct against women.

CLARIFICATION AND EXPLANATION OF TERMS

This presentation is limited to sexual violence perpetrated by priests and brothers in the Roman Catholic Church in the Philippines. This does not in any way imply that sexual violence in churches or faith communities happens only within the Roman Catholic Church. Sexual violence as treated in this work is an act of violence and aggression against another person, be it psychological or physical or both.[1]

The CBCP identified different forms of sexual violence depending on the circumstances that surround the act. They can be as follows:

> Sexual abuse generally refers to sexual contact between a cleric and a minor or "vulnerable adult" as defined by law, as well as suggestive verbal behavior.[2]

Examples of this are: pedophilia, ephebophilia,[3] exhibitionism, molestation, rape.

"Sexual exploitation" in particular, refers to sexual contact between a cleric and someone receiving pastoral care from the church. The term may include sexually suggestive verbal behavior such as a prolonged hug when the customary behavior is a brief hug. Sexual exploitation is fundamentally a betrayal of trust in the professional relationship by using one's personal, professional, and/or physical power to develop a romantic relationship with someone under one's care or to use that person for one's own sexual stimulation and satisfaction.

Sexual harassment refers to unwanted sexualized conduct or language between co-workers in the church setting. Examples: Risqué jokes, verbal innuendo, unwelcome visual contact, undesired physical contact (lap-sitting, kissing, hugging, pinching, as well as intentional touching of breasts, genitals, buttocks), comments or questions about clothing or physical appearance, seductions, requests for social engagements, or displaying derogatory posters, drawings or cartoons.

Women and men, boys and girls have been victims of the above forms of sexual violence. It is to be noted, however, that except in the case of child abuse, most of the victims are women. Sexual violence in general is in fact a manifestation of the traditional inequality between the sexes, and of women's subordination to men. Moral theologian Carol Adams explains: Sexual violence is "both a practice and an index of inequality between the sexes, both a symbol and an act of women's subordinate social status to men."[4]

ROOTS OF VIOLENCE AGAINST WOMEN IN THE PHILIPPINE CATHOLIC CHURCH

Understanding violence against women in the Catholic Church in the Philippines necessitates understanding of the larger context of violence in Philippine society including the history of colonialism in the country.

The Story of Women during the Colonization of the Philippines

Around the 16th century, Spain came to colonize the Philippines and brought with it Christianity and Western civilization. While it cannot be fully claimed that precolonial Philippines was matriarchal, it is fair to say that the Filipino women enjoyed egalitarian status with men. A historian, F. Landa Jocano, wrote:

The idea and practice of gender inequality that we talk about today were introduced by the colonizers—the Spaniards and the Americans. These were not part of our indigenous tradition....[5]

Referring to the Filipino myth that the first woman and man came out of the bamboo at the same time, Jocano explains that our ancestors believed that male and female were created simultaneously. They were both co-equal.... The female was meant to be the partner of the male— endowed with the same status, rights and roles in society.[6]

The introduction and imposition of a patriarchal society and a system of governance dominated by men, drastically affected Philippine society, especially women's status therein. Woman's participation in daily life gradually changed. She was deprived of her right to inheritance, autonomy in production, and the right to lead in rituals and cultic practices as priestess or *babaylan*. Believed to possess the knowledge of natural and herbal healing, the *babaylans* were methodically and systematically demonized by the friars and made objects of ridicule.

The Filipino woman's dignity was taken away from her as she was subjugated and became a sex object of the colonizers including the Spanish friars. She was reconstructed by the Spaniards into the image of the "good woman of the Judaeo/Christian mythology," a woman who is submissive, docile and subservient. This ideal made the *mujer indigina* vulnerable to sexual abuse and exploitation even within the walls of the churches.

Many stories of our ancestors indicate that the arrival of the Spanish colonizers in the Philippines coincided with experiences of clerical sexual abuse against women. In "Scars ARE History: Colonialism, Written on the Body," Rachel Bundang said:

The Spanish period in the Philippines was nothing short of a friarocracy. Imported clerics of all orders—primarily Augustinians, Dominicans, Franciscans and Jesuits—then sought to reshape their newfound world in the image and likeness of the one back home. Imitating their ideal of a "totalitarian economy of divine mercy," they controlled bodies by controlling the spaces in which they lived. . . . As they controlled bodies and space, the friars likewise controlled minds (and souls) by controlling language. . . . They modeled Filipina girls after the Spanish women of the Iberian society of their time, where their life style did not differ much from that of a contemplative nun today . . .[7]

Today we still hear of the yearning for the ideal Filipinas, "the sweet, shy, docile, and pious" Maria Claras modeled after one of the women in the life of the "national hero" Jose Rizal and described in his book, "Noli Me Tangere." Being an illegitimate child of a Spanish friar, and not wanting to bring shame to her loved ones, in the novel Maria Clara retreats from society and becomes a nun. Eventually she becomes insane and commits suicide. There are other similar stories and these all have become part of the Filipino Woman's Story.

The reconstructed *mujer indigina* was affirmed by subsequent colonizers who patronized the "sweet, submissive and caring" native woman. The general struggle, however, against the economic, political and cultural deprivation inflicted by the invaders has been felt more intensely by women especially the poor and less privileged. Prostitution flourished as the colonizers plundered and controlled the resources of the country. Luis Camara Dery, a historian, said: "The male foreigners' 'passing passion' and the benefits they bestowed on the impoverished native women led to the formation of "temporary or permanent alliances" between them. Even members of the clergy succumbed. "Some of the young women impelled by the desire of obtaining (their) good graces" led some members of the clergy to forget their vow of chastity.[8]

Women carry the extra weight of humiliation and degradation because they are commodified, abused and exploited locally and abroad. Women have become socialized to accept the cultural norms concerning their own body and sexuality, and this has usually made them silent accomplices of male violence. "ilent suffering has been the most prevalent female response to male violence. . . ."[9]

It is unfortunate that despite all its power and influence as an institution, the Philippine Church has not helped to alleviate this subordinated status of women. It has in fact reinforced the silencing of women victims of violence in the home and in the Church. As one columnist of a daily paper wrote when clerical misconduct was the focus of media coverage:

> The Church has a history of cover-ups, "a subculture of secrecy"; a disposition to suppress, subtly; or to silence directly. "Excommunication" which we thought had disappeared with the Inquisition, still crops up to this day![10]

In a country where Catholics are the majority, women confide their experiences of violence at home to their confessor (usually a priest). The recent past has shown that these "men of the cloth" are not the safest persons to go to as they themselves could be perpetuators or perpetrators; perpetuators in that they inculcate self-sacrifice and forgiveness based on a theology that women are supposed to give unconditional love to their husbands and serve them and their children, "till death do us part;" perpetrators because some priests and brothers are themselves culpable of sexual abuse, sexual exploitation or sexual harassment.

Religio-cultural Roots of Violence Against Women

Many priests and male religious have yet to learn to see women as full human beings with equal dignity and potential. Men continue to be socialized to consider themselves superior to women, and having "the right to maintain their authority over women—especially their women... As a defense against helplessness, pain or need, men tend to resort to power, control and domination.[11]

Attitudes and belief systems about women as Eve, the temptress, and the cause of man's fall need to be eliminated. Attitudes and structures reinforced by doctrines and theological constructions of the Church Fathers during the patristic and medieval times and the Church hierarchy of today ought to be re-examined and corrected when these tend to keep women in subordination and perpetuate sexual violence against women. Examples of these doctrines and theological constructions are as follows:[12]

John Chrysostom, a 4th Century theologian, had this to say: "Among all savage beasts, none is found so harmful as women."[13]

Tertullian (155-245) wrote: "Do you not know that you are Eve? . . . You are the devil's gateway...How easily you destroyed man, the image of God. . ."[14] (PL 11418b-19a. De cultu feminarum, libre duo 1, I)

St. Thomas Aquinas, one of the acknowledged Great Doctors of the Church, also had much to say about women. Excerpts of his statements are:

> Different kinds of temptations make war on man in his various ages, some when he is young and others when he is old: but woman threatens him perpetually. Neither the youth, nor the adult, not even the saint is ever safe from woman.[15]

These teachings and comments about women reverberate to present times. While said differently, what is heard today nevertheless carry a common tone, a common attitude revealing the sexist mind-set that still predominates within the clerical hierarchy today. In response to media coverage of clerical sexual abuse, a prominent Church authority in the Philippines recently told about turning down a woman's proposal to sleep with him while he was a young priest. The article went on to say that:

> They (women) advertise themselves before the object of their affection. And priests, many of whom are no different from men driven by testosterone, respond to the advertising. So these men give in to their desires, rejecting [this Church person's] advice of either taking a cold shower or using white flower, a liniment, to control their sexual urges.[16]

Negative portrayals of women by the Church have definitely influenced and reinforced the subordination and violence against women in society. It is not surprising that violence against women is socially sanctioned in many ways. Too often, when a woman complains of rape or sexual abuse, the immediate response even from family members includes questions and comments like: "How were you dressed?" "Where were you?" "Why did you go with him anyway?" "You know he is a womanizer. . . Don't tell it to anyone, it is embarrassing."

Dealing with male abusers who have victimized women is dealing, not only with an individual's misconduct or pathology, but with an entire set of social, cultural and religious beliefs. In the Philippines are the "culture of silence" and the fear of *Karma* or *Gaba* (curse in English). A shameful experience is better kept within the family circle. *Hiya* (shame) is still evident in our culture. The opinion of others or what others would think is very important.

Where offenses by clergy are concerned, people continue to be influenced by the fear of karma or gaba (Bisayan term). It is believed that speaking ill of a priest or a nun brings bad luck to the family. That is why, even if a person has had a painful experience, he or she is not to talk against the servant of the Church because they would experience bad luck.

The CBCP in its document "Pastoral Care of Victims and Offenders"[17] has acknowledged that when the abuser is from the clergy or religious, the community tends to remain silent because accusing a religious person imbued culturally with holiness and divine authority can disturb the peace of society. There is that lurking fear that victims (and/or those who will talk) will be blamed for challenging the culture's superpowers.

The CBCP also states, "In addition to an individual's upbringing, personality disorders and social maladjustment, some elements of our Filipino culture might contribute to situations of sexual abuse, especially by the clergy and religious. . . ." One is touching. "It is acceptable in our culture for persons to touch one another. Touching can manifest caring and nurturing. But when boundaries are not clear, touch can lead to malice...There are touches that give mixed signals and the children and other vulnerable persons cannot always read the signals until it is too late." Another element is the understanding of family. "Family is defined loosely and broadly in our cultures to include many people other than biological relations. A cleric is usually a welcome member of the Filipino family. . . . Our culture also sees the clergy as more than ordinary human, possessing extraordinary powers and so with the Church that they represent... Some women are drawn to members of the clergy more than other males because they are associated with mystery and spirituality... associated with caring and nurturing. . . ."[18] These cultural aspects make women easy objects of abuse by an irresponsible clergy.

Like any other men in various sectors of society, priests and male religious have the responsibility to maintain professional ethics and moral standards in their field of discipline. Many in the Church have yet to learn what it means to enter into a just or mutual relationship especially with a woman. There remains a great challenge to see and respect women as full human beings with equal dignity and potentials and as partners in ministry; not as inferior, not as commodities, not as temptresses. There remains a challenge to reconstruct Adam as a creature equally gifted as Eve with wisdom and courage to face realities and to assume all corresponding responsibilities.

RESPONSE TO CLERGY SEXUAL
MISCONDUCT IN THE PHILIPPINES

Clergy sexual misconduct is not a new phenomenon. In the Philippines, records about sexual exploitation of women by Spanish friars have been found in the *Ramo Inquisicion in the Archivo General de Nacion in Mexico*.[19] When I was still in high school, I've heard of sexual abuse by priests. But we never talked about them publicly and as freely as we do now. These were our so-called "secrets." The fact is, these cases of sexual abuse and exploitation existed long before we even dared speak publicly about them.

Today, the issue of clerical abuse and misconduct has finally come out into the open and is staring everyone in the face. The issue has to be dealt with; justice and truth need to surface. To remain silent or to silence victims is complicity to the sin of violence against women and children. Jesus said to those who would rather keep things quiet, "I tell you, if they keep silent, the stones will cry out!"(Luke 19:40).

In the last three years the Catholic Church in the Philippines could no longer dodge the issue of sexual abuse by its clergy and religious. In this section I will describe the responses from the faithful in general and specific responses of the Church hierarchy and the religious sector in particular.

The general response I have encountered during the first two years is aptly described by Marie M. Fortune and James Poling in their article entitled "Calling to Accountability: The Church's Response to Abusers."

They name these responses as "temptations" which one typically falls into when a victim discloses abuse:[20]

1. The temptation of disbelief. For instance, when sexual abuse of women by priests and brothers was included in the report of a women's group about violence against women in the Philippines, the bishops' general response was disbelief. Some said that if there are sexual abuses done by priests these are isolated cases, and allegations about this were influenced by western feminism.

2. The temptation to protect the Church's image. Even if there has been some private acknowledgment, there is often public denial or minimization. When an acceptance is made that there are erring priests, such acceptance or acknowledgement is often followed by rhetoric that majority of the priests are faithful to their commitment. The abused woman is usually encouraged to keep quiet, given money for studies, or if she is pregnant, she is sent away or sometimes put in the care of groups that care for unwed mothers until she gives birth.

3. The temptation to blame the victim. Churches are notorious for thinking that the victim brought on the destruction by her/his own behavior. "Eve blaming" is very common among church people and the society in general. It is often claimed that priests are only human and vulnerable to temptation, or that it is the women who go after the priests. The woman's reputation and character immediately come under scrutiny. The belief and attitude that women victims are temptresses and that men fall into temptation continue to prevail.

4. The temptation to sympathize with the abuser. The focus is on the pain, which the accusation causes the abuser, the possible damage to the abuser's career, etc. The tendency is to give as much time as possible to the priest abuser to make a graceful exit from his parish or area of assignment. While the erring priests are given tearful departures, the women victims (including their families) are often ridiculed, isolated and estranged from their parishes. A church leader allegedly told a woman impregnated by a priest to stay away from the priest because he has a bright future.

5. The temptation to protect the abuser from the consequences of his/her behavior. This leads to avoidance and secret keeping. It has

been a practice among church leaders that if priests are accused of abuse, they are transferred to other parishes or assignments, or they are sent for further studies or mission abroad. In some cases, other leaders would claim that the priest already left or is considered "AWOL (absence without leave)." In cases such as these, the aggrieved woman is often left with no recourse.

6. The temptation of cheap grace. If and when a congregation does acknowledge that a member or pastor is an abuser, there is an immediate move to forgive and forget. There is a practice in the Philippine Church that erring priests are sent for a retreat for 30 days or so or "rehabilitation." If after the retreat or "rehabilitation" the priest decides to remain a priest, he is accepted back. "Priest fathers" who have sired one child may remain a priest if he decides to do so after attending a "Program of Rehabilitation." His obligations include giving support to his child until he/she reaches adulthood. The mother of the child must receive moral and spiritual help, especially through counseling or spiritual direction.[21]

The temptation of cheap grace needs clarification. This, according to Fortune and Poling is bad psychology and, worse, bad theology. It has no basis in either Hebrew or Christian scriptural teaching. They explain that the purpose of judgment is always to bring someone to confession and then repentance. The substance of repentance is always "... a new heart and a new spirit." (Ezk. 18:31). Repentance always begins with acknowledgment to oneself, one's victim(s), and one's community of responsibility for the harm done. Forgiveness before justice cannot contribute to authentic healing and restoration to wholeness for the victim or for the offender. It cuts the healing process short and may well perpetuate the cycle of abuse. It also undercuts the redemption of abusers by preventing them from being accountable for their abusive behavior, and from self-transformation especially regarding their attitude to women. It also undercuts transformation within the Church from a patriarchal to a more inclusive and egalitarian community.[22]

Public interest and the reactions generated by the media prompted the Church hierarchy, as well as, leaders of religious congregations in the Philippines, to be more attentive and responsive to charges of sexual abuse by the clergy. The Philippine Catholic Bishops formulated the document that has been referred to earlier the "Pastoral Guidelines on Sexual Abuses and Misconduct of the Clergy."[23] It states that the CBCP, through the Episcopal Commission on the Clergy, has been conducting programs for priests, one of which is designed for those involved in sexual abuse. It is a program that offers "intensive renewal that includes treatment and spiritual guidance." With these programs priests might have come out "renewed" or 'treated" but has sexual abuse or clergy misconduct stopped? Do the programs contribute to the transformation of the priests' attitude toward women? Do they underscore transforming patriarchal attitudes and systems toward inclusivity and mutuality of relationships within the Church?

In the education of church workers and seminarians on relevant issues, who are called or accepted to teach or facilitate? In seminaries and theological schools especially where priests and deacons enroll, are women theologians and women biblical scholars invited to teach? If and when Gender Issues or Sexuality are discussed, whose point of view is conveyed? Are women's voices or perspectives listened to or heard?

The Church hierarchy, religious congregations, and societies of women and men still need to recognize how the patriarchal and hierarchal structures, systems and practices reinforce unjust relationships and perpetuate violence against women in the Church. In dealing with complaints of clerical misconduct, the CBCP says: "In cases involving priests or deacons, the diocesan bishop will entrust the preliminary inquiry to one or more of the following persons: the vicar general, the chancellor, and the chairman of the Commission on Clergy. As deemed necessary, other committees will be set up to implement and monitor the stages of the process. In the case of a bishop offender, the ecclesiastical superior will initiate the appropriate process." There is a need for the Church to look seriously at the composition of these bodies. Are the investigating bodies composed of women and men who will be neutral to the parties involved? If the respondent is a member of the Church, is justice likely to be attained if the investigating body is composed of members of the same Church more so members who are in authority, such as bishops, vicars, leadership team, chancellors, and parish council, majority of whom are men?

On the part of the offenders, it is important that they realize and accept what they have done and the injury that they have inflicted. They need to be held accountable for their actions and whatever rehabilitation is possible.[24] They need to become aware of men's socialization for violence. The use of power by the clergy has to be studied, analyzed and critiqued. There is also a need to recognize that priests are like any other professionals, subject to the professional standards, subject to laws on abuse and exploitation of employees and workers, the abuse of power and authority, betrayal and violation of trust of those who go to them in their professional capacity. Indeed, the clergy need to understand and be constantly and intentionally conscious that their ministry is both a vocation and a profession.

BREAKING THE SILENCE AND
TURNING *GABA* INTO BLESSING

More and more women are now sharing their painful stories of abuse and violence. They have slowly emerged from the silent cocoon and into the light of truth ushering a new life and new beginning for these women of courage who have endured humiliation and shame. When a victim tells her story, and is listened to with compassion and openness, she is healed somehow and gains strength. To be able to share with another compassionate human being one's painful experiences is a step toward healing.

Many victims are still in the process of remembering and reconstructing in their own minds events that they would rather forget. Time for mourning might be needed by some. Painful experiences bring about loss of bodily integrity, a void in relationships with friends, community and even family. All of this requires recognition and grieving. Judith Herman, in her book "Trauma and Recovery," says: "Reclaiming the ability to feel the full range of emotions, including grief, must be understood as an act of resistance rather than submission to the perpetrators' intent... Only through mourning everything that she has lost can the patient discover her indestructible inner life..."[25]

The process toward healing takes time. The difference is, now these women are not alone. They feel supported by those who have reclaimed their voice and continue seeking truth, seeking justice. As Herman says, "Groups provide the possibility not only of mutually rewarding relationships but also of collective empowerment."[26] With the voices and courage of those who have reclaimed their voices many others are being empowered and becoming proclaimers of the gospel of life. This has to be sustained by communities of faith.

The call is for communities of faith to bond with these women survivors to work for change in society and Church. In the story of Jairus's daughter (Mark 5:41), Jesus said to the young daughter: Get up! Come alive. And the girl stood up and began to walk about. Doing so, she claimed her rightful space in society as any other member should have a right to do regardless of age, sex, class, race or religion. The Gospel challenges Church leaders and men in general to allow the woman to freely "walk about," claim her place in the Church and society, develop her potential and have access to resources afforded to any human being. And to drive his point even deeper, Jesus said to the community: Give her something to eat. What is Mark's message here? Mary Ann Tolbert, a biblical scholar, sees this as Jesus re-incorporating the twelve-year-old daughter into the human and family circle.[27] And this would mean for the community to assume responsibility, to see to it that the girl is cared for, that she is kept alive. The call does not stop at allowing the woman to walk about, giving her space. There is a further call to feed her. Let her live. Sustain that life in her.

How do we sustain life, the life in abused women? Don't they deserve the fullness of life? In my ministry with abused women, I, together with the Women and Gender Commission-Association of Major Religious Superiors in the the Philippines, was led to facilitate the setting up of "Talitha Cum," a temporary home for abused women. As its name suggests, the goal is to help the women to rise up from their pain, from their sleep, even from their entombment, and seek justice, reclaim their dignity, and be healed. I recognize, however, that the ministry does not end there. There is a need to journey with the women further as they re-integrate into society and the church community. To do so involves reflection that also leads to transformation on the part of the faith communities.

A true beginning is facing and not denying the realities in our midst, the realities of injustice, of abuses and misuse of power even within our Church and religious organizations. In doing so we can begin authentic collaboration in building a sanctuary of life as has never been seen before in our midst. And we women in the church, with this conference and similar gatherings, have begun the process. Indeed, the reign of God is at hand. "I am about to do a new thing; now it springs forth, do you not perceive it?"(Isaiah 43:19).

NOTES

[1]   Marie Marshall Fortune, *Sexual Violence, The Unmentionable Sin: An Ethical and Pastoral Perspective* (Ohio: The Pilgrim Press, 1983), 5. Marie Fortune is a church minister, and the founder and executive director of the Center for Prevention of Sexual and Domestic Violence in Seattle, Washington.

[2]   Catholic Bishops' Conference of the Philippines, "Pastoral Guidelines on Sexual Abuses and Misconduct by the Clergy" (Manila: CBCP, 2004).

[3]   While pedophilia refers to sexual abuse of pre-pubescent children aged thirteen and below, ephebophilia is sexual abuse of pubescent males or females between thirteen and eighteen years of age.

[4]   Carol Adams, "Toward a Feminist Theology of Religion and State," in *Violence Against Women and Children: A Christian Theological Sourcebook*, ed. Carol J. Adams and Marie M. Fortune (New York: Continuum, 1998), 18.

[5]   F. Landa Jocano, *Filipino Prehistory: Rediscovering Precolonial Heritage* (Metro Manila: Punla Research House, 1998), 104-5.

[6]   Ibid., 104.

[7]   Rachel Bundang, "Scars are History: Colonialism, Written on the Body" in *Feminist/Womanist Perspectives on Religion, Colonization, and Sexual Violence*, ed. Nantawan Boonprasat Lewis and Marie M. Fortune (New York: The Haworth Pastoral, 1999), 58.

[8]   Luis Camara Dery, *A History of the Inarticulate* (Quezon City: New Day, 2001), 133.

[9]   Reinhild Traitler-Espiritu, "Violence Against Women's Bodies," in *Women Resisting Violence: Spirituality for Life,* ed. Mary John Mananzan, J. Shannon Clarkson and Letty Russell (Maryknoll: Orbis, 1996), 66-79.

[10] Asuncion David Maramba, "The Church 'Close-Open'," *Philippine Daily Inquirer*, May 2002, 9.

[11] Pamela Cooper-White, *The Cry of Tamar: Violence Against Women and the Church's Response* (Minneapolis: Fortress Press, 1995), 208.

[12] Amelia Vasquez, "Toward Fullness of Life," *East Asian Pastoral Review* 41, no. 3 (2004): 275-77.

[13] Cooper-White, *The Cry of Tamar,* 52.

[14] Mary Daly, *The Church and the Second Sex* (Boston: Beacon, 1985), 87.

[15] Mary John Mananzan, ed., *Woman and Religion* (Manila: Institute of Women Studies, 1998), 8.

[16] Juan Sarmiento, "Talk of the Town," *Philippine Daily Inquirer*, 26 May 2002, 10.

[17] CBCP, "Pastoral Care of Victims and Offenders: Handling Cases of Sexual Abuse and Misconduct by the Clergy," 2003. This document was later revised and entitled "Pastoral Guidelines on Sexual Abuses and Misconduct by the Clergy."

[18] Ibid.

[19] Mary John Manzanan, "The Filipino Woman Before and After the Spanish Conquest of the Philippines," in *Babaylan*, Issue No. 1 (Quezon City: Center for Women Resources, 1984), 18.

[20] Marie M. Fortune and James Poling, "Calling to Accountability: The Church's Response to Abusers," in *Violence Against Women*, ed. Carol J. Adams and Marie M. Fortune (N.Y.: Continuum Publishing Company, 1998), 452-53.

[21] CBCP, "Pastoral Guidelines."

[22] Mary Potter Engel, "Historical Theology and Violence Against Women: Unearthing a Popular Tradition of Just Battery," in Violence *Against Women*, ed. Adams and Fortune, 252-53.

[23] CBCP, "Pastoral Guidelines."

[24] Cooper-White, *The Cry of Tamar*, 209.

[25] Judith Herman, M.D.. *Trauma and Recovery* (New York: Basic Books, 1992), 188.

[26] Ibid., 216.

[27] Mary Ann Tolbert, "Mark," in *Woman's Bible Commentary: Expanded Edition*, ed. Carol E. Newsom and Sharon H. Ringe (Kentucky: Westminster John Knox, 1998), 35.

BIBLIOGRAPHY

Adams, Carol. "Toward a Feminist Theology of Religion and State." In *Violence Against Women and Children: A Christian Theological Sourcebook*. Edited by Carol J. Adams and Marie M. Fortune, 15-35. New York: Continuum, 1998.

Bundang, Rachel. "Scars are History: Colonialism, Written on the Body." In *Feminist/Womanist Perspectives on Religion, Colonization, and Sexual Violence*, 53-70. Edited by Nantawan Boonprasat Lewis and Marie M. Fortune. New York: The Haworth Pastoral, 1999.

Camara Dery, Luis. *A History of the Inarticulate*. Quezon City: New Day, 2001.

Catholic Bishops' Conference of the Philippines. "Pastoral Guidelines on Sexual Abuses and Misconduct by the Clergy." Manila: CBCP, 2004.

Cooper-White, Pamela. *The Cry of Tamar: Violence Against Women and the Church's Response*. Minneapolis: Fortress, 1995.

Daly, Mary. *The Church and the Second Sex*. Boston: Beacon, 1985.

David Maramba, Asuncion. "The Church 'Close-Open'." *Philippine Daily Inquirer*, May 2002, 9.

Fortune, Marie M. and James Poling "Calling to Accountability: The Church's Response to Abusers." In *Violence Against Women*, 451-63. Edited by Carol J. Adams and Marie M. Fortune. N.Y.: Continuum Publishing Company, 1998.

Herman, Judith, M.D. *Trauma and Recovery*. New York: Basic Books, 1992.

Landa Jocano, F. *Filipino Prehistory: Rediscovering Precolonial Heritage.* Metro Manila: Punla Research House, 1998.

Mananzan, Mary John, ed. *Woman and Religion.* Manila: Institute of Women Studies, 1998.

Mananzan, Mary John. "The Filipino Woman Before and After the Spanish Conquest of the Philippines," in *Babaylan* , Issue No. 1 (Quezon City: Center for Women Resources, 1984), 13–21.

Marshall Fortune, Marie. *Sexual Violence, The Unmentionable Sin: An Ethical and Pastoral Perspective.* Ohio: The Pilgrim Press, 1983.

Potter Engel, Mary. "Historical Theology and Violence Against Women: Unearthing a Popular Tradition of Just Battery." In *Violence Against Women and Children: A Christian Theological Sourcebook*, 242–61. Edited by Carol J. Adams and Marie M. Fortune. New York: Continuum, 1998.

Sarmiento, Juan. "Talk of the Town." *Philippine Daily Inquirer*, 26 May 2002, 10?.

Tolbert, Mary Ann. "Mark." In *Woman's Bible Commentary: Expanded* Edition. Edited by Carol E. Newsom and Sharon H. Ringe. Kentucky: Westminster John Knox, 1998.

Traitler-Espiritu, Reinhild. "Violence Against Women's Bodies." In *Women Resisting Violence: Spirituality for Life*, 66-79. Edited by Mary John Mananzan, J. Shannon Clarkson and Letty Russell. Maryknoll: Orbis, 1996.

Vasquez, Amelia. "Toward Fullness of Life." *East Asian Pastoral Review* 41, no. 3 (2004): 270-87.

Queer Revisions of Christianity

Sharon A. Bong

14

The lesbian body is the pregnant text of feminist-postmodernist engendering: the contentious site of foregrounding and problematizing the dialectical tension between sex and gender:

> "There is no sex . . . [it] is oppression that creates sex."[1]
> "One is not born, but becomes a woman."[2]
> "We are not born heterosexual. We are taught to become heterosexual."[3]

The ambivalence of the postmodern condition to feminism, as either collaborative or antithetical, stretches the limits of both theoretical frameworks and political agendas (feminist and postmodernist).[4] Without dismissing postmodernist existential despair, the "critical constant,"[5] that affords the connecting thread, indeed, symbiotic link between these discourses (including lesbian/gay) is anti-foundationalism.

From an anti-foundationalist perspective, the text that I have selected to analyse is "Pope John Paul II's Letter to Women"[6] written in conjunction with the United Nation's Fourth World Conference on Women, Beijing, 1995, and in reaction to the weight of feminist scholarship and activism of which that global event is the apotheosis. Though the Pope's letter purports a corrective, even apologetic and liberating disposition towards women, it unwittingly betrays the prejudices of Christianity, traversed through centuries of ascetic misogyny. The document is a reflection of the Church's most contemporary and congenial (indeed concessive) stance towards the perception, treatment and status of women. It is an indefatigable defence not only of naturalized but also divinely sanctioned categories of sex and gender. The deconstruction of these categories is thus "naturally" embodied in the configuration of lesbians from an ideological (re-constructed by theory and theology) and material (in cognizance of their historical and cultural constructs) perspectives. To illustrate the above contention, three focal points will be used: the lesbian mother, the lesbian nun, and butch/femme stylization to evince a sex/gender distinction, its de-stabilisation and essentially, its parody. Within a primarily Western Christian tradition, the (presumed) hegemonic matrices of motherhood, womanhood and heterosexuality (respectively) will be contested.

LESBIAN MOTHER

The Christian image of motherhood is over-determined: it is premised on the formulation of biology-is-destiny. As such, the simplistic equation of sex/gender/desire contingent on the perpetuation of patriarchy is afforded: a woman born is naturally female and desirous of femininity as conveyed in her compliance with societal codes, circumscribed roles, and gender demarcations. The preamble to the pope's letter thus emphatically acknowledges the Church's incalculable debt to women, albeit not on their own esteem, but as appendages: as mothers, wives, daughters and sisters. Cursory gratitude is typically accorded to autonomous women: those who work and are consecrated.[7] Notable is the relative hierarchization of mothers in the Church's lofty scheme of designating positions and dispensing favors. The late Pope laments that "the gift of motherhood is often penalized rather than rewarded... [and that] much remains to be done to prevent discrimination against those who have chosen to be wives and mothers."[8] The latter sentiment is ambivalent at best, as it both challenges the de-valuing of mothers (through inadequate support systems) by our present technologically advanced societies, as well as reprimands, I suspect, feminist pro-choice advocates (i.e., Catholics For A Free Choice), among other women's non-governmental organizations (NGOs), who were particularly vocal at both the World Conference on Women and its corollary, the NGO Forum. The glory of motherhood is also conferred on women who unselfishly devote themselves to Christian education: as "they exhibit a kind of *affective, cultural and spiritual motherhood*."[9] Mothers are ultimately aggrandized through their affinity with "*Mary the highest expression of the 'feminine genius*.'"[10] I contend that the late pope's adulation of women as mothers, as predicated on her essentialised nature and in emulation of the "feminine genius" of the Virgin Mother, unwittingly risks de-humanising women (not all women are desirous of becoming mothers).

Against this backdrop of seeming acquiescence to male dictates through fear or favor, the lesbian mother thwarts the patriarchal expediency of sex/gender/desire. She paradoxically approximates yet invalidates the iconic Virgin/Mother—Mary's celebratory "'virginity *in partu* and *post partum*,' the belief that her physical integrity was not damaged during or after the birth of Jesus."[11] Clerical obsession with the contrivance of Mary's blessed preservation from phallic penetration, both penis and baby, inadvertently underscores her self-containment. The lesbian mother is no less self-sufficient, as she is invested with self-determination and agency in her controversial choice of parenthood (in contrast to Mary's pliancy to God's will). As a consequence of such deviancy, some lesbian mothers are given the derogatory appellation of "lipstick lesbians" [having been] accused of having babies merely as a "fashion accessory" and are "forced to parade their man-loving credentials" to appear less threatening to the status quo.[12] As such, the lesbian mother deprives men control over her body and sexuality and imbibes motherhood with its uniqueness as surpassing a woman's mere atonement for her lack, her naturally defective state of being. Instead, the relatedness and mutuality (and not merely complementarity) between the sexes become redemptive: a "model of at-one-ment."[13]

The lesbian mother embodies Irigayan embrace of a woman's auto-eroticism which translates into her sexuality, Imaginary (Lacanian concept of self), and language: she "'touches herself' all the time . . . for her genitals are formed of two lips in continuous contact. Thus, within herself, she is already two."[14] The self-sufficiency of her pleasure, the plurality of her sexuality, and the joyfulness of her womanhood, risk co-optation if valued in phallocractic terms: she would be reduced to "a virgin mother."[15] In transgressing the symmetry of sex/gender/ desire (a woman born, is naturally female, and desirous of femininity), she radically departs from "the exhausting labour of copying, miming. Dedicated to re-producing—that sameness in which we have remained for centuries, as the other"—she is not only woman, female and feminine:[16]

> Sex itself is a gendered category . . . gender is not to culture as sex is to nature: gender is also the discursive/cultural means by which "sexed nature" or "a natural sex" is produced and established as "prediscursive," prior to culture.[17]

The categories of sex and gender were initially consolidated to refute the biology-is-destiny formula (which obliterated sex/gender differences), thus resulting in a sex/ gender distinction. Sex is naturalized where gender is constructed: hence the former is foundational and upon it the latter is predicated, the one seemingly intractable, the other suggestively fluid. Judith Butler then characteristically unsettles that binary by relocating sex from its privileged (uncontested), "prediscursive" position by stipulating that it, in actuality, is the effect of gender.[18] What ensues is not simply an inversion of the sex/ gender dichotomy but a deconstruction that is exemplified by the configuration of the lesbian mother in her rejection of the "[doctrinal] 'script' of gender."[19] Espoused is a "feminist theology of friendship" that reclaims the ethics of mutuality and community, honesty and non-exclusivity, flexibility and other-directedness as embodied by lesbian conceptions of God, humanity and the world at large, respectively.[20] The lesbian mother potentially liberates herself from male libidinal economy that appropriates and domesticates her body and sexuality as a procreative vessel within the confines of sanctioned motherhood vis-à-vis a heterosexual, monogamous union of incomplete halves. Her relish of her own sexual pleasure as an end in itself, and her prophetic role in "redeeming education" for her children,[21] are re-visions of a relational (not merely maternal), sensual self. In so doing, the lesbian mother challenges the over-determinism of motherhood as articulated in the pope's Letter.

LESBIAN NUN[22]

> As a shifting and contextual phenomenon, gender does not denote a substantive being, but a relative point of convergence among culturally and historically specific sets of relations . . . a complexity whose totality is permanently deferred.[23]

Butler's assertion above is contested by the biology-is-destiny standpoint of the Church that has remained impervious to permutations of engendering subjectivities through the centuries. The late pope deems it fitting even at the turn of the third millennium, to reiterate the circumscribed ministerial role of "consecrated women" bound within male "economy of 'signs'": her divine exclusion from priesthood. That this essentialized correlation of man/male/masculine as "being an 'icon' of [Christ's] countenance as 'shepherd' and 'bridegroom' of the [feminine] church"[24] prevails, is symptomatic of the Church's indefatigable adherence to the expedient conflation of sex/ gender/ desire (a man born, is naturally male, and desirous of masculinity). Despite the "signs of the times," the Church's insistence on essentialism strikes one as not only antiquated but also embarrassing. Endemic to such hierarchical compartmentalizing, is the Church's de-personalization of "womanhood" as imbued with the sublimation of Mary who has been transformed into an icon of contradictions: a Virgin and Mother.

> "Womanhood" . . . especially in a woman who is "consecrated," a kind of inherent "prophesy" . . . a powerfully evocative symbolism, a highly significant "iconic character," aptly expressed the very essence of the church as a community consecrated with the integrity of a "virgin" heart to become the "bride" of Christ and "mother of believers."[25]

The flight from society to the cloister, at the outset, is ironically liberating: a religious woman's exemption from the secular and inferior observance of sex/gender/desire, primarily through her negation of her corporeal nature, is tolerated. She seemingly inverts her otherness to loftier ends—that of servitude to God not man. At the risk of romanticizing her ambivalent disposition, the cloistered nun paradoxically comes out, thus approximating, albeit nominally, the lesbian political stance. The configuration of a lesbian nun accentuates that emancipation of body, sexuality and self that is absent from the parameters of masculinist signification for she is defiantly other than Other, refusing (token or otherwise) recuperation from the margins:

> *She is neither one nor two*. . . . She resists all adequate definition. . . she has no "proper" name. And her sexual organ, which is not *one* organ, is counted as *none*. The negative, the underside, the reverse of the only visible and morphologically designatable organ . . . the penis.[26]

In the lesbianism (committed erotic relationship) between Benedetta Carlini, an Italian Theatine nun of the seventeenth century and her lover Bartolomea, the former envisioned that she was transformed into a male angel during love-making.[27] This illustrates Luce Irigaray's postulation of woman's essential plurality (as woman is the "sex which is not one"), her opacity and autoeroticism that defy the inadequacy and irrelevance of male representation within the hegemonic discourse of identity. A lesbian nun thus constitutes a paradox: she is invisible yet multiple.

Carter Heyward as a lesbian-feminist-ordained minister compounds the problem of definition, exacerbating the impasse of the postmodern condition—that welcomed prelude to the dismantling of categorical designations that are naturalistic, immutable and exclusive. Her theology posits a relational, historical and contextual God—beyond dichotomous confines, such as "God is light. God is *not* death" and from the declamatory certainty of "I AM WHO I AM" (however provisional, it is an extension of totalization)[28] to "I AM BECOMING WHO I AM BECOMING."[29] God, as an extension of women's fluidity of being, justifiably (and in accordance to Scripture) becomes the "unrepresentable," "unconstrainable" and "undesignable"[30] within "phallologocentrism."[31] Hence, Heyward's bold, almost blasphemous assertion of "when we love, we god"[32] is a testimony to the sanctity of women's bodies and sexualities, created as they are in the image of God. That woman,

> [i]s definitely other in herself. . . . Within themselves means *within the intimacy of that silent, multiple, diffuse touch.* And if you ask them insistently what they are thinking about, they can only reply: Nothing. Everything.[33]

Woman attests to her propensity to elude even self-definition and her embodiment of autoeroticism of which the lesbian nun is the apotheosis. Through the paradoxical "unrepentant"[34] and redemptive configuration of her being, she thus evinces an eroticized spirituality and a spiritualized eroticism. In a lesbianised or radicalized Christianity, "the feminist word is made flesh": "redeemed bodiliness" and "redemptive mutuality" are reinstated[35] and "her [and the church's] very being—proud and gay—is a sign of new religion/new consciousness/ new faith."[36] The essential recuperation of its biblical "love ethic" as intrinsic to Christianity (as opposed to the exclusive "sex ethic"),[37] has as its revolutionary praxis; "a more reconciled embodiment [which is] eschatological," an adoption of "sexual theology: the movement from Christian faith to sexuality"[38] and ultimately, a celebratory re-vision, re-enactment and re-creation of the embodied Word made flesh. In so doing, the lesbian nun configuration deconstructs the sex/gender distinction as reinforced in the pope's Letter.

BUTCH/ FEMME STYLIZATION

The "lesbian butch and femme gender stylization" concretizes the lesbian/feminist aphorism of the turn of the century; that "gender is *performative.*"[39] Butler's insubordinate de-stabilizing of the sex/gender construct parallels the dismantling of the heterosexual/homosexual regime. To recapitulate, the feminist-postmodernist permutations of engendering subjectivities are thus expressed:

> Gender ought not to be construed as a stable identity or locus of agency from which various acts follow; rather, gender is an identity tenuously constituted in time, instituted in an exterior space through a *stylized repetition of acts.*[40]

The privileging of gender as malleable, derivative of, and distinguishable from sex, its pre-discursive other, affords a temporary sanctuary (psychic relief and political platform) for feminists to resuscitate their truncated selves from the insidious normativity of woman/female/ feminine. The presumed antecedence, coherence and stability of sex (upon which the biology-is-destiny formula is predicated), ironically foregrounds women's self-agency, in their re-appropriating the cultural constructs of gender within the interests of their personal and political agendas. The anti-foundational discourse which de-naturalises sex/ gender categorical assumptions, inadvertently undermines woman as subject; where gender, displaced from its binary dialectic, amounts to "a constituted *social temporality,*" the "*appearance of substance*" and is "phantasmatic, impossible to embody."[41] But this breakdown of identity is paradoxically a breakthrough, as the self is liberated from the limits of circumscription, regulation and conformity.

In a similar vein, Butler thus systematically deconstructs the dichotomous heterosexual/lesbian artifice. Firstly, that,

> [c]ompulsory heterosexuality sets itself up as the original, the true, the authentic; . . . being lesbian is always a kind of miming, a vain effort to participate in the phantasmatic plenitude of naturalized heterosexuality which will always and only fail.[42]

Reminiscent of the polarization of sex/gender, lesbianism is relegated as an inferior, even transgressive copy of divinely sanctioned heterosexuality in this instance. Butler then strategically inverts this ontological privilege in postulating that:

*[g]ender is a kind of imitation for which there is no original. . .
in other words, compulsory heterosexual identities . . . are
theatrically produced effects that posture as grounds, origins,
the normative measure of the real.*[43]

With the pre-discursive limits of heterosexuality thus exposed and
its primacy denied, the apparent derivativeness of lesbianism is re-
deployed as "a copy of a copy"—the logical conclusion of which would
reinstate "homosexuality [as] the origin and heterosexuality the copy."[44]
The configuration of butch/femme in their parodic performance of
heterosexuality consolidates the above dislocation of prior claims to
truth. It constitutes a paradigm shift.

In antithesis are the central tenets of Christianity that are endemic
to the perpetuation of heterosexuality as a divinely conferred bias:

Womanhood and manhood are complementary *not only from
the physical and psychological points of view*, but also from the
ontological. It is only through the duality of the "masculine"
and the "feminine" that the "human" finds full realization.[45]

The Church's idealization and institutionalization of the
complementarity of the sexes, confer onto husband/wife (not man/
woman per se), the sacred duty not only of "procreation and family
life, but the creation of history itself."[46] Evident is the conflation of
sex/gender/desire that in itself is not necessarily debilitating but its
exclusivity and unremitting retribution (for the audacious few who
digress from this ordained path) are so. Bereft of a holistic self, one is
susceptible to this seemingly divine "relational 'individuality.'"[47]

In contrast, Irigaray justifiably refutes such indoctrination and
romanticization of heterosexuality, predicated as it is on the physical,
psychological and ontological circumscription of women:

We are women from the start. That we don't have to be turned
into women by them, labeled by them, made holy and profaned
by them... Their properties are our exile. Their enclosures, the
death of our love. Their words, the gag upon our lips.[48]

Her feminist-postmodernist theorizing that (inadvertently) disclaims transcendent, ahistorical and acontextual biblical (mis)interpretations, more closely embodies the "redemptive mutuality" of "female friendship" or "gyn/affection":[49]

> Our whole body is moved. No surface holds, no figure, line, or point remains. No ground subsists. But no abyss, either.... Our depth is the thickness of our body, our all touching itself.... Everything is exchanged, yet there are no transactions.[50]

The absence of rigid boundaries (straightness) is not lamentable, as it dislocates immutable frames of identity and releases the (pinioned) subject/woman from vacillating between claustrophobic binary oppositions, such as "virginal/deflowered, pure/impure, innocent/experienced."[51] More significantly, the challenge to heterosexuality redefines "spirituality [as] depth of relatedness [and] redemption as making right relation," thus re-inscribing a passion and compassion for social justice that is the cornerstone of the Eucharist, indeed, of Christianity itself.[52]

In consideration of the Church's discriminatory and irrevocable aggrandizing of heterosexuality, the configuration of butch/femme, that incomparable duo, is rebellious and revolutionary. The butch/femme configuration re-appropriates Monique Wittig's radical "'j/e' or coupled self," which is differentiated from a divided self (as posited by dominant psychoanalytic discourse), thus ingeniously "replacing the Lacanian slash with a lesbian bar."[53] In addition, they recuperate a "space of seduction," not merely an inconspicuous "lesbian subculture," however dissident, and affect a "hypersimulation of woman" in parody of essentialist engendering of subjectivities.[54] Seeking to exhaust the (limits of) permutations within a male libidinal economy, the butch "proudly displays the possession of the penis, while the femme takes on the compensatory masquerade of femininity."[55] They exemplify Butler's controversial thesis that "there is no performer prior to the performed, that the performance is performative, that the performance constitutes the appearance of a 'subject' as its effect."[56] They stretch the dialectical tension between heterosexuality/ lesbianism: the "'providing' butch who seems *at first* to replicate a certain husband-like role . . . [is implicated] in the most ancient trap of feminine self-abnegation."[57] Whilst the femme, who at the outset, appears subordinate, in actuality, imbibes the negotiating power to orchestrate and eroticize her own sexual exchange.[58] The paradox of butch/ femme as "both evidence of a failure of the cultural imaginary and its most symptomatic recuperation,"[59] simultaneously complicit and transgressive within phallocentricism, does not undermine the political lesbian stance, but ironically, strengthens its subversive potential. Thus, its excessive de-naturalizing (with carnivalesque flair through usurpation, mimicry, performance), suspends indefinitely, the consolidation of sex/gender categories. In so doing, the butch/femme configuration parodies the sex/gender distinction that is the foundational basis of complementarity of the sexes as reinstated in the pope's Letter.

In conclusion, Wittig's tacit allusion to the limits of a lesbian discourse, is noteworthy, as she argues: that "without gender, categories of sexuality are meaningless"[60]—the dialectic of heterosexual/ lesbianism informs and inadvertently authenticates the other. A lesbian identity, however pluralistic and divergent, is potentially divisive, as it imbibes the danger of privileging its own existence, an instance of a holier-than-thou disposition.[61]

One also appreciates Adrienne Rich's prophetic insight, even at the risk of redeeming "sisterhood" (from the fringes of feminism):

> A lesbian continuum as a political affiliation [can] reestablish those lost same-sex loyalties by uniting women—heterosexual, bisexual, and lesbian—in a mutual woman-focused vision.[62]

As postmodernist feminists (for those of us who claim this subjectivity), we integrate a dynamic and progressive "theology of gender" with gender theories at an interdisciplinary level: encompassing ontology, subjectivity, epistemology, agency and teleology.[63] As Christian postmodernist feminists, there is a greater imperative to realize a transformative faith and praxis that re-claims difference as an index to inclusivity, mutuality and hope: it embraces an *"ecclesia* of lesbians and gay men . . . [the] *community at the margins."*[64] In genuine reconciliation, those who engage with theologizing impacted by postmodernist-feminist theorizing acknowledge that lesbians and gay men are "an expression of the true church of Jesus as one, holy, catholic and apostolic."[65] And it is this community at the margins, this *ecclesia* of lesbian mothers, lesbian nuns and butches and femmes that challenges us to concretize our faith by embracing them lovingly in imitation of Christ Jesus who eschewed the discriminatory center himself by standing in solidarity with the despised.

NOTES

1 Monique Wittig, *The Straight Mind and Other Essays* (Hemel Hempstead: Harvester Wheatsheaf, 1992), 2.
2 Simone de Beauvoir, *The Second Sex*, trans. H M Parshley (New York: Bantam, 1949), 249.
3 James B. Nelson and Sandra P. Longfellow, eds., *Sexuality and the Sacred: Sources for Theological Reflection* (London: Mowbray, 1994), 393.
4 The postmodern condition heralds the demise of Man, History and Metaphysics: the de-legitimisation of absolutism, ahistoricity and transcendental discourse respectively. Feminist counterpoints to such absence of foundational thought are thus delineated: as the demystification of the male subject of reason, engendering of historical narrative and feminist scepticism towards the claims of transcendent reason. Yet, a critical distance by feminists is warranted as the logical conclusion of such confluence (feminism/postmodernism) witnesses the deconstruction of women's agency, her-story and gendered narratives. Seyla Benhabib *Situating the Self: Gender, Community and Postmodernism in Contemporary Ethics* (Cambridge: Polity, 1992), 212–13.
5 Esther D. Reed, "Whither Postmodernism and Feminist Theology?" *Feminist Theology* 6 (1994): 20.
6 John Paul II, "Letter To Women;" available from http://www.vatican.va/holy_father/john_paul_ii/letters/documents/hf_jp-ii_let_29061995_women_en.html; Internet, accessed Aug. 2004.
7 Ibid.
8 Ibid.
9 Ibid.
10 Ibid.
11 Marina Warner, *Alone of All Her Sex: The Myth and Cult of the Virgin Mary* (London: Weidenfeld and Nicolson, 1976), 43.
12 Alison R. Webster, *Found Wanting: Women, Christianity and Sexuality* (New York: Cassell, 1995), 106–7.
13 Mary Grey, *Redeeming the Dream: Feminism, Redemption and Christian Tradition* (London: SPCK, 1989), 170.
14 Luce Irigaray, *This Sex Which is Not One*, trans. Catherine Porter (Ithaca, N.Y.: Cornell University Press, 1985), 24.
15 Ibid., 30.
16 Ibid., 207.
17 Judith Butler, *Gender Trouble: Feminism and the Subversion of Identity* (New York: Routledge, 1990), 7.
18 Ibid., 7.
19 Elaine Graham, *Making the Difference: Gender, Personhood and Theology* (London: Mowbray, 1995), 216.

20 James B Nelson, *Embodiment: An Approach to Sexuality and Christian Theology* (London: SPCK, 1994), 179–81.

21 Mary Grey, *Redeeming the Dream: Feminism, Redemption and Christian Tradition* (London: SPCK, 1989), 166.

22 See also Rosemary Curb and Nancy Manahan, eds., *Lesbian Nuns: Breaking Silence* (London: Women's Press, 1993), x, for a "definition" of nuns as resting on a continuum: encompassing lay as well as religious women who (un)officially embrace the vows of chastity, poverty and obedience and their poignant insights and sharing of personal stories, of breaking the silence.

23 Butler, *Gender Trouble*, 10, 16.

24 John Paul II, "Letter To Women."

25 Ibid.

26 Irigaray, *This Sex Which is Not One*, 26.

27 Nelson and Longfellow, *Sexuality and the Sacred*, 370–71.

28 Judith Butler, "Imitation and Gender Insubordination," in *Inside/ Out: Lesbian Theories, Gay Theories,* ed. Diana Fuss (New York and London: Routledge, 1991), 15.

29 Carter Heyward, *Our Passion for Justice: Images of Power, Sexuality and Liberation* (New York: Pilgrim Press, 1984), 36, 43.

30 Butler, *Gender Trouble*, 9.

31 Phallologocentrism is a neologism that condenses the primacy of the phallus and logos (Word) in Western thought and construction of subjectivities. Women devoid of such phallic representation and alienated from a logocentric/ masculine disposition are thus marginalized. Rosemarie Tong, *Feminist Thought: A Comprehensive Introduction* (London: Routledge, 1992), 217.

32 Carter Heyward, *Our Passion for Justice: Images of Power, Sexuality and Liberation* (New York: Pilgrim Press, 1984), 140.

33 Irigaray, *This Sex Which is Not One*, 28–29.

34 Heyward, *Our Passion for Justice*, 39.

35 Grey, *Redeeming the Dream*, 162, 173.

36 Heyward, *Our Passion for Justice*, 39.

37 Nelson and Longfellow, eds., *Sexuality and the Sacred*, 379.

38 Nelson, *Embodiment*, 273, 200.

39 Butler, "Imitation and Gender Insubordination," 24-25.

40 Butler, *Gender Trouble*, 140.

41 Ibid.

42 Butler, "Imitation and Gender Insubordination," 20-21.

43 Ibid., 21.

44 Ibid., 22.

45 John Paul II, "Letter To Women."

46 Ibid.

47 Ibid.

48 Irigaray, *This Sex Which is Not One*, 212.
49 Grey, *Redeeming the Dream*, 162.
50 Irigaray, *This Sex Which is Not One*, 213.
51 Ibid., 212.
52 Grey, *Redeeming the Dream*, 171, 174.
53 Carter 283.
54 Ibid., 285, 297.
55 Ibid, 291.
56 Butler, "Imitation and Gender Insubordination," 24.
57 Ibid., 25.
58 Ibid., 25.
59 Judith Roof, *A Lure of Knowledge: Lesbian Sexuality and Theory* (New York: Columbia University, 1991), 245.
60 Ibid., 250.
61 Webster, for instance, arguably deems lesbian relationship to be "qualitatively superior to heterosexual ones in terms of mutuality, equality, intimacy, communication and sexual pleasure," in Webster, *Found Wanting*, 27.
62 Henry Abelove, Michèle Aina Barale and David M. Halperin, eds., *The Lesbian and Gay Studies Reader* (New York and London: Routledge, 1993), 239.
63 Graham, *Making the Difference*, 222-31.
64 Nelson and Longfellow, eds., *Sexuality and the Sacred*, 398.
65 Ibid., 400.

BIBLIOGRAPHY

Abelove, Henry, Michèle Aina Barale and David M Halperin, eds. *The Lesbian and Gay Studies Reader.* New York and London: Routledge, 1993.

Benhabib, Seyla. *Situating the Self: Gender, Community and Postmodernism in Contemporary Ethics.* Cambridge: Polity.

Butler, Judith. *Gender Trouble: Feminism and the Subversion of Identity.* New York: Routledge, 1990.

Butler, Judith. "Imitation and Gender Insubordination." In *Inside/Out: Lesbian Theories, Gay Theories*, 13–31. Edited by Diana Fuss. New York and London: Routledge, 1991.

Curb, Rosemary and Nancy Manahan, eds. *Lesbian Nuns: Breaking Silence.* London: Women's Press, 1993.

De Beauvoir, Simone. *The Second Sex.* Translated by H M Parshley. New York: Bantam, 1949.

John Paul II, "Letter To Women." Available from http://www.vatican.va/holy_father/ john_paul_ii/letters/documents/hf_jp-ii_let_29061995_women_en.html; Internet, accessed August 2004.

Graham, Elaine. *Making the Difference: Gender, Personhood and Theology.* London: Mowbray, 1995.

Grey, Mary. *Redeeming the Dream: Feminism, Redemption and Christian Tradition.* London: SPCK, 1989.

Heyward, Carter. *Our Passion for Justice: Images of Power, Sexuality and Liberation.* New York: Pilgrim Press, 1984.

Irigaray, Luce. *This Sex Which is Not One.* Translated by Catherine Porter. Ithaca, N.Y.: Cornell University Press, 1985.

Nelson, James B. *Embodiment: An Approach to Sexuality and Christian Theology.* London: SPCK, 1994.

Nelson, James B. and Sandra P. Longfellow, eds. *Sexuality and the Sacred: Sources for Theological Reflection.* London: Mowbray, 1994.

Reed, Esther D. "Whither Postmodernism and Feminist Theology?" *Feminist Theology* 6 (1994): 15–32.

Roof, Judith. *A Lure of Knowledge: Lesbian Sexuality and Theory.* New York: Columbia University, 1991.

Warner, Marina. *Alone of All Her Sex: The Myth and Cult of the Virgin Mary.* London: Weidenfeld and Nicolson, 1976.

Webster, Alison R. *Found Wanting: Women, Christianity and Sexuality.* New York: Cassell, 1995.

Wittig, Monique. *The Straight Mind and Other Essays.* Hemel Hempstead: Harvester Wheatsheaf, 1992.

VI

Images of God's Body

Bodily Representations of Hindu Goddesses: A Feminist Perspective

A. Metti, SCC

15

The wedding celebration I recently attended shook the very core of my being. There was no semblance of any parity between the newlyweds: the bridegroom walked around majestically with his head held high, the bride followed her head bent. The bridegroom wore a simple suit, while the bride was bedecked with ornaments aplenty—chains, necklaces, nose rings, earrings, anklets, toe rings, bangles, *tilak*,[1] and flowers. Her wedding garment was studded with precious stones and threads. She was a work of art and an object of male desire. But as a person, she was a "nobody," a woman symbolically "chained" in marriage.

Today, in Indian culture, femininity is bound up closely with how we perceive and represent the female body. Centuries of religious symbolism and imagery, literature and art equate feminine qualities with the supposed frailty of women's bodies. While men are assessed by their social status, intellect, achievements, and material prosperity, women are defined by their physiological appearance and relationship to men. The visual is important in the definition of femininity because of the significance attached to images in culture and tradition and as woman's character and status are judged by her physique.

Definitions of femininity and female sexuality are reproduced in cultural forms that circumscribe a woman's role, duties, and accessible "spaces" in society. As with all cultural forms, meanings are not fixed, but produced in specific historical and social contexts by "readers" whose own experiences and knowledge construct meanings. The woman's body has always been visible as an object within culture. Only rarely have women been acknowledged rightfully as subjects of cultural production.

Bombarded with images portraying female bodies as expendable, women either passively absorb this thinking or vehemently resist it. This article explores one such image, that of the goddess as depicted in Hindu temples. Looking into the visual representations of four major goddesses, viz., *Lakshmi, Saraswati, Parvati,* and *Kali,* I ask, how does religion typify or portray goddess images in temples? What is their role as goddesses? What are the implications for contemporary Indian women and men? This work also attempts to capture the impact of these goddess images on Christian women and men.

VISUAL REPRESENTATION OF GODDESSES IN INDIA

Worship of the Mother Goddess moved down in history through kingdoms and culture, the cult changing and adapting to the particular requirement of each time.[2] India is one of the few civilizations that still uphold goddess worship and present it as a vital aspect of religio-cultural life. The cult of Goddess worship has a long history as old as the scriptures in the Hindu religion based on the Vedas, the Puranas, the Tantras,[3] the epics and other allied scriptures.[4]

The Hindu tradition believes that:

[T]he source and sustenance of all creation, whether at the level of matter or life or mind, is one and only one. It is *Sakti* (energy). Brahman (the absolute) of the Vedanta and *Sakti* of the Tantras are identical. When that "energy" is in a static condition, with neither evolution nor involution, when the universe to be created is not even in a seed-form as it were, it is called Brahman. When it starts evolving into this creation, sustains it and withdraws it back into itself, it is called Sakti.[5]

If Brahman is fire, Sakti is its burning power. They are inseparable: one in two and two in one.[6] Moreover, in Hindu mythology, this energy or Sakti is ever pictured as female deity, as the consort of male deity. Each member of the Trinity[7] has Sakti as his consort; for example, Parvati of Siva, Saraswati of Brahma and Lakshmi of Vishnu. However, the mother cult evolving over centuries is predominantly centered round Parvati, Siva's consort.

We shall see here below how each goddess is depicted in images.

Goddess Saraswati

Goddess Saraswati is considered as *Sakti* (power), representing the power and intelligence of her consort, Brahma the Creator. Saraswati means "the flowing one," denoting fertility and purification. She represents intelligence generating organized creation.[8] She is portrayed as fair-skinned, the goddess of learning, all creative arts, and sciences. Wearing a crescent moon on her brow, riding a swan or a peacock, or seated on a lotus, she is a goddess of sensual love, creativity, and beauty. She promotes learning and teaching. Knowledge is the antithesis of the darkness of ignorance. Hence, she is depicted in pure white. "Since she is the representation of all sciences, arts, crafts and skills she has to be extraordinarily beautiful and graceful," says Swami Harshananda.

Saraswati's brilliant fairness shows that her intellectual power is stupendous and absolutely pure. She holds in her four hands a *Vina* (lute),[9] *aksamala* (rosary) and *pustaka* (book). The book represents all secular sciences. The *Vina* she plays shows the need to cultivate fine arts. The rosary symbolizes all yogic sciences—*tapas* (austerities), meditation, and *japa* (prayer). Swan or Peacock is her carrier. In modern India, she is worshipped primarily by school children and those involved in education and arts.[10]

Goddess Lakshmi

Bedecked with jewelry and clad in a rich silk sari, goddess Lakshmi personifies wealth and abundance, beauty and good fortune.[11] The power and consort of Vishnu the preserver, hers is the power of multiplicity and fortune, ingredients of preservation. Her gleaming eyes and glowing appearance personify beauty. Her face sheds moon rays, eyes beholders. Elephants are on either side, emptying pitchers of water over her. She has four colors—black, white, golden yellow, and pink—on diverse occasions. Sitting or standing on a red lotus, she holds lotuses in her hands. The lotuses in various stages of bloom represent the worlds and beings in stages of evolution.[12] Plates full of fruits like pomegranate, citron, wood apple and coconut are placed before her. Fruits represent the products of human labor. The coconut with its shell, kernel and water means that three levels of creation originate from her—gross, subtle, and extremely subtle. A pomegranate or citron signifies that various created worlds are under her control. The wood apple fruit stands for *moksa* (heaven).

Lakshmi's palms drop gold coins because she personifies all wealth, power, and glory a living being can aspire for. Owl (signifying Indra, the king of gods),[13] which is considered an inauspicious bird, is her carrier.[14] Lakshmi is preferred to Saraswati. In contemporary Hinduism she is popular among businessfolks who believe that material prosperity can only be found with Lakshmi's presence and blessing.[15]

Goddess Parvati

Goddess Parvati, whose names are too many to mention, is the power and consort of Siva, the god of destruction.[16] She is always decorated with gold and flowers, and at all times shown with Siva, never alone. Parvati has two hands, the right one holding a blue lotus and the left hanging loosely. Though most goddesses are variations of Parvati and all female deities are called *Saktis* of their male counterparts, the words *Sakti* and *Devi* are more particularly—or even exclusively—used to denote the *Sakti* of Siva, the innumerable aspects of Parvati.[17] Parvati's principal role is to attract Siva (an ascetic deity) into marriage. She brings into the world the immense spiritual and sexual energy he accumulated through his asceticism for the world's benefit.[18]

Kali

In the amalgamation of the North and South Indian religious trends, some feminine and masculine names of gods were fused. An example is *Kortravai*, the Tamil goddess, more popularly known as Kali and also as Uma, Siva's Sakti. Kali is portrayed as god's terrifying aspect. Her shrine is found in village outskirts, with no fence around her. The background of her image is a burial ground or war-field, strewn with mutilated and dead bodies. There, black and broad-chested, her luxuriant hair disheveled, Kali's terrifying figure stands formidably on a dead body, that of her spouse Siva. Her four hands stretch out in four directions: one hand clutching a tyrant's bloody head, a sharp knife in the grip of the second, in the third a flag symbolic of fearlessness, and the fourth hand showing the goddess bestowing grace. A victorious smile glitters in her three eyes; blood drips from her protruding tongue; her legs are dancing.[19]

The name Kali may be from Greek, with a Sanskrit root that means "to rotate," "to turn around." The designation may mean time as the destroyer. Perhaps Kali was the consort of Kala, Eternal Time, later denoting death.[20] Representing the state where time, space, and causation have disappeared sans trace, she is depicted as black. The hands represent capacity for labor, kinetic energy. Her garland of fifty skulls corresponds to the fifty letters of the Sanskrit alphabet from where the sound of creation emanates. The skulls signify destruction, the garland shows that manifestation of creation is withdrawn. Being the supreme energy for dissolving the created universe, Kali's form naturally creates awe and fear but she is worshipped for her inherent powers.

There is evidence to prove that Kali and similar fierce goddesses were worshipped widely in India.[21] Originally belonging to a subaltern tradition, Kali worship was absorbed slowly into the Brahmanical tradition.[22] Married to Siva in Brahmanical myths, her popularity grew gradually. She has retained her malevolence and original fierceness, her delight in bloody sacrifices,[23] and her destructiveness.[24] As war-goddess, she has to protect gods and human beings from their enemies. Thus, her very anger blesses humanity. But Kali is a destructive goddess and when she labors to help gods and annihilate demons, she is uncontrollable. She destabilizes cosmic order and has to be restrained from destroying the world. Kali is therefore the opposite of Parvati in her relationship to Siva. She induces Siva into destructive frenzy, whereas Parvati pacifies him.[25]

A FEMINIST CRITIQUE OF GODDESS IMAGES

The present-day image of the Hindu woman is endowed with a long history. This past is constituted basically from two elements, the first known as the Vedic age, the second associated with the *Manusmrti*.[26] Indian society appropriated ideas from these textual traditions to produce its own images and icons for the establishment and maintenance of the social structure it envisaged.[27] The patriarchy which resulted has been mediated structurally and ideologically by systematically perpetuating the feminine identity as norm for women.

Visual representations (statues, icons, and paintings) have helped shape social ideals of femininity. "The underlying social attitudes and assumptions are expressed often in extreme form"[28] in these representations of goddesses. Now for a closer look.

Impressive Descriptions

It is notable that these goddesses are on par with their husbands in power and position. When goddesses withdraw their Sakti from their husbands, their husbands become mere *savam* (corpses), meaning powerlessness. The great Siva becomes impotent without his consort, his Sakti. As a Christian interviewee rightly puts it, "The creation of the world is not one male god's business but the work of both male and female gods." [29]

In the case of Saraswati, the goddess of learning, it is encouraging to see that a woman is portrayed as the source of knowledge and wisdom. Moreover, Saraswati's symbolic rosary is a reminder that each Indian woman is in possession of these extraordinary powers of knowledge and wisdom, enabling her to live optimistically even when beaten up and abused. When empowered, women rebel against patriarchal oppression. When asked for the meaning of sakti, many said it is power like the ability to act, to make others act, to make things happen, etc. Of the goddess Lakshmi, Mallika, an uneducated woman said: "Whatever you want to happen, she will make it happen. If you believe that she can do it, she will do it." "When something acts, it is Sakti; when it just is, it is Siva," said another woman. The tradition of goddess-worship empowers every Indian woman spiritually as well as generatively. The belief in a goddess has another and deeper meaning: that there is an essential unbreakable unity among women themselves. The *Sakti* or power of solidarity is the synergy engendered by gathering together. This is the central significance of the doctrine that the goddess *Sakti* has and her power consists in this union of many.[30]

Off-putting Imageries

Though most Hindu men and women whom I interviewed were happy and positive in their goddess-experience, they were aware of the contrasts in these various goddess depictions and the reality of Indian women. We shall see some of them.

Women deprived of Basic Education

Though goddess Saraswati is honored as the goddess of learning, one can never forget that for a long time in the history of India, women were denied basic education and educating them was considered wasteful expenditure. The 2001 statistics reveal that only 40 percent of women have had basic education. Women are made to believe that wealth is more important than learning. A Hindu woman said, "Women usually pray to Lakshmi more often than to Saraswati. We pray for wealth and fortune."

Bharati, a staunch devotee of Goddess Saraswati, describes Saraswati as follows:

(She) is enthroned on a white lotus and arrayed in glory; she holds in her hand the lute, which is a riot of sweets; her eyes represent the Vedas and her forehead the moon. . . .disputation and logic are her twin-ears; resolution is her earrings; illumined knowledge is her nose; the multifoliate *Sastras* are her mouth; imagination has formed her honeyed lips; the great epics are her gemmed breasts; all arts starting with sculpture are her flowery hands; and the tongues of the poets are her feet.[31]

However, he adds that these descriptions have not improved women's education and the real worship of Saraswati should promote education at all levels without any discrimination of caste,[32] creed and religion, especially among the downtrodden.[33] Though symbolically Saraswati represents Brahma's intelligence and power, in real life most of the women are treated as if they have no power or intelligence. Even today in many Indian houses one hears a husband say, "You don't know anything. Keep your mouth shut and do what you are to do as a wife."

"The goddess of learning, Saraswati, did not write any book as the Brahmins never allowed women to write their texts. Nowhere does she speak even about the need to give education to women. How is it that the source of education is herself an illiterate woman?" asks Kancha Ilaiah.[34] Though he speaks in *Dalitbahujan* context,[35] what he says applies to most Indian women. In addition, "knowledgeable women who question or rebel against patriarchy are called aberrations, unnatural, unattractive, unisexual, unnaturally sexed, and man-haters."[36]

Ritual Space

Holding the rosary, goddess Saraswati symbolizes spiritual knowledge and all spiritual sciences. The *Rig Veda* consists of over a thousand hymns of which those attributed partly or wholly to women seers do not number more than twelve or fifteen, that is approximately 1 percent. This is an indication of women's severely limited access to the construction of prestigious and sacral traditions.[37] Indian women are deprived of ritual participation and their body is considered impure at menstruation and childbirth. They have numerous *vratas* (fasting) to make for their husbands and family but cannot perform *poojas* (rituals) in temples. Rather "serving the husband is equated with the period of studentship and the performance of household duties is identified with the worship of the sacred fire."[38] Their ritual space is scant. Men decide and dictate their spirituality.

Denied Property Rights

Goddess Lakshmi denotes wealth. Ground reality is, women are deprived of the rights to possess wealth. It is fitting to quote here the repeated words of Savithribai Phule,[39] "Brahmins were so cunning that they have assigned to Lakshmi the role of being the source of wealth and property while all Brahmin women are denied the right to property."[40] While women had a right to own some property or possessions including *stridhana*, literally women's wealth (jewelry, utensils, clothes, etc.), the relations of kinswomen and kinsmen to property were asymmetrical (*Manusmrti* IX.119). The extent of the difference becomes obvious if one compares the means of acquiring wealth legitimately open to men and women. The former were granted access to inheritance, profit, purchase, the fruits of victory, interest on loans, gifts (*Manusmrti* X.115) whereas women could only receive gifts from kinsfolk during marriage (*Manusmrti* IX. 194) and were not allowed to accumulate wealth without their husbands' permission (*Manusmrti* IX. 199).[41] Not only Brahmin women but all women are denied their property rights.

Woman's Body as Property of Men

Women's bodies are treated as men's personal property. A UNICEF report (1998) said that each day, 12 women are killed in India for bringing insufficient dowries. While 40 percent of women reported physical abuse by husbands or in-laws, another 43 percent complained of psychological abuse, a study done by *India Safe, 2000* revealed. The worst was that 50 percent of women said abuse occurred during pregnancy, a period when we expect they are treated well.[42] Recent nationwide surveys by *International Council for Research on Women* (ICRW) estimate that up to 60 percent of married women, regardless of caste, class, and education, experience domestic violence. "Except for a few sensational cases, day-to-day physical abuse of women in their own homes remains largely hidden," say ICRW reports on domestic violence.[43]

Beauty Myth

Images of Saraswati, Lakshmi, and Parvati reinforce the concept of beauty which is perpetuated through the icons of the goddesses. 'The forms of worship include giving women ornaments, clothes and food on festive occasions' (*Manusmrti* III. 59). All these goddess images sport a big golden crown, earrings, nose rings, bangles, and garnishing from head to foot, while a woman devotee who prays to her may not even have a half sovereign of gold to make herself a marital ring. When a woman dresses up well with all frills, she is considered as goddess.[44] The well-dressed woman is the perfect model for an Indian woman who worships her goddess. These goddesses sit or stand comfortably on a lotus flower or travel atop delicate birds, viz., swan or peacock or owl for they are delicate and light in weight. And this is what is expected of an ideal woman; a slim, fair, and tall figure.

Freedom of Bodily Movements

Their very posture reveals the ideal woman's space in society. They are either made to sit or stand keeping the legs together in modesty—and this is what is expected of every Indian woman. Besides, all these Brahmanical goddesses depend on their consorts for power and the roles which they perform are also ordained by their consorts. They do not and cannot exist independently.

By creating images like those of Lakshmi, Parvati, and Saraswati, the patriarchal Brahmanical system maintained its supremacy over women. These figures influence all women enormously and today's media, through different tele-serials and films taken on goddesses, reinforces these all the more.

Impact of Kali

Now for another look at the subaltern goddess Kali.[45]

Freed from Brahmanic tradition's constraints, Kali is intimately associated with villagers' daily life. She contrasts with beautiful, rich, and serene Brahmanic goddesses, who are consorts. Kali is unassociated with any male deity, and if at all, she is linked with Siva, inciting him to dangerous, destructive behavior, destabilizing the cosmos.

On the surface, Kali is menacing and cruel, mystifying observers by her malefic nature. Studied in-depth, the truth that she embodies emerges and certain meaning evolves from the meaningless chaos. She stands for rebirth after death and for fresh life from pain and suffering. She confers no birth and life without pain. All deities in their destructive attitude are thus seen to give release to those who break natural laws, and go against established social structures.[46] Isn't this divine paradox? The majesty of her posture is indescribable and speaks volumes of her unrestrained freedom. The disheveled hair speaks of her untrammeled freedom.

Kali's figure combines the terror of destruction with the reassurance of motherly tenderness, for she is the cosmic power, the totality of the universe, and a glorious harmony of the "pairs of opposites." She deals out death, as she creates and preserves. Her three eyes strike dismay into the wicked yet ooze affection for devotees; her third eye is the divine wisdom; She is *Prakriti*, the procreatrix, nature, the destroyer, and the creator. Nay, she is something greater and deeper still for those who have eyes to see.[47] Sri Ramakrishna says, "I am the machine and she is the Operator. I am the house and she is the Indweller. I am the chariot and she is the Charioteer. I move as she moves me; I speak as she speaks through me."[48]

Kali is rarely pictured as mother. She stands in contrast to the archetypal mother goddesses who are heavy-hipped and heavy-breasted to signify their association with beauty and fertility. As Kali appears emaciated, she draws people, not because of beauty but because of her role.

According to Kancha Ilaiah, the images of village goddesses "function to create a common cultural ethic, one that re-energises the masses so that they can engage in productive activity."[49] Kali is a goddess who is not locked within four walls. Rather she is found at the entrance or at the exit of the village. She has no daily *pooja*.

> The people can approach her without priestly mediation. They talk to the Goddess as they talk among themselves: "Mother," they say, "we have seeded the fields, now you must ensure that the crop grows well, one of our children is sick it is your bounden duty to cure her . . ."[50]

Kali is independent. She does not depend on others, especially men. Her very posture and her nude body is a powerful threat to the patriarchal view of woman's body. Kali's body is freed from all accompaniments like jewels, flowers, silk saris, etc. She is so dark that one does not feel bad about one's color.

Lakshmi or Saraswati, typifying the goddesses who have power and status due to their marriage, reflect the higher-class women and they are termed the space goddesses. Kali represents the lower class women, autonomous in her position, not dependent on any marital status.[51] Kali therefore stands as a symbol of freedom and valor.

IMPACTS OF GODDESSES ON
CHRISTIAN MEN AND WOMEN

Even though Christians in their day-to-day life maintain good relations with people of other religions, their attitude towards non-Christian gods and goddesses is very narrow.

Coming from a traditional Catholic family, though there was a temple close to our house, I did not enter a temple dedicated to a goddess till I completed my religious formation. This experience was not only mine, it was shared by the Christian men and women with whom I chatted over this issue.

"As a college-going girl, I remember that whenever we were to taken to different places during tours, we Christian girls used to remain in the bus especially when they stopped to visit temples," says Joicy.[52] This is a clear evidence of the Church's attitude towards other religions in general. Though the Church speaks of inter-religious dialogue and developing healthy relationships with people of other faiths, the residue of traditional attitudes continues to influence Christian thinking patterns.

The four main reasons, which Indian Christians[53] cite as hindrances to approaching Hindu goddesses are as follows:

Exclusivist Attitude
Christianity has kept away from Hindu religious practices. It has considered Hinduism as something evil and shunned it completely. "Why should we go to other religions when our religion is the best?" says Stephen. The notion that we have the truth and salvation within the Catholic Church continues to dominate Christian religious practices. In consequence, most of the Christians do not pay visits to the Hindu temples and even consider it sacrilegious to do so.

Androcentric Attitude
As Judaeo-Christian tradition is patriarchal, the view of God as male is another reason for its lesser involvement with Hindu tradition, which speaks of the feminine half in God and calls that feminine half *Sakti*, making her the consort of God.[54] The same *Sakti* is identified with the

Supreme Being and is conceived as having different personifications. Although in recent years feminists have identified and brought to light the female image of God in Sophia, the traditional Christian theology still holds on to the androcentric God image in the church.

Christianity expresses God as male through masculine metaphors, images and symbols. Bede Griffiths observes: "The Hebrew tradition was patriarchal and Christianity has preserved only a masculine concept of God. The Father and the Son are masculine in their very names, and even the Spirit, which is neuter in Greek, has been given masculine character."[55] All the same we do find expressions of the Divine Feminine in the Judaeo-Christian tradition but these do not attract attention.

Negation of Body

Often, Christian understanding of body and sex has been highly one-sided and afflicted with a pessimistic outlook of sexuality, rooted in misogyny. This view is contrasted with positive views of sexuality found in the Hindu religion where gods do not function alone but have their consorts with them. Besides, Christianity has often given importance to virginity over marriage. Whether in the case of mother Mary or other women saints, virginity is highlighted. "Sexual renunciation was linked with higher holiness for the Christians not only of late Patristic and medieval era"[56] but of today.

Therefore, Christians in general focus on the negation of the body and its needs. For Christians, that God became human to make us divine was the ancient understanding of incarnation, not to celebrate but to overcome the frailties of the flesh that tied it to corruptibility and death. Therefore, their understanding of spirituality, of poverty or simplicity, etc., flows from this perception. They do not even bother to look at Goddess Kali in her black complexion, disheveled hair, and her naked body. The Hindu tradition, on the other hand, maintains that the body is meant for celebration and "it has a more radical vision of its potential for transformation."[57]

Centralised Ritual and Sacramental Power

Mariamman, a Dalit who changed her name to Mary when she converted to Christianity shares: "In Christianity, there is no god that threatens or challenges you. Mother Mary is humble and obedient and seen as a boon-giver whereas when I go into the presence of Kali, I get a new energy and she awakens my dormant energy within me to become a person of valor." [58] She continues, "Even before coming to Christianity, I used to get the power of Kali and people used to come to me for blessings and guidance. But after coming to the Catholic Church, I see that only men, and that too only ordained priests, can give blessings and guidance and can bring about the sacramental presence of God."

In Christianity, ritual and sacramental power is concentrated more in the clergy than in the laity. Though theoretically sacramental power is available to all, in reality it is commonly and legitimately tapped and transmitted more by the clergy than others. Meanwhile, worshippers of Kali feel that any body (male or female) can be possessed by goddesses and prove to be a promising agent of effective divination.

Some Christians who are recent converts from Hinduism do approach these goddesses for their need. Sahaya Mary, a Dalit by origin, shared with me saying, "What is wrong in going to Mari Amman temple? Mari Amman is like our mother Mary." [59] All the same, she said that she has visited the Amman temples when her children had smallpox. Fearing punishment by Mari Amman, they (some new converts) visit and offer prayers to her.

Adverse Impacts on Christians

Though they seem indifferent to goddess-worship, the bodily representation of goddess with all its frills has had an adverse impact on Christians. Christian spirituality promotes simplicity of life but this ideal has not entered into the homes of Christians. "A woman must be dressed up like Lakshmi (goddess). Then only will she look beautiful," says Catherine. Besides, the concept of beauty and the desire for ornaments and cosmetics depicted in Hindu goddesses have had an impact on Christians' image of Mother Mary who has been adorned as well with jewels, flowers, silk *saris*, etc.

Even though Christianity favors theoretically and scripturally the equality of men and women, gender-based discrimination is prevalent. The existing hierarchy perpetuates such acts. Indian Christians are taking up the ideal feminine characters reinforced by the goddesses and women are considered even today as "helpmates" who will be partners to their husbands.

CONCLUSION: TOWARDS DECONSTRUCTION AND ABSORPTION

My proposals for proactive living:

Decode Goddess Myths

We must seriously consider the deconstruction of oppressive goddess-myths that perpetuate the ideal feminine, and underscore instead the liberative elements in these goddesses. Certain representations of goddesses, such as Kali, symbolize freedom, for instance. Promoting local goddesses with empowering representations can be encouraged in every village among the Hindu sisters and brothers.

Re-emphasize Inclusive Language

The subaltern tradition can help to bring out another aspect of the godhead, the concept of God as female. Christianity needs to re-examine her language of God and start addressing God in inclusive images, both male and female. In the context of inculturation, the Church in India also needs to include female images for God.

Re-consider the Portrayal of Images

The Church ought to re-examine its images of the Divine and encourage symbols that challenge the faithful. These should not make Christians more submissive and passive but rather, re-energize them in their daily lives.

Celebration of Body

It is necessary that the Church insists on holistic approaches and attitudes towards body. Being body-persons, we need to relate to God, others, and ourselves through our bodies, thus celebrating the gift of body in loving relationships.

Consciousness of the Inner Power
In goddess-worship, the devotee realizes the Sakti within, and activates the same to face life. In its religious cult and practices as well as spirituality, the Church today should emphasize this consciousness and activation of the power within. Jesus while empowering the woman who suffered from haemorrhage for twelve years gave expression to his inner power.[60]

Away with Ornaments
Though most images we have of the Virgin Mary are simple, the Church has absorbed, by acculturation, the ornamentation of the deity from goddess-worship. Thus one finds the image of Mother Mary adorned with jewels. This is practiced not only in India but in other countries without Hindu tradition as well. The church should do away with this practice, which has a negative impact on the devotee in today's context of consumerism.

Decentralise Ritual Power
The worshippers of Kali feel that any body (male or female) can be possessed by a goddess and be a promising agent of effective divination. In the Church too, theoretically, sacramental power is available to all and scripturally all receive the gifts of the Holy Spirit.[61] However, in practice, this power is commonly and legitimately tapped and transmitted more by the clergy (only male) than others. As an effort to build a reign of God based on the values of Christ Jesus, it is high time that the Church thinks in terms of decentralizing ritual and ministerial power to both men and women.

NOTES

1 *Tilak* is a powder like (usually red) which an Indian Hindu woman uses on her forehead. It is also used by Catholic women as well as by Hindu men today.

2 Indira S. Aiyar, *Durga As Mahisasuramardini: A Dynamic Myth of Goddess* (New Delhi: Gyan, 1997), 79.

3 Tantras are a vast body of Hindu religious literature devoted to expounding the cult of the Divine Mother.

4 David Kinsley, *Hindu Goddesses* (Delhi: Motilal Banarsidass, 1987), 1; H. Krishna Sastri, *South Indian Images of Gods and Goddesses* (New Delhi: Asian Educational Services, 1986).

5 Swami Harshananda, *Hindu Gods and Goddesses* (Mysore: Sri Ramakrishna Ashrama, 1982), 97–98.

6 Ibid.

7 As in Christianity, the Hindu tradition also believes in a Trinity. And the gods are addressed as Siva, Vishnu and Brahma, each one with a different function.

8 A. G. Mitchell, *Hindu Gods and Goddesses* (London: Victoria and Albert Museum, 1982); Harshananda, *Hindu Gods and Goddesses*, 99.

9 *Vina* is one of the ancient musical instruments of India.

10 Mircea Eliade, *The Encyclopedia of Religion* vol. 6, s.v. "Gods and Goddesses" (New York: Macmillan, 1987), 52; N. N. Bhattacharya, *Indian Mother Goddess* (Calcutta: Indian Studies Past and Present, 1971); S. Sen, *The Great Goddess in Indic Tradition* (Calcutta: Papyrus, 1983); Kailash Nath Seth, *Gods and Goddesses of India* (New Delhi: Diamond Pocket Books, 1986).

11 Nath Seth, *Gods and Goddesses of India*, 106.

12 U. N. Dhal, *Goddess Lakshmi: Origin and Development* (New Delhi: Oriental Publishers, 1978).

13 The word in Sanskrit for owl is Uluka. Uluka is also one of the names of Indra, the king of gods. Hence Lakshmi being the goddess of fortune could not have found a better person to ride on than the king of gods, who personifies all the wealth, power, and glory that a living being can aspire for in life.

14 Harshananda, *Hindu Gods and Goddesses*, 108.

15 R.P. Sharma, *Woman in Hindu Literature* (New Delhi: Gyan, 1995); Eliade, s.v. "Gods and Godesses," 52.

16 Literally, Siva is one in whom the universe "sleeps" after destruction and before the next cycle of creation. All that is born, must die. All that is produced must disintegrate and be destroyed. This is an inviolable law. The principle that brings about this disintegration, the power behind this destruction, is Siva.

17 E. O. James, *The Cult Of the Mother Goddess: An Archaeological and Documentary Study* (New York: Thames and Hudson, 1959); Margaret Shanthi and Corona Mary, *We Dare To Speak* (Trichy: Worth, 1994), 62–85; Harshananda, *Hindu Gods and Goddesses*, 118.

18 Eliade, s.v. "Gods and Goddesses," 52.

19 David Kinsley, *The Sword and the Flute: Kali and Krishna, Dark Visions of the Terrible and the Sublime* (Los Angeles: University of California, 1975); Joseph Sebastian, *God as Feminine* (Tiruchirapalli: St.Paul's Seminary, 1995), 89–90.

20 P. K. Agarwala, *Goddesses in Ancient India* (New Delhi: Abhinav), 120; Vidyadhar Sharma Guleri, *Female Deities in Vedic and Epic Literature* (Delhi: NAG, 1990).

21 M. C. P. Srivastava, *Mother Goddess in Indian Art, Archaeology and Literature* (Delhi: Agam Kala Prakashan, 1979); Aiyar, *Durga as Mahisasuramardini*, 163.

22 The Brahmanical tradition was originally known as Great Tradition in India.

23 H. Whitehead, *The Village Gods of South India* (New York: Garland Publishing, 1980); Aiyar, *Durga As Mahisasuramardini*, 163.

24 Aiyar, *Durga As Mahisasuramardini*, 176.

25 Ibid., 177–78.

26 The focus on these two areas of the past is by no means accidental. The *Vedas* are the earliest textual sources available in India, and are, by definition, sacred and by extension sacrosanct. The *Manusmrti*, on the other hand, is amongst the most well-known prescriptive texts of early India.

27 Tanika Sarkar and Urvashi Butalia, eds., *Women and the Hindu Right* (New Delhi: Kali for Women, 1995), 11; Amaury De Riencourt, *Woman and Power in History* (New Delhi: Sterling, 1989), 161–85.

28 David Dean Shulman, *Tamil Temple Myths* (Princeton: Princeton University Press, 1980), 140.

29 The quotation is from Agnes, a Christian whom I had interviewed for the purpose of this article.

30 Susan S. Wadley, ed., *The Powers of Tamil Women* (New Delhi: Manohar, 1991), 27. Also see A. S. Altekar, *The Position of Women in Hindu Civilization* (Delhi: Motilal Banarsidass, 1987).

31 Subramania Bharati, *Panjali Capatam*—Parts 1 & 2 (Madras: Bharati Prasuralayam, 1924), 3–5. Bharati is a Tamil Freedom fighter and a poet.

32 Caste divides the Indian population into four major groups: the *brahmin* (priestly class) at the top, followed by the *kshatriya* (warrior caste) then the *vaishya* (traders and artisans) and at the bottom the *sudra* (agricultural labourers) some of whom are beyond the pale of caste and are known as untouchables.

33 Sebastian, *God as Feminine*, 102–3.

34 Kancha Ilaiah, *Why I Am Not a Hindu* (Calcutta: Samya, 1996), 74.

[35] *Dalitbahujan* means "people and castes who form the exploited and suppressed majority."

[36] Kiran Prasad, "Contemporary Mass Media and Gender Justice," *Journal of Dharma* 29, no. 2 (Apr.-June 2004): 153.

[37] Sarkar and Butalia, *Women and the Hindu Right*, 14.

[38] G. Jha, *Manu-Smrti,* vol. 2 (Calcutta: Penguin, 1932), 67.

[39] Savithribai Phule is the first woman who worked to provide education for all women in India in the mid-nineteenth century, wife of Jyotirao Phule, who is one of the freedom fighters of India who also fought for the liberation of women.

[40] As quoted by Ilaiah, *Why I Am Not a Hindu*, 76. Preeti Sharma also shares the same opinion in her book on *Hindu Women's Right to Maintenance* (New Delhi: Deep and Deep Publications, 1990), 25–26.

[41] Sarkar and Butalia, *Women and the Hindu Right*, 19.

[42] *Asian Age,* 5 Sept. 2000, cited in *Women's Link* 7 (Jan.-Mar. 2001): 57.

[43] Shiela Reddy, "Domestic Violence," *Women's Link* 7 (Jan.-Mar. 2001): 3.

[44] In South Indian films there are so many songs that address young beautiful well-dressed up woman as goddess Lakshmi. Even in normal conversation a well-dressed woman is addressed as Lakshmi or *Devatha* (Goddess).

[45] This Kali is different from "*Kali*" who is the same as "*Durga*" in West Bengal.

[46] Aiyar, *Durga as Mahisasuramardini*, 184.

[47] *The Gospel of Ramakrishna,* abridged ed., trans. Swami Nikhilananda (New York: Ramakrishna-Vivekananda Center, 1988), 11–12.

[48] Ibid., 616.

[49] Ilaiah, *Why I Am Not a Hindu*, 91.

[50] Ibid.

[51] Aiyar, *Durga as Mahisasuramardini,* 179.

[52] Joicy, a staunch Christian, is a college professor today. She shared this in a personal interview at her house.

[53] When I say "Indian Christians" I speak of those men and women whom I had interviewed for the purpose of this paper. They belong to different category viz., married and unmarried laity, priests, religious, etc.

[54] Sebastian, *God as Feminine,* 306.

[55] Bede Griffiths, *The Marriage of East and West: A Sequel to the Golden String* (London: Collins, 1982), 191.

[56] Rosemary Radford Ruether, "Sex in the Catholic Tradition," in Lisa Isherwood, *The Good News of the Body: Sexual Theology and Feminism* (New York: New York University Press, 2000), 37.

[57] Ibid.

[58] The term *Dalit* means "suppressed and exploited people." For further details, see Kancha Ilaiah, ibid., viii.

[59] Mari Amman is a patron goddess of sickness like small pox, chicken pox, etc.
[60] Jesus said, "Someone touched me; for I noticed that power had gone out from me" (Lk 8:43–48).
[61] Acts 4:31–33. ". . . they were all filled with the Holy Spirit and spoke the word of God with boldness."

BIBLIOGRAPHY

Agarwala, P. K. *Goddesses in Ancient India*. New Delhi: Abhinav, 1978.

Aiyar, Indira S. *Durga As Mahisasuramardini: A Dynamic Myth of Goddess*. New Delhi: Gyan, 1997.

Altekar, A. S. *The Position of Women in Hindu Civilization*. Delhi: Motilal Banarsidass, 1987.

Asian Age. 5 Sept. 2000. Cited in *Women's Link* 7 (Jan.-Mar. 2001): 57.

Bharati, Subramania. *Panjali Capatam*—Part 1 & 2. Madras: Bharati Prasuralayam, 1924.

Bhattacharya, N. N. *Indian Mother Goddess*. Calcutta: Indian Studies Past and Present, 1971.

De Riencourt Amaury. *Woman and Power in History*. New Delhi: Sterling, 1989.

Dhal, U. N. *Goddess Lakshmi: Origin and Development*. New Delhi: Oriental Publishers, 1978.

Eliade, Mircea. *The Encyclopedia of Religion*. Vol. 6. s.v. "Gods and Goddesses." New York: Macmillan, 1987.

Griffiths, Bede. *The Marriage of East and West: A Sequel to the Golden String*. London: Collins, 1982.

Harshananda, Swami. *Hindu Gods and Goddesses*. Mysore: Sri Ramakrishna Ashrama, 1982.

Ilaiah, Kancha. *Why I Am Not a Hindu*. Calcutta: Samya, 1996.

James, E. O. *The Cult Of the Mother Goddess: An Archaeological and Documentary Study*. New York: Thames and Hudson, 1959.

Jha, G. Manu-Smrti. Vol. 2. Calcutta: Penguin, 1932.

Kinsley, David. *Hindu Goddesses*. Delhi: Motilal Banarsidass, 1987.

Kinsley, David. *The Sword and the Flute: Kali and Krishna, Dark Visions of the Terrible and the Sublime*. Los Angeles: University of California, 1975.

Mitchell, A. G. *Hindu Gods and Goddesses*. London: Victoria and Albert Museum, 1982.

The Gospel of Ramakrishna. Abridged edition. Translated by Swami Nikhilananda. New York: Ramakrishna-Vivekananda Center, 1988.

Nath Seth, Kailash. *God and Goddesses of India*. New Delhi: Diamond Pocket Books, 1986.

Prasad, Kiran. "Contemporary Mass Media and Gender Justice." *Journal of Dharma* 29, no. 2 (Apr.-June 2004): 153–62.

Radford Ruether, Rosemary. "Sex in the Catholic Tradition." In Lisa Isherwood, *The Good News of the Body: Sexual Theology and Feminism*. New York: New York University, 2000.

Reddy, Shiela. "Domestic Violence." *Women's Link* 7 (Jan.-March 2001), 3.

Sarkar, Tanika and Urvashi Butalia, eds. *Women and the Hindu Right*. New Delhi: Kali for Women, 1995.

Sastri, H. Krishna. *South Indian Images of Gods and Goddesses*. New Delhi: Asian Educational Services, 1986.

Sebastian, Joseph. *God as Feminine*. Tiruchirapalli: St.Paul's Seminary, 1995.

Sen, S. *The Great Goddess in Indic Tradition*. Calcutta: Papyrus, 1983.

Shanthi, Margaret and Corona Mary. *We Dare To Speak*. Trichy: Worth, 1994.

Sharma Guleri, Vidyadhar. *Female Deities in Vedic and Epic Literature*. Delhi: NAG, 1990.

Sharma, Preeti. *Hindu Women's Right to Maintenance*. New Delhi: Deep and Deep Publications, 1990.

Sharma, R.P. *Woman in Hindu Literature*. New Delhi: Gyan, 1995.

Shulman, David Dean. *Tamil Temple Myths*. Princeton: Princeton University Press, 1980.

Srivastava, M. C. P. *Mother Goddess in Indian Art, Archaeology and Literature*. Delhi: Agam Kala Prakashan, 1979.

Wadley, Susan S., ed. *The Powers of Tamil Women*. New Delhi: Manohar, 1991.

Whitehead, H. *The Village Gods of South India*. New York: Garland Publishing, 1980.

The Universe as Body or Womb of God

Theologizing on Difference and Interdependence

Jeane C. Peracullo

16

We grasp that body-talk is crucial if we need to establish new ways of understanding our bodies that will liberate us from the shackles of exclusion. We have become suspicious of any view, especially that which looks at the biological body as innocent and natural. On the contrary, we hold that the body is historically and politically read and shaped. The body is historical, plural and culturally mediated form.[1] This implies that any understanding of body is never a direct, un-constructed, and unmediated knowledge about our bodies. For Susan Bordo, we are always reading our bodies according to various interpreted schema. Thus, language is one of mediating factors with which we understand body. The idea is provocative for feminists because it establishes two things: firstly, that language is a legitimizing tool to perpetuate the exclusion and oppression of women when body is understood as part of "semantic grids," that is, the A/non-A rhetoric, where it finds itself in the right or bottom of the equation, and is cloaked in metaphors that are deemed to be fixed and natural; secondly, that language becomes a liberating tool when we regard it simply as a representation of the body and not a direct knowledge of it.

When we change our metaphors about the body, we change the way we understand it. Similarly, who God really is, is as incommensurable as the body is. We cannot know God directly and so we rely on metaphors that are culled from our daily mundane experiences, to describe our understanding of God. For Sallie McFague, all religious language is metaphorical; language about God does not describe God's being but attempts to articulate human experience of God.[2] When we change our metaphors on God, we change the way we see God.

JOINING THE DANCE OF INTERACTION

New language is demanded by a new way of seeing, feeling and perceiving the world. Aware of this, feminist epistemologists who reject androcentric notions regarding objectivity and knowledge hold that what we learn about our environment is mediated through our bodies. We experience the world by using our bodies. Every knower, however, is a situated knower—present here and now, contingent and limited. A situated knower[3] is one who takes into account one's interest in the inquiry, one's emotional involvement, background assumptions, and character as well as one's material, historical and cultural circumstances.[4] Metaphors such as "dance of interaction" and "world-traveler" are terms that are often used to describe the sensibilities of this knower.

What does "dance of interaction" connote? Firstly, it connotes a stage where this dance occurs. A stage signifies temporality, concreteness and situatedness. Music for this particular dance suggests that time is a crucial element measured by beats. When music and stage are present, the dance exists in time and space characterized by distance and intimacy. The movement of the dancers suggests fluidity as well as complexity, which seem boggling in relation to the obvious weightiness of bodies. Harmony is achieved when these elements come together. The dance acquires a motif: unity of the whole. Wholeness is crucial here because it is not understood as the blurring of the individual components to annihilation but as each player—varied, nuanced and distinct uniting with others to achieve a goal. We may perceive the whole, the dance, but trained senses are able to pick up each individual component.

These trained senses are what we bring to become world-travelers. To be so, we need to be mindful not only of the differences of the culture and situation of the places we are visiting but also of the similarities among them and our places of origin. Bordo and Maria Lugones write that thinkers who are genuine world-travelers have the desire and ability to explore reality "wearing the other's shoes."

> This means recognizing, whenever and wherever one goes, that the other's perspective is fully realized and is not merely a bit of exotic "difference" to be incorporated into one's world. The world-travelling thinker is prepared not only to appreciate the foreign, but also to recognize and nurture those places. And the world-traveling thinker will always be ready to abandon familiar territory when human understanding and communication seem to require it. [5]

To take in the stance of a foreigner, a world-traveler, a willing dancer in the dance of interaction, requires that one develops a depth of perception that sees diversity. Yet, it seems that in celebrating diversity, one is not really emphasizing differences, an attitude that can be a basis for intolerance and bigotry, but rather one is actually recognizing similarities. It is as if the difference becomes apparent only if one takes in the whole—the community of humans, nonhuman beings, the entire universe. Similarly, the trained senses (sight, smell, taste, hearing, touch) establish that the whole becomes visible because of the teeming diversity of subjects. Acknowledging these realizations helps us to see these metaphors as neither upholding dualism nor nihilism; rather, they exist in a continuum by which the pleasure of difference is upheld and the newer understanding of interdependence is appreciated.

DIVERSITY AND INTERDEPENDENCE OF BODIES

Sallie McFague recognizes that the dilemma of body-talk is it unmasks two minds: it reinforces the stereotypes that have oppressed women for centuries and, on the other hand, it liberates and redeems women. To operate in either position is to fall into a trap of the "'the either-

or' rhetorical trap" which is of course dualism. Aware of this trap, McFague proceeds to discuss the notion of body in a way that is not to be understood solely as gendered. Thus, instead of speaking of "body," which is highly politicized, she speaks of "bodies" to highlight the fact that body does not refer only to women's or men's bodies but also to Earth, our planet; to "heavenly bodies," or stars, planets and galaxies; to "bodies" of water. The word also refers to bodies of all life forms in our planet. McFague draws attention to this idea when she writes that the "body" of God is not a human body or that God "has" a body but that this "body" is the universe itself, understood as the diversity of bodies.[6] This does not mean that there is no more use for the gendered reflection on the body. On the contrary, the actuality of the female body is a site of conflict where we see both loathing and worship. It is not mere coincidence then that women and nature are both identified as bodies. When we speak of women's bodies, we also speak of other bodies that exist in the same space and time in the universe.

Emphasis on a non-gendered understanding of the body including the reality that it is socially constructed, suggests that we can look at it in ways that avoid falling into dualism. One way is to recognize that we may have focused on a notion of "body" that contributes to its being problematic:

> What we mean by body is a set of associations and stereotypes that are often assumed to be "natural" or obvious but instead are complex, highly nuanced networks of values and interests controlled implicitly (and at times explicitly) by those in power.[7]

McFague's pronouncement effectively placed her conception of the body outside of the essentialism/difference discourse that characterizes Western feminist reflections on the body as she claimed that our understanding of the body, however varied, is just a construction—it is not in any way fixed and immutable. Since this is so, McFague suggests that we can change the way we see and understand the body. In the *Body of God*, she proposes not dualism but continuum, an epistemological stance that takes in the diverse bodies in the universe but at the same time is cognizant of their interdependence.

Embodiment as Awareness of Difference

When we try to examine the connotations of the body, we come up with the following representations: solidity, concreteness, presence, and contingence. These representations are crucial in the task of discarding the general disdain over the body and recovering that which will liberate both women and nature from identification with the body. McFague holds that when we abandon the dualistic mindset which regards the body and everything connected with it as inferior, secondary, and less important than soul or spirit (and everything identified with it), we grasp that embodiment, literally, made flesh, makes perfect sense. She agrees with the feminist notion of situated knowing. Here knowing is not removed from feeling and doing. Hence we can say that embodiment connotes simultaneity of thinking, feeling and doing. She holds that whatever we say about that part of ourselves we call brain, mind or spirit, that part evolves from and is continuous with our bodies.[8] This implies that the body is the spring of identity because of its presence and solidity—it invites the other to neither dismiss it nor pretend that it does not exist. Its very concreteness demands this awareness. To assume embodied feeling, knowing, and doing is to be acutely sensitive to the presence of other bodies. Embodiment then is paying attention to difference.

In *Super, Natural Christians*, McFague uses the imagery of maze to show how to pay attention by "getting into our knees and touching the earth."[9] The use of the maze as a metaphor of knowing nature implies close attention to details and the predisposition to look closely, interestedly, and responsively. Embodiment further signifies that appreciation of multiple perspectives that arise from varied bodies (each one solid, concrete, present and contingent) is the starting point for knowing and doing. And doing in this sense is rightly understood as response, *praxis*, which embodiment embraces and which invites us to "love and honor the body, our bodies and the bodies of all life forms in the planet," without forgetting that although "it gives us so much pleasure, it also gives us so much pain."[10] Here McFague calls attention to the poignancy of our relationship with our bodies.

Embodiment as Awareness of Interdependence

McFague maintains that embodiment is not just awareness of the differences of bodies; it is also consciousness that they exist in relation to one another. The crucial question to ask is, "How should we speak of unity that connects the ongoing array of a diverse, complex, and intricate universe?"[11] She responds by proposing a model she calls organic. Organic at this juncture suggests growth, flourishing, and of course, life. The model is culled from reflecting on the Big-Bang theory and other creation stories, which have a running common thread: the body of the earth, teeming with variety is but a tiny cell in the body of the universe that includes matter in all its form. This realization is radical (literally a "going back to one's roots") a term she cherishes, since it implies that matter is not a collection of things that are excluded, negated, and denied—a particular view of a mechanistic model that operates on "dis-embodied thinking and dis-embodied doing."[12] Further, the model posits a unity—a coming together of different elements that eventually formed each body that is not only manifested in the parts but also in the whole. To grasp this is to understand why it makes sense to say, "We are all made of stardust!" The implication of the coming together is a common beginning and the absence of an originator, an intelligent mind, standing apart from the body and directing this unity. To illustrate ecological unity, McFague uses the imagery of the Earth, which, if viewed from outer space, seems to be a solitary, enclosed system. However, the Earth is really teeming with a tremendous number of bodies. It is not just one body formed by interrelated parts, it is an entity in itself, with individual bodies, each distinct but interdependent.

Is there a place for Gaia, another way of seeing the Earth in McFague's organic model? The Gaia Hypothesis also regards the Earth, as an individual as a subject in its own right. It proposes that our planet functions as a single organism that maintains conditions necessary for its survival. Earth is understood to be "possessing organized, self-contained look of a live creature; a single cell."[13] Gaia's emphasis on the interdependence of things or elements in Earth echoes, to some extent, McFague's organic model. Furthermore, the hypothesis calls for similar praxis that springs from a different understanding of the Earth as a body that sustains us all. McFague recognizes this when she writes:

The evolutionary, ecological perspective insists that we are in the most profound way, "not our own." We belong, from the cells of our bodies to the finest creations of our minds, to the intricate, ever-changing cosmos. We both depend on the web of life from our own contained existence, and, in a special way, we are responsible for it, for we alone know that life is interrelated and we alone know how to destroy it.[14]

Though not exactly referring to Gaia, McFague is aware of the "dance of interactions" among ecological perspectives that operate on organic models. Nonetheless, Gaia is not exactly like McFague's organic model in the sense that its notion of interdependence sees the whole but not the individuals in it. This is apparent in the understanding of the Earth as a "single living entity"; a "single cell." In other words, the Earth is a body, but all entities in it are not. They are by-products of a living entity that sustains itself. Proponents of Gaia use the analogy of a human body to illustrate how seemingly different parts come together to enable the human to survive but these "different parts" are just processes defined by their physiological functions. They are not by themselves distinct— they are realized only in their relationship with the body. This is a different take on interdependence in McFague's organic model, which cultivates the senses into an awareness of the idea that the self only exists in radical interrelationship and interdependence with others and that all living and nonliving beings exist in continuum.

THE UNIVERSE AS THE BODY OF GOD

McFague's insistence that body should be rightly honored, respected, and even loved, finds its fullest expression in her proposal for a new image of God that takes into account our present ecological situation and the reality of the different yet connected oppression of the poor, women and nature. Feminist theologians have worked to dismiss a patriarchal imagery of God, especially images that cement the dualistic mindset. In so doing, these theologians paved the way for God to be understood/seen/perceived differently. Reflecting on nature demands that we see God in a different light, one that reveals God as concerned and loving over the entire creation and these love and concern are mediated through bodies.

Images of God do not describe God but express ways, experiences, of relating to God. We must use what is familiar to talk about the unfamiliar; so we turn to events, objects, relationships from ordinary, contemporary life in order to say something about what we do not know how to talk about—the love of God. We have been given central responsibility to care for God's body, our world. If we thought of the world as God's body, would we not begin to think of the world as somehow sacred ground, not as something to be used and misused but treasured and protected just as we treasure and protect the bodies we love?[15]

McFague uses the metaphor for the universe as "body" of God. God's body in this metaphor is not one body, but all the bodies, from subatomic to galactic ones. This has special import to Christianity, an embodied religion, because of the primacy of the belief in God's incarnation manifested in Christ. However, the traditional understanding of the "body of Christ" is paradigmatic—it refers to a specific body—a human body (and male at that) so that the realities of other bodies are not emphasized. This view suggests sameness not difference, the latter being the product of reflecting on the sheer diversity of bodies in the universe.[16]

What are the implications of this metaphor? Firstly, it proposes that God is both immanent and transcendent. An organic, ecological perspective does not do away with the notion of a transcendent God; rather it directs our attention to the other model of God, God as imminent in the world. McFague holds that these two views are not mutually exclusive—on the contrary they are interrelated. It suggests that God is "physical" and therefore more personal and accommodating as opposed to a God that is distant, monarchical—a being-in-itself and therefore unrelated or standing apart from creation. Yet, God is also transcendent because there is no sense in operating from a mind/body, spirit/matter, and culture/nature mindset when we function from an evolutionary, ecological perspective. To see the world as God's body brings us close to God. God is not far off in another place, a king looking down, as it were, on his realm, but here, as a visible presence. The world is the bodily presence, a sacrament of the invisible God.[17] Put in another way, the universe is "God's self-expression." The theological message is that God, the incarnated God, does not look at the body as dirty, nonsensical, unworthy. It also revolutionizes the way we regard redemption or salvation, that is, salvation, which is not hinged on spirit/body split but encompasses all aspects of human reality: political, economic, spiritual, and social.

THE UNIVERSE AS THE WOMB OF GOD

"Womb" is also a poignant imagery, especially for Hindus and Vietnamese whose songs, dances, myths and stories are replete with images that depict women as "affirmers of life," "life-givers," and the like.[18] To reflect on the metaphor, universe as womb of God emphasizes the centrality of the female body to the crafting of new images of God. Use of the metaphor "universe as the womb of God" seems to be a rejection of McFague's position that body-talk needs to be situated outside of the essentialist/difference debate on women's identity. This is because the image of womb is a particular female imagery, evoking as it does, symbols that resonate in the deepest parts of our being, which represent life and continuity.

Is the centrality of the female body in the metaphor, universe as womb of God, a rejection of McFague's metaphor? It seems to be but it is not actually different, or a discontinuity. It is not even a different metaphor, but a continuum of the metaphor, the universe as the body of God. To talk of the womb is to talk of the body—the womb is a body part; it does not exist apart from the body. What the metaphor invites us to do is to look at the prevailing image of God as creator and see whether the image is in consonance with the ecological perspective.

Reflecting on a Lotus Flower
According to McFague, Genesis's creation stories posit a model of God as an artistic creator.[19] However in the organic model, God as creator is not an artist looking at creation from a distance and declaring it "good," but God is the source of life; the "ground of being."[20] What better way to illustrate God's creative power than imagining God as one "who gives birth" to the universe? In her work in Tantric Buddhism, Miranda

Shaw posits that Queen Maya, the mother of Gautama Buddha, rightly deserves to be understood as the originator of things. She is also known as the Goddess Prajnaparimata, Perfect Wisdom:

> Queen Maya's womb attained cosmic proportions. Universes streamed forth from her body while everything in this universe was in turn visible in her womb. All the worlds, lands, and buddhas were visible in each of her pores. The Birth-Giver is greater than the one who is born.[21]

A mandala, or sacred circle, is a representation of the Buddhist universe. In Buddhism, the circle or mandala is taken to symbolize the perfection of totality, also known as the union of opposites, which may seem distinct but are actually interrelated like the part to the whole and the whole to the part. Mandala's shape suggests space and is empty. However, emptiness is not to be understood as nothingness, but as fullness of everything. Because it suggests space, mandala is also used as imagery for the womb, and as such, as a symbol for female. The interlocking circle suggests the dynamic encounters of parts to the whole.[22]

The Lotus flower is also a symbol for the womb, an embodiment of mandala. This flower emerges from polluted pond waters fully, half-submerged, or submerged. It is so beautiful that it is known as "jewel in the lotus"—a being emerging from the Cosmic Womb.[23] The imagery is very significant for Asian women. Firstly, it recognizes that the womb is home for new life. Life here is not limited only to human life, it includes everything that requires tremendous creative power to emerge, e.g., books, poetry, stories, songs, etc. Secondly, it honors what women in Asia traditionally do: food gathering, garden keeping, homemaking, and even fishing and farming. The lotus flower's sheer beauty and luminosity elevates the everyday, mundane experiences of women into something spiritual, which has emerged, either fully, semi-fully or is even still half-submerged. Thirdly, it connotes interdependence and interrelatedness. The flower is not a separate entity from the plant and the pond. Although the flower rises up above the plant, it is still attached to the latter that itself is rooted in the pond. Lastly, the lotus depicts an image of God as Mother, whose compassion and love is so encompassing, they penetrate even the "dirty" pond, enabling it to nurture a plant from which a "jewel" emerges. For McFague, the model of God as a mother is a continuity of the model, the universe as God's body, but one that expands it and inflames it because it is not yet fully considered in mainstream Christian tradition.[24] For one thing, God as a mother gives Christianity a new image of God (God as female) that rejects patriarchy.

Kinship: Interdependence and Difference

So, God gives birth to a universe. And if everything comes from the same womb, how are we to understand interdependence and difference? To answer this question, we further dwell on the significance of the womb. The womb is said to be empty but emptiness here should not be equated with nothingness. Rather, emptiness is to be understood as being full of everything because things are interdependent. Buddhism gives us some insights regarding its nature.

The understanding of the nature of Emptiness, also known as void or zero, rests on the recognition that all things do not have permanent, independent, immovable essences that remain forever. So much suffering has been caused by the belief that there is in a thing something permanent and immovable. This notion led to discrimination and intolerance of what is considered as the "other." Understanding emptiness leads to the insight that all beings are interdependent and related in such a way that the existence of something implies that all other things must exist. This is not to posit solipsism, where there is no reality but the self, or nihilism, where there is nothing at all. To use the analogy of waves in the sea: the individual waves are our selves yet cannot be removed from the water. We can say that form is the wave and emptiness is water. The nature of emptiness cuts through the delusion of dualism, especially Cartesian dualism. Shaw holds that all things are born out of emptiness; emptiness is the fertile womb of reality.[25] McFague herself recognizes that "Universe as the Womb of God" is a powerful imagery to highlight interdependence and interrelatedness of all life. It is because we all come from our mothers and we were fed by our mothers.[26]

Does reflecting on interdependence discard difference? Let us turn to the words of a mother reflecting on her pregnancy:

> In pregnancy, a woman's body is not her own. The primary occupation of that body is the housing and growing of a baby. The mother, as the residence for this other being, is filled with a sense of its value, which is apart from her own sense of value. Though intricately bound up with this being, she is distinct from it. The two are one, and herein lies the paradox. The pregnant woman is both herself and this other being. The two are distinct from each other, though they are not separate.[27]

This is a powerful insight shared by all pregnant women regardless of race, culture and religious affiliations. A pregnant woman is literally possessing two bodies—distinct yet interdependent. In every change in their bodies, women note that the baby is slowly but surely announcing its presence. It is this "intrusion" that makes pregnancy a highly charged event and the ensuing birth, the cause of so much pain for both mother and child. The pain may be from the violent way unity was severed or from the realization that each now has to begin the process of individuation.

Using the analogy above and applying it at the cosmic level, we can say that we all came from the same womb. Though we may be born from the same womb, we are still distinct from the mother. Mother here is God, thus stressing difference as well from God. We possess our own bodies; we may come from our mother's bodies but we are not entirely hers. However, we retain some affinity with her; we are products of her body so we resemble her to some extent. This makes sense if we are to account for the diversity of bodies in the universe. So reflecting on interdependence does not discard difference.

Kinship becomes the manifestation of the metaphor "the universe is the womb of God." This insight is evident in Vietnam where, regardless of religious beliefs, they call each other *dong-bao*, which means, "born of the same womb," suggesting belongingness. For Nguyen Ngoc Binh, the health and integrity of every community, its creativity and growth, depends on the sense of belonging. Forgiveness is a necessity from this perspective; it is the very fabric of the universe.[28] Extending this ethic to nature, we say that all entities are "born of the same womb."

Implications of the Metaphor to Asian Context

Asia is characterized by diversity, complexity, and variation. However, undeniably one of the things that many Asians share is the experience of poverty in varying degrees. If the woman is malnourished because of lack of access to land, in which she can plant and grow food, then her children will be as equally malnourished as she is. This is where the image of God as Mother of the Universe acquires deep significance for Asian women. This is a powerful image, one that resonates in the deepest part of their beings because it highlights the passionate love, which they have glimpsed and experienced in motherhood. In the face of abject poverty and extreme difficulty, mother and the child persist anyway, as if enlivened by deep faith that God is the God who cares and loves deeply and the same God that nourishes all beings. It is no surprise that Buddhism emphasizes compassion as this singular trait of *Boddhisatvas*, who delay their entry to Nirvana until all suffering beings are brought there.[29]

Compassion is like the love McFague has in mind when she underscores that the image of God as mother of the universe stresses God's love as so encompassing that there is joy in the birth of every body. God declares joyfully: "It is good that you exist!" The mother and child relationship can be very problematic but not so with God and the universe. It is because God is the creator of the latter, which comes forth from God's very being.

This love highlights the interdependence of life in all forms, the desire to be with other beings in both their needs and joy. God as a Mother of the universe is concerned with the nurture and fulfillment of life, not just with birth.[30]

CONCLUSION: METAPHORS IN CONTINUUM

As I posited early in this article, both metaphors, "Universe as the Body of God" and "Universe as the Womb of God," exist in continuum and both operate in the framework of an organic model. This makes sense when we grasp the meaning of metaphor as not dyadic but multiple; not oppositional but interactive. Metaphors are from the familiar things we encounter in our daily lives. When we accept that we are interdependent yet at the same time distinct from the other, surely metaphors we use will reveal the paradigm, with which we see and interpret God and the universe.

These metaphors acquire greater significance at a time when our planet, Earth, is experiencing unprecedented environmental destruction; nonhuman beings especially species of plants and animals are disappearing; and large numbers of humanity are experiencing acute poverty. However, these terrible phenomena also allowed new sensibilities to appear to respond to these challenges. One very remarkable sensibility is the reflection on wholeness. We see an explosion of literature inviting us to take a closer look at wholeness, wholism, holism. And we declare, "There must be something in this discourse that takes us closer to what the truth is" and then we begin to examine our very own paradigms and see whether they have contributed to the destruction (fragmentation?) in our midst.

I tend to see and interpret McFague as someone who has reflected on wholeness. Her reflection on the universe as the body of God will prove this. How can someone who declares herself "feminist" be able to operate from outside that epistemological lens?

Further, it is very difficult to reflect on the body, whether represented by a womb or other parts. It is because as women, we have an ambivalent relationship with our bodies. It is a love-hate relationship and an excruciatingly passionate one. For so long, we have been identified with our bodies and the negative connotations ascribed to it reflect ultimately on us, bearers of these bodies. Is it any wonder that most women hate their "protruding" breasts and stomachs? These parts that form the locus of our being female are viewed as "obtrusive," "untamed," and "uncivilized." However, there are women who declare that we need to own these parts because they are the locus of our identity. Yes, we see how problematic body-talk could be.

But she did and in so doing, was able to escape the trap with which some Western feminists find themselves—caught in the essential/difference discourse.

An expanded self is the product of acquiring an ecological perspective. This self is now able to see how a new image of God can be revolutionary, radical, and contribute significantly to sow compassion towards all bodies in the universe.

NOTES

[1] Susan Bordo, *Unbearable Weight: Feminism, Western Culture and the Body* (Berkeley: University of California Press), 288.

[2] Sallie McFague discusses in length the value of metaphors in God-talk in her book, *Metaphorical Theology: Models of God in Religious Language* (Philadelphia: Fortress Press, 1982).

[3] Ibid.

[4] Lorraine Code, "Taking Subjectivity into Account," in *Feminist Epistemologies*, ed. Linda Alcoff and Elizabeth Potter (New York and London: Routledge, 1993), 26.

[5] Maria Lugones, "Playfulness, World Traveling, and Loving Perception," in *Women, Knowledge, and Reality: Exploration in Feminist Philosophy*, ed. Ann Garry and Marilyn Pearsall (New York and London: Routledge, 1996), 428.

[6] Sallie McFague, *The Body of God: An Ecological Theology* (Minneapolis: Fortress Press, 1993), 37.

[7] Ibid., 15.

[8] Ibid., 16.

[9] Sallie McFague, *Super, Natural Christians: How We should Love Nature* (Minneapolis: Fortress Press, 1997), 67.

[10] Idem, *Body of God*, 16.

[11] Ibid.

[12] Ibid., 15.

[13] Author Unknown, "The Remarkable World," available from http://www.oceansonline.com/gaiaho.htm; Internet, accessed October 2004.

[14] Sallie McFague, "The World as Body of God," *The Christian Century* (July 20-27, 1998): 671-73, available from http://www.religion-online.org/showarticle.asp?title=2324; Internet, accessed October 2004.

[15] Ibid.

[16] Idem, *The Body of God*, 37.

[17] Idem, "The World as God's Body," available from http://www.religion-online.org/cgi-bin/relsearchd.dll/showarticle?item_id=56; Internet, accessed July 2002.

[18] Aruna Gnanadason, "Towards a Feminist Eco-Theology for India," in *Women Healing the Earth: Third World on Ecology, Feminism, and Religion*, ed. Rosemary Radford Ruether (Marynoll, N.Y.: Orbis Books, 1996), 75.

[19] Sallie McFague, *Models of God: Theology for an Ecological, Nuclear Age* (Philadelphia: Fortress Press, 1987), 105.

[20] Ibid.

[21] Miranda Shaw, "Blessed are the Birth-Givers," *Parabola* 23, no. 4 (Winter 1998): 48-53.

22 Author Unknown, "Chapter II The Meaning of the Mandala: The Eternal Circle," available from http://web.ukonline.co.uk/phil.williams/index.htm; Internet, accessed October 2004.

23 Hindus also regard the lotus as a symbol for womb. The Taittiriya Brahmana describes how Prajapati, desiring to evolve the universe, which was then fluid, saw a lotus-leaf, pushkara parna, coming out of water. It is described that when divine life-substance was about to put forth the universe, the cosmic waters grew a thousand-petalled lotus flower of pure gold, radiant like the sun. This was considered to be a doorway, or an opening of the mouth of the womb of the universe. See Trilok Chandra Majupuria, *Trilok Chandra Majupuria* (Lashkar, India: M. Gupta, 1989).

24 McFague, *Models of God*, 105.

25 Shaw, "Blessed are the Birth-Givers," 48-53.

26 McFague, *Models of God*, 105-6.

27 Rachel Richardson Smith, "Pregnancy and Childbirth: A Theological Event," available from http://www.religion-online.org/showarticle.asp?title=1271; Internet, accessed October 2004.

28 Nguyen Ngoc Binh, "The Power and Relevance of Vietnamese Myths," in *Vietnam: Essays on History, Culture, and Society* ed. Asia Society (New York: Asia Society, 1985), 61-77; available from http://www.askasia.org/frclasrm/readings/r000061.htm; Internet accessed October 2004.

29 "Bodhisattva (Skt.): literally, "wisdom-being" or "hero"; anyone who, having attained enlightenment, dedicates himself to helping others do the same. Originally, bodhisattva referred to any of the most highly developed disciples of Shakyamuni Buddha or to a being in the final stage of enlightenment." Roshi Philip Kapleau, *Zen: Merging of East and West* (New York: Anchor Books, Doubleday, 1989), 290.

30 McFague, *Models of God*, 102.

BIBLIOGRAPHY

Bordo, Susan. *Unbearable Weight: Feminism, Western Culture and the Body*. Berkeley: University of California.

"Chapter II The Meaning of the Mandala: The Eternal Circle." Available from http://web.ukonline.co.uk/phil.williams/index.htm; Internet, accessed October 2004.

Code, Lorraine. "Taking Subjectivity into Account." In *Feminist Epistemologies*, 15-48. Edited by Linda Alcoff and Elizabeth Potter. New York and London: Routledge, 1993.

Gnanadason, Aruna. "Towards a Feminist Eco-Theology for India." In *Women Healing the Earth: Third World on Ecology, Feminism, and Religion*, 74-81. Edited by Rosemary Radford Ruether. Maryknoll, N.Y.: Orbis Books, 1996.

Kapleau, Roshi Philip. *Zen: Merging of East and West.* New York: Anchor Books, Doubleday, 1989.

Lugones, Maria. "Playfulness, World Traveling, and Loving Perception." In *Women, Knowledge, and Reality: Exploration in Feminist Philosophy,* 419–33. Edited by Ann Garry and Marilyn Pearsall. New York and London: Routledge, 1996.

Majupuria, Trilok Chandra. *Trilok Chandra Majupuria.* Lashkar, India: M. Gupta, 1989.

McFague, Sallie. *Super, Natural Christians: How We should Love Nature.* Minneapolis: Fortress Press, 1997.

McFague, Sallie. *The Body of God: An Ecological Theology.* Minneapolis: Fortress Press, 1993.

McFague, Sallie. *Models of God: Theology for an Ecological, Nuclear Age.* Philadelphia: Fortress Press, 1987.

McFague, Sallie. *Metaphorical Theology: Models of God in Religious Language.* Philadelphia: Fortress Press, 1982.

McFague, Sallie. "The World as Body of God." *The Christian Century* (July 20-27, 1998): 671-73; Available from http://www.religion-online.org/showarticle. asp?title=2324; Internet, accessed October 2004.

McFague, Sallie. "The World as God's Body." Available from http://www.religion-online.org/cgi-bin/relsearchd.dll/showarticle?item_id=56; Internet, accessed July 2002.

Ngoc Binh, Nguyen. "The Power and Relevance of Vietnamese Myths." In *Vietnam: Essays on History, Culture, and Society,* 61-77. Edited by Asia Society. New York: Asia Society, 1985. Available from http://www.askasia.org/frclasrm/readings/r000061.htm; Internet accessed October 2004.

"The Remarkable World." Available from http://www.oceansonline.com/gaiaho. htm; Internet, accessed October 2004.

Richardson Smith, Rachel. "Pregnancy and Childbirth: A Theological Event." Available from http://www.religion-online.org/showarticle.asp?title=1271; Internet, accessed October 2004.

Shaw, Miranda. "Blessed are the Birth-Givers." *Parabola* 23, no. 4 (Winter 1998): 48-53.

Index

Abesamis, Marilen, 64

Abortion, forced, 72n 12

"Absentee mothers," 62

Abuse: in children, 7, 9: gendered responses, 8; physical and sexual, 7, 66; verbal, 8

"Adult voluntary prostitution," 76

Adult women prostitutes, 85

Adultery: among men, 84; in Ezekiel 16, 113–15; in migration context, 63

"Aesthetic resistance", 54n 16

Aging, 12, 201, 206–7; and beauty, 208; women, 208: religious, 203

Agni, 43

AIDS, 11

Alcibiades, 36

Alzheimer's, 12, 25, 26

AMRSP, Association of Major Religious Superiors in the Philippines, 229

Anagnorisis, 162

Animism and psychosomatic unity, 131

Anthropocentrism, 93, 96

Anthropology, theological: Christianity, 173–74, l98; Tantrism, 44, 46

Antinomianism, 123, 124, 129

"Apotheosis of the mother," 142

Aristotle, 6

Artificial contraception, 14

Asceticism, 9: extreme, Pauline view, 123–24, Hellenistic, 123, 129

Asian Migrant Center, 67

Asian Migrant Coordinating Body, 65

Atman, 141

Atr-smriti, 142

Augustine, St.: anthropology, theological, 93; on faith and doubt, 13; on the sacramental bond, 14–15

Autism, 22–23, 26–27

Ayyal Kuttam, 55n 35

Babaylans, 219

Bagchi, Jasodhara, 35

Balabanski, Vicki, 195

Banmui, 68, 72n 21

Beauty, 66, 82–83, 260

Berry, Thomas, 97

Bhakti, 41, 43, 54n 16

Bhushan, Madhu, 142–43

Bible: bent-over woman, 139, 144–49, 176; body in 1 Corinthians, 120–32; hemorrhaging woman, 176–77; Jairus's daughter, 229; leper's healing, 175; metaphorical woman in Ezekiel, 104–17; Tamar, 84–85; women standing near the cross, 157–63

Birthing, 187

Blood, shedding, 191–92

Bodiliness, 173, 174, 178–81

Body of Christ: as church, 130–31; in 1 Corinthians, 126, 127–30; and women, 178–81

Body: abuse, 7; Asian context, 131; in Buddhism, 132, 136n 41; in Christianity, negative view, 1; correspondence with building/temple, 123, 132; as constructed, 19–20, 21; in Gospels, 173; imagery in 1 Corinthians, 121, 122–23; importance, 120; as

inscribed, 2; as language, 19, 154–56;
lesbian, 234; marking of, 6; meaning
of, 19; as microcosm of universe,
for Tantrics, 41; as Other, 5; Pauline
perspective, 129–33; and self identity,
6–11, 18–19; in Semitic anthropological
view, 131; of sexuality, 14; as symbol of
society, 175; transcendence, 3, 11–14,
95; women's, 3, 155–56, 203, 208–9
Book of Manu, 142, 151n 1.
Bordo, Susan, 273
Bridadaranyaka Upanishad, on men and
women, 141
Brock, Rita Nakashima. *Casting Stones,* 34
Brown, Peter. *The Body and Society,* 14
Buddhism, 98, 282: emptiness, 283;
mandala, 282; Queen Maya/Goddess
Prajnaparimata, 282; stupa, 132; zen
meditation, 137n 41
Budhi, 157
Bundang, Rachel. *Scars ARE History:
Colonialism Written on the Body,* 219
Butler, Judith, 238, 241

"Candela," 142
Cannon, Kathleen, 178
Capitalism: global, 109–10, 141; industrial,
92–93
Caste, 269n 32: Dalit, 270n 58; upper,
traditionalists, 54n 16
Catholic Church, 9–10: Philippines, 217,
224, 226
CBCP, Catholic Bishops' Conference of the
Philippines, 217, 223, 227
CBCP, "Pastoral Care of Victims and
Offenders," 223
CBCP, "Pastoral Guidelines on Sexual
Abuses and Misconduct of the Clergy,"
227
Celibacy, priestly, 2
"Cell phone mothers," 63
Chakras, 38, 41
Chang, Kimberly, 64
Chang, Kuei-Ying, 78

Charismata, 127
Chittister, Joan, 156
Christa, 185n 25
Christian community: reading text as, 114–
15, 116; as "body of Christ," 127–29
Christian theology, 35, 37, 44, 155: fertility,
51; human eros, 51; on dignity of
domestic workers, 68–69
Christianity: and anthropocentrism,
96; boundaries of, 182; naturalized
categories, 235; syncretism, 123; temple
(church) and human body, 132
Christic-ness, 182–83, 184n 2
Christology, high and low, 131
Chronic illness, 9–11
Chrysostom, John, 221–22
Chung, Hyun Kyung, 68
Class system, 140
Clergy sexual misconduct, 219, 222,
224–28
Coles, Robert, 205
Collective Of Sex Workers And Supporters
(COSWAS), 75–76, 85–86
Collins, Mary, 194
Colonization, Philippine, 218–20
Community, Corinthian, 120, 122-23, 126
Complementarity, of sexes, 242
Constructionist model, 5
Corley, Kathleen, 153, 157-59; "Death and
Burial Ceremonies of the Ancient Roman,
Greek and Jewish Customs," 157–58;
"Role of Women during the Death and
Burial Rituals of Jesus's Time," 153–54
Corpus, Ray, 63
C.O.Y.O.T.E. (Call Off Your Old Tired
Ethics), 79
Creation story, in 1 Corinthians, 130
Culpepper, R. Alan, 162
"Culture of silence," 223
Czajka, Maya, 76, 79

Daiuonion, 37
Dakshinachara, 39
Dalit women, 143

Damasio, Antonio. *Descartes' Error,* 23, 26
Dance: as aesthetic resistance, 53n 1, 53n
16, 54; "dance of interaction," 274–75,
279
Dangco, Lilia, 66
Devadasi system, 143
De Beauvoir, Simone, 37
De las Casas, Bartolome, 6
Dery, Luis Camara, 220
Dewey, Joanna, 177
Difference(s), 98, 127, 275–79, 283: of sex,
126–27
Disability, 9–11
Diversity, 51, 275–76: in unity, 127
Domestic workers, migrant, 60–68:
and lesbianism, 64; and motherhood,
62–63; objectification, 67–68, 69;
and "Sabbath," 69
Douglas, Mary. *Purity and Danger,* 175
Dowry murders, 53n 6
Dualism, 123, 127, 134n 8: Classical (stoic
or Christian), 5, 34, 93–94; effect of, 35,
38; model, 4–5, 11; soul/body dualism, 3
Durga, 39

Ecological crisis, 90–91:
and demographics, 16
Ecological spirituality, 98–99
Education, models of, 55n 32
Embodiment, 68, 98, 240, 277
Elderly women, pastoral program for,
210–12
Emotions: abuse, 8;
gendered recognition, 23
Enlightenment, 19, 45, 92
Ephebophilia, 231n 3, 217
Epistemologies, feminist, 97, 274, 277
Equality, 179
Erikson, Erik. *Eight Ages of Man,* 204
Eros, 35–38, 45: and Mother Teresa,
51–52; and Nietzsche, 35; and Plato,
36; and St. Jerome, 35; as Sakti in
Tantric philosophy, 38–40, 46; in Greek
philosophy, 36–38
Eskēnōsen, 154
Essentialism, 5, 238, 276

"Ethic of service," 64
Ethnic societies, 6
Eucharist, 194–95: and women's daily
lives, 187–98; and women's ordination,
193–98
Eve, 35, 222, 224
Executive Yuan Committee for the
Promotion of Women's Rights, 75
"Exploring the Erotic Policy of Taiwan:
Research, Movement, and Feminism," 77
Ezekiel, chapter 16, 106–8, 109 table, 116:
"pedagogy," 110, 111, 113

Family, and clergy, 223
Feminism, 42–44: and postmodern thought,
244–45, 246n 4; ecofeminism, 94–95,
98; epistemology, 96; Indian culture,
252–53; liberal, 94; and materialism,
5; postmodern, 234; radical, 94; and
spirituality, 154
Feminist theology, 44, 46, 49, 174–75, 179
"Feminization of poverty," 198
Fidelity, in sexual ethics, 25
Filipino domestic helpers : "from airport to
airport," 66; gendered transitions,
62–64; gendered violence, 64–66;
"For Hong Kong Only" affair, 64;
married, 62–63; physical abuse,
66; physical appearance, 65–66;
relationships, 64; sexual abuse, 66;
sexuality, 63, 64; single, 63; working
conditions, 67–68, 72n 16
Filipino migration, 61–62
Filipino socialization, 61
Fiorenza, Elisabeth Schüssler, 46, 47, 49:
In Memory of Her, 178
Flesh, 154; sins of, 35
Foreign domestic helpers (FDH), in
Hong Kong, 65
Forgiveness, 226
Fortune, Marie M., 224
Fourth Gospel, 162, 154
Fowler, James, 204–5
Fox, Matthew, 97
Frank, Frances Croake, 193
Fundamental option, 22

Gaba, 223, 228
Gaia hypothesis, 278–79
Gender, 16–17, 106, 241: identity, 105–106, 115, 116; socialization pattern, 8
"Gender, Psychology, and Culture—The Development of Native Feminism," 77
Gendered migration, 61–62
George, K. M., 190
Gifts of the Spirit: and effective contraception, 14; in Paul, 126–28
Globalization, 110: women in, 61
Gnosticism, 14, 123, 129–30
God: as female (Sophia) 264; inclusive language for, 266; as mother, 188: of the universe, 275–76, 279, 281–82, 285; visual representations/images of, 11–17, 112–15, 117, 266, 280, 281. *See also* Islam, names of God
Goddesses, India: feminist evaluation of visual representations, 253–54, 257–67; impact on Christian men and women, 263–67; Kali, 255–56, 261–62, 264–65; Lakshmi, 254–55, 257, 259, 260, 261–62, 265, 268n 13, 270n 44, 270; Mari Amman, 270n 59; Parvati, 255, 260, 261; Sakti, 38–39, 253–54, 263–64; Saraswati, 254, 257, 258–59, 260, 261–62
Greek philosophy, 123, 129
Grief, manifestation of, 157
Griffiths, Bede, 264

Hawking, Stephen, 11
Healing: in the gospels, 175–77, 182; of abused women, 229
Hellwig, Monika. *The Eucharist and the Hunger of the World*, 198
Herman, Judith, *"Trauma and Recovery,"* 228–29
Heterosexual/lesbian artifice, 241–44
Heterosexuality, 240–44
Heyward, Carter, 239–40
Hinduism, 39, 141: Atman, 141; Devadasi system, 143; *Manusmrti* or The Laws of Manu, 141–42, 146, 151n 1, 257, 269n 26; marriage as preferred vocation, 16.

See also Womb, Lotus flower
Hinduism, tantric: history, 40–41; purpose, 41–42; Sakta philosophy, 39, 42; Shakti/Sakti as energy, 38, 42–44; Siva –Sakti, 42–43; tantra(s): meaning, 39, 268n 3; Vamacara, 39–40. *See also* Yoga, Bhakti, Goddesses, India
Hiya, 223
Holism, 91
Holler, Linda. *Erotic Touch: The Role of Touch in Moral Agency*, 22–23
Homosexuality, 17. *See also* Lesbian
Hooker, Evelyn, 17
Human beings: in image of God, 173–74
Human body: woman, 92: sacred and holy, 131
Human rights, 20. *See* Rights.
Human sexuality, 82. *See also* Sexuality
Human work: and church teachings, 79, 86
Hwang, Shu-Ling, 77

Ilaiah, Kancha, 262
Illness, chronic, 9
Images, 115–16: of God in human, 132, 174; with Jesus, 115
Incarnation, 68–69, 73n 24, 129, 174–75, 183
Inculturation, 266
Indian Church, 35
Indian patriarchy, 139–40, 149
Infanticide, female, 53n 6
"Inner depths," 20–21
Interdependence: and organic model, 278–79; and kinship, 283–84
Irigaray, Luce, 236, 239, 242
Isis, 155–56
Islam: marriage as preferred vocation, 16; names of God, 116

Jerome, St., 35
Jerusalem as woman, 106–7, 115
Jesus: as mother, 189; and social outcasts, 151n 10
Jih, Huey-Wen, 78
Jocano, F. Landa, 218–19
Johannine crucifixion, 158

John Paul II, Pope: on labor, 79, 86;
on women, 234–35
Johnson, Elizabeth. *She Who Is*, 115
Judaism: 145, 151n. 8, 160, 176; marriage
as preferred vocation, 16; *ochlos*, 145
Jung, Patricia, 15

Kali, 39, 46, 188
Kama Sutra, 41
Kang, Eu-Jin, 204
Karma, 223
Kaulajnana-nirnaya, 41
Keller, Helen, 11
Kinsey, Alfred, 17
Knowledge as power, 48–49
Korean elderly women, 204
Kothar, Rajni, 51
Kundalini, 38, 41, 44

Labor, 49: gender division of, 61–62;
conditions of foreign domestic workers,
67, 72n 16
"Laborem Exercens—On Human Work," 79
Lament rituals, of women, 158
Late modern culture. *See* Postmodernity
Laws of purity, 142
"Left-Hand Path," see *Vamachara*
Lesbian, 234, 235–45: butch/femme
stylization, 240–45; motherhood,
235–38; nun, 238–40; relationships
among migrants, 64
Liberal feminism, 94
Loevinger, Jane, 205
Logos, 154, 155, 157
"Long-term meal ticket," 84
Lorde, Audre. *The Erotic as Power,* 45

Madonna (organization), 76, 79
Mahasaka, 43
Man: in Ezekiel 16, 113–14
Manusmriti, 141, 146, 151n 1, 269n 26. *See
also* Book of Manu
Maria Clara, 220
Marital sex, 15

Marriage, 83–84: in Ezekiel, 104, 115;
with foreign brides, 83; imagery, 106,
108; prohibition for widows, 142, 151n
4; with man "in-between," 83; for single
domestic workers, 63; for St. Augustine,
14–15
Mary, Virgin: among women standing
near the cross, 153, 166n 1; expression
of feminine genius, 236; and
Hindu goddesses, 265, 267; icon of
contradiction, 238; negation of body, 264
Maslow, Abraham, 204
McAllister, Julian, 64
McFague, Sallie, 97, 275–80
Menstruation: and shame, 142; and
Eucharist, 191–92
Mezirow, Jack, 95–96
Mies, Maria, 142
Migration, feminization of, 62
Moksada, 43–44
Morality, double standard, 84
Motherhood, 16, 187: in Hinduism, 142;
John Paul II, 235; transnational, 63
Mulackal, Shalini, 51
Mutuality: difference as an index to, 244; in
female friendship, 236–37, 240, 243–44;
norm for relationships, 83, 98, 227
Myerhoff, Barbara, 205

Nature: Asian animistic view, 132; and
human being, 130–32; shift from
medieval organic to mechanistic vision
Nayaka, 54n 16
"Neither 'Saints' Nor 'Prostitutes': Sexual
Discourse in the Filipina Domestic
Worker Community in Hong Kong," 64
Nietzsche, Friedrich, 35
Nymphomaniac harlot, in Ezekiel 16,
104, 114

Ochlos, 145
Old age, 202, 208, 212. *See also* Aging
Our Bodies, Ourselves, 4–5

Pain: role of touch in alleviation, 10; and self, 3, 9

Parvathi, 39

Passion: and passions, 191: narrative, 161; women's testimony, 162–63

Pativrata, 142

Patriarchal: Judaism, 145, 148, 151n 8: society, 179, 197: Philippines, 19, 227; structures, 93; theology, 38, 45

Patriarchy, 93, 96, 140, 142: definition, 93, 140

Peacock, Arthur, 90

Pedophilia, 231n 3, 217

Pedophilia, clergy, 2

Phallologocentrism, 247n 31

Philippine Church, 220–21

Plato. *Symposium,* 36–37

Platonic thought, 36–37, 92

Poling, James, 224

Poor: in Asia, 182; as vicars of Christ, 181. *See also* Poverty

"Pope John Paul II's Letter to Women," 234–35

Porete, Marguerite. *The Mirror of Simple Souls,* 4

Postmodernity, 246n 4: and feminism, 234, 239–41; *See also* Self, Postmodern

Poverty, feminization, 64, 86, 189

Power, 46: inner (Sakti), 257, 267; and knowledge, 47–49; Mahasaka 43; sacramental, 196, 265

Pratt, Geraldine, 68

"Princess of public relations," 78

Property rights, 140

Prostitute movement, 75

Prostitution: adult voluntary, 76, 80–81, 84, 85; Hindu women, 143; legalization, 80, 81; Philippines, 220; sexual romanticist and libertarian views, 79; teen, 79; theological readings, 84–85; and women, 64, 71n 11, 75–86; as work, 81–82

Race, 6, 13

Racial bodies, 6–7, 13

Rahner, Karl, 196, 183

Ramo Inquisicion in the Archivo General de Nacion in Mexico, 224

Rasa, 54n 16

Recognition, literary genre, 162

Reeves, Christopher, 11

Reign of God, 146, 147, 148, 150, 182

Reincarnation, 21

Reproduction, of male sons, 83, 142: for migrant domestic workers, 65

Resurrection, 14, 131: of the body, 128

Rig Veda, 259, 269n 26

"Right-Hand Path," 39

Rights: and sex work, 75, 79, 81: human rights in late modern culture, 20; property, 140, 142, 259–60; reproductive, 72n 12; of women in pre-colonial Philippines, 219

Ritual participation of women: in Catholicism, 143, 193–98, 267: in Hinduism, 142, 259; in pre-colonial Philippines, 219

Rolheiser, Rolan. *The Holy Longing–the Search for a Christian Spirituality,* 51

Romance and Resistance: The Experience of the Filipina Domestic Workers in Hong Kong, 63

Rose, Renate, 195

Ross, Susan, 195–96

Ruether, Rosemary Radford, 92, 173

Sabbath, 69, 145–48

Sacramental bond, in marriage, 15

Sacrament, in ordinary life, 195

Saivings, Valerie, 94

Sakti/Shakti: creative energy from God, 38–39, 41–44; creation-centered, 52; dignity of women, 50; goddess, 39; 41; knowledge in, 48-49; as power, 254, 257-58; and Siva 46; spirituality, 45; supreme power, 141; female energy, 190

Salvation, 123, 129, 130–31, 145, 175

Santiso, Teresa, 156

Sarx, 130, 154

Scarry, Elaine. *The Body in Pain: The Making and Unmaking of the World,* 9

Schillebeeckx, Edward, 195
Self: and aging, 1–5, 12, 27, 141; and
    Alzheimer's disease, 12, 26; and body,
    4–5, 23, 27; and brain, 4: trauma, 26;
    and chronic illness, 9–10; constructionist
    models, 21; developmental, 5, 22; as
    discontinuous, 21–22, 24–25; ecological,
    97; identity, 4, 7, 8, 11, 24; and inner
    depths, 20–21; materialist view, 5;
    modern, 3–4, 19–20; postmodern, 3–5,
    18–23; pre-modern, 3, 4, 20; as soul, 4.
    See also Atman
Self-actualization, according to Maslow, 205
"Selling of the body," 80
Sensitivity, to emotion, 23
Sensuality, 35, 42
Sepulveda, Juan, 6
"Service Work," 78
Sex, 16–18: abstinence, 134n 8, 135n 12;
    as a school for love, 15; as biologically
    given, 106, 237, 241; as socially
    constructed, 17–18, 237; in Tantra,
    41–42
Sex/gender construct, 240–42
"Sex Work," 78. *See also* Prostitution
Sex workers, 75, 77–78: human rights, 81,
    82
Sexual abuse, 7–9, 66, 217, 218
Sexual desire/passion: as pre-moral good,
    14–15; as enemy of the holy, 34n 8
Sexual exploitation, clergy, 217–18
Sexual harassment in church setting, 218;
    and forgiveness, 110
Sexual identity, 4, 18
Sexual intercourse, with low-caste partner,
    41
"Sexual libertinism," 123
Sexual orientation, 16, 17, 105–6, 116
Sexual pleasure, 15
Sexual violence, 218, 221–24. *See also*
    Sexual abuse
Sexuality, 24, 35, 42, 63, 64, 82, 155, 166n
    1: commercial, 77; and ethics, 24; and
    experience of God, 42, 155; of women,
    91–93, 107: beauty, 82–83

Shame, 107–8, 110–11, 223
Shringara, 54n 16
Siva/Shiva, 41–43, 46, 268n 16
Skenos, 154
Slavery, African, 6–7
Snowdon, David, 203
Soares-Prabhu, George, 49
Socrates, 36
Soma, 43, 130, 131
Spirituality, 51, 98 130: ecological, 98–99;
    of aging, 205–8; of warfare, 38; for
    women, 195
Sprout: Taiwan Catholic Sprout Women
    – Concerns Association, 87n 1
Sringara, 41
St. James, Margo, 79
Stupa, 132
Super Natural Christians, 277
Sringara, on women, 141
Swidler, Leonard, 143
System of multiple discrimination, of
    women, 141

Taboo-breaking, 41, 85, 143
"Talitha Cum," 229
Tantra(s), 40–42, 268n 3
Tantrism, 38, 39, 45–46, 52: knowledge in,
    48–49
Taylor, Charles. *Sources of the Self,* 3
Teilhard de Chardin, 207–8
Teresa, Mother, 51
Tertullian, 222
Theology: and anthropology, 177–78:
    embodying, 70; Sakti, 44–52;
    of suffering, 69, 177–78; Theology
    and metaphors: beyond image, 115–17;
    biblical hermeneutics, 47;
    1 Corinthians, 122–23, 129;
    epistemology, 274, 286; metaphorical,
    97; woman in Ezekiel, 104;
Thomas Aquinas, Saint, 93, 196, 223
Tolbert, Mary Ann, 229
Touch, 10–11, 223. *See also* Pain

Uluka, 268n 13
Unity in diversity, 127
US Catholic Bishops, 82

Vamachara, 39–40
Vedanta, 141
Vicar(s) of Christ, 181–82
Victim-blaming, 2, 225
Violence: against women, definition, 142;
    culture of, 142–43; domestic 2, 260
Virginity, in Christianity, 14, 16, 264
Vyasa Samhita, 142

Walby, Sylvia, 140
Webb, Val, *In Defense of Doubt,* 196
WHISPER (Women Hurt in Systems of
    Prostitution Engaged in Revolt), 79
White, David Gordon, 38
White, Lynn, 96
Whitehead, Alfred, 95
Widow marriage, 142, 15n 4
Wilfred, Felix, 50
Winter, Gibson, 97
Witchcraze, 180–81
Womanhood, 192
Womb, 188, 192, 194, 282: and Lotus
    Flower, 281–82, 289n 20; *dong-bao*
    (Vietnam), 284

Women: according to John Chrysostom,
    221: according to St. Paul, 126;
    according to Tertullian, 222; and aging,
    202, 208: pastoral program, 209–11;
    Asian, 164–65; in Christian tradition,
    179–80; commodification, 92, 220; Dalit
    143; as disciples, 153–54, 159, 163–64;
    domination, 140; in Eucharistic ritual,
    187–88, 190; in Indian Church, 139,
    143–44; in Jewish tradition, 160; in
    Johannine community, 159–60; lament
    rituals, 158; in postmodern India, 139;
    and nature, 91–93; ordination, 194–97;
    pre-colonial Philippines, 219; religious,
    202–3, 238–39; role, 157, 160; sexual
    abuse, 216, 228; spirituality, 194–95,
    196; trafficking, 176, 184n 10; value, 83;
    violence against, 35, 53n 6, 221–24
Women and Gender Commission –
    AMRSP, 229
"World as God's body," 97–98

Yasuo Yuasa, 131
Ybanez, Rita, 67
Yoga, 39, 40, 98: Bhakti. 40; Buddhist, 40
Youth culture, 18, 19

Zikaron, 195

Editors and Contributors

LEONILA V. BERMISA is a member of the Maryknoll Sisters and is currently the Congregational Vocation Ministry Director. She is also a Candidate for Doctor in Ministry at the San Francisco Theological Seminary, California. She was the Dean of the Institute of Formation and Religious Studies, Quezon City, Philippines from 2000 to 2004. (Lbermisa@mksisters.org)

SHARON A. BONG received her Ph.D. from the Department of Religious Studies, Lancaster University, United Kingdom, in 2002. She was a specialist writer with the New Straits Times Press and a Programme Officer (publications) at ARROW, the Asian-Pacific Resource and Research Centre for Women. She presently lectures at Monash University Malaysia and her main research interests include women and religious studies in postcolonial contexts. (sadelbong@yahoo.com)

AGNES M. BRAZAL is full-time faculty member at the Maryhill School of Theology, Ecclesia of Women in Asia 2004 coordinator and vice-president of the Catholic Theological Association of the Philippines (DAKATEO) from 2002-2006. She has published articles on liberation, feminist, intercultural and migration theologies in local/international journals and collections of essays. She is married to Emmanuel S. de Guzman, a lay theologian, and has a son named Nathanael. (abrazal2001@yahoo.com)

MARY CECILIA CLAPAROLS is a member of the Religious of the Assumption. She has a DUER (Diplome Universitaire pour les Etudes Religieuses), M.A. Religious Education, Masters in Theological Studies (with concentration on Biblical and Christian Spirituality) and is doing her Doctorate in Ministry at the Pacific School of Religion, Graduate Theological Union, Berkeley. She is involved in Buddhist-Christian Dialogue on Spirituality and Social Transformation. (smarycee@yahoo.com)

CHRISTINE GUDORF is professor at the Department of Religious Studies, Florida International University. She spent two years in Indonesia, as a Fulbright Senior Scholar teaching Gender in World Religions in Spring 2002 and as a Fulbright Serial Scholar in 2003. Her book *Body, Sex, and Pleasure: Reconstructing Christian Sexual Ethics* won the Midwest Book Achievement Award in 1995. She obtained her Ph.D. in theology at the Columbia University/Union Theological Seminary. (gudorf@fiu.edu)

ANTOINETTE GUTZLER is a member of the Maryknoll Sisters of St. Dominic. She comes from the United States and is presently living and working in Taiwan where she serves as associate professor of theology at Fu Jen University, Taipei. She has a Ph.D. degree in systematic theology from Fordham University, New York, U.S.A. She dedicates her paper to the memory of William V. Dych, SJ. (ngutzler@yahoo.com)

DZINTRA ILISHKO is from Latvia, Eastern Europe and holds a doctorate in theology. She is a member of the International Board of the European Society of Women in Theological Research (ESWTR) and is in charge of ESWTR's international contacts and relationships. (dilisko@hotmail.com)

PUSHPA JOSEPH is a religious of the Franciscan Missionary of Mary. She is teaching and post-doctoral fellow at the Department of Christian Studies, University of Madras. She obtained her doctoral degree in theology in the University of Madras. She was Ecclesia of Women in Asia 2003 coordinator. (pushpajoseph@yahoo.co.in)

ANDREA LIZARES SI holds a Master's in Divinity from the Asian Theological Seminary and is currently finishing her Master's of Education on Marriage and Family at the John Paul II Institute for Studies on Marriage and Family, Bacolod City, Philippines. A lawyer by profession, she specializes in women's issues and has been President of the Development through Active Women Networking Foundation since 1993. (lizaresandrea@yahoo.com)

ASTRID LOBO GAJIWALA holds a Doctorate in Medicine and is the head of The Tissue Bank in Tata Memorial Hospital. She is a founding member of the Satyashodhak, a Mumbai based group of Christian feminists and is a member of the CBCI Commission for Women, Mumbai Women's Desk Core Team. Astrid has published articles in journals such as *In God's Image, Daughters of Sarah, Magnificat, Women's Link, The Month, Vidyajyoti, Jnanadeep*, as well as, in collections of essays. (lobogajiwalaa@tmcmail.org)

A. METTI is a member of the congregation of the Sisters of the Cross of Chavanod. She is a full-time research scholar in the Department of Christian Studies, University of Madras, Chennai in India. She obtained her masteral degree in theology at Vidya Jothi, Delhi. She works for the cause of women's concerns. She is also involved in theologizing at Theologates in Trichy and Chennai. (mettiamir@yahoo.co.in)

NOZOMI MIURA is a sister of the Religious of the Sacred Heart. She obtained her masteral degree in theology at the Loyola University, USA. She is currently a teacher of high school students. (sismiura@hotmail.com)

EVELYN MONTEIRO is a member of the Congregation of the Sisters of the Cross of Chavanod. She is on the Faculty of Theology at Jnana-Deepa Vidyapeeth, Pontifical Institute of Philosophy and Religion, Pune, India and head of the Department of Systematic Theology. She holds a doctorate in Theology from Centre Sèvres, Facultès Jèsuites de Paris and is author of *Church and Culture: Communion in Pluralism*. (evelynm@vsnl.net)

JULIA ONG SIU YIN is a member of the Institute of the Sisters of the Infant Jesus. She obtained an MA in Education, major in Religious Formation from the De La Salle University, Manila. She taught at secondary schools, worked in centers for children and was the Pastoral Associate of five secondary schools before she was appointed Deputy Director of Religious Education for Catholic Schools in Singapore. (ijj2005@yahoo.com.sg)

JEANE C. PERACULLO teaches Philosophy and Theology at various universities in the Philippines. She holds an MA in Theological Studies from the Maryhill School of Theology and is presently a PhD in Philosophy candidate from De La Salle University-Manila. She is an active advocate for environmental issues. (peracullojeane@yahoo.com)

HAN SOON HEE is a sister of the Society of the Sacred Heart of Jesus. She teaches at the Department of Religious Studies at the Catholic University of Korea. She finished an MA in Pastoral Studies, major in spirituality, at the Loyola University, USA. (hanrscj@catholic.ac.kr)

GEMMA TULUD CRUZ holds an M.A. in Religious Studies from the Maryhill School of Theology in the Philippines and a PhD in Intercultural Theology at Radboud University Nijmegen, the Netherlands. She has published a number of articles in international journals and collections of essays and is a regular contributor to the Global Perspective column of the National Catholic Reporter. (serenity3_99@yahoo.com)

THERESA YIH-LAN TSOU is a member of the Sisters of Social Service of Los Angeles in Taipei, and secretary-general of the Taiwan Catholic Sprout Women-Concerns Association. She is a psychiatrist at Ming-En Mental Hospital, Yingko, Taipei Hsien, with a postgraduate training in Physical Medicine and Rehabilitation from State University of New York at Buffalo Affiliated Hospitals (SUNYAB). (ssstpe@ms46.hinet.net)